THE LEAST YOU SHOULD KNOW ABOUT ENGLISH

Form A
First Canadian Edition

TERESA FERSTER GLAZIER

PAIGE WILSON

CANADIAN EDITOR:
KATHLEEN A. WAGNER

Harcourt Canada

Harcourt Canada

Toronto Montreal Fort Worth New York Orlando
Philadelphia San Diego London Sydney Tokyo

Canadian Cataloguing in Publication Data

Glazier, Teresa Ferster
    The least you should know about English: form A

1st Canadian ed.
Includes index.
ISBN 0-7747-3710-7

1. English language – Rhetoric. 2. English language – Grammar 3. Report Writing.
I. Wilson, Paige. II. Wagner, Kathleen A. III. Title

PE1408.G59 2002   808'.042   C99-932978-2

Acquisitions Editor: Anne Williams
Developmental Editors: Rebecca Conolly/Lise Dupont/Eliza Marciniak
Production Editor: Laurie Thomas
Production Co-ordinator: Cheri Westra

Copy Editor: Trish Letient
Permissions Editors: Mary Rose MacLachlan/Cindy Howard
Cover Design: Rivet Design
Typesetting and Assembly: Christine Gambin
Printing and Binding: Transcontinental Printing Inc.

Cover Art: Picking Shadows by Dawne Stevenson, Colour Slide, 1996. Reprinted by permission of the artist.

Harcourt Canada Ltd.
55 Horner Avenue, Toronto, ON, Canada M8Z 4X6
Customer Service
Toll-Free Tel.: 1-800-387-7278
Toll-Free Fax: 1-800-665-7307

This book was printed in Canada.
1 2 3 4 5   05 04 03 02 01

This book is for students who need to review basic English skills and who may profit from a simplified "least you should know" approach. Parts 1 to 3 cover the essentials of spelling, sentence structure, and punctuation. Part 4 on writing teaches students the basic structures of the paragraph and the essay, along with the writing skills necessary to produce them.

Throughout the book, we try to avoid the use of linguistic terminology whenever possible. A conjunction is a connecting word; gerunds and present participles are *ing* words; an infinitive is the *to* ___ form of a verb. Students work with words they know instead of learning a vocabulary they may never use again.

There are abundant exercises, including practice with writing sentences and proofreading paragraphs—enough so that students learn to use the rules automatically and thus *carry over their new skills into their writing*. Exercises consist of sets of ten thematically related, informative sentences on such subjects as the first Canadian woman astronaut, the invention of the snowmobile, British Columbia's Ice Man, the Canadian national anthem, and vending-machine dating in Japan. Such exercises reinforce the need for coherence and details in student writing. With answers provided at the back of the book, students can correct their own work and progress at their own pace.

For this new edition, we have completely revised Part 4 on writing, which covers the writing process and which stresses the development of the student's written "voice." Writing assignments follow each discussion, and there are samples by both student and professional writers. Part 4 ends with a section designed to help students with writing assignments based on readings. It includes articles to read, react to, and summarize. Students improve their reading by learning to spot main ideas and their writing by learning to write meaningful reactions and concise summaries.

The Least You Should Know about English functions equally well in the classroom and at home as a self-tutoring text. The simple explanations, ample exercises, and answers at the back of the book provide students with everything they need to progress on their own. Students who have previously been overwhelmed by the complexities of English should, through mastering simple rules and through writing and rewriting simple papers, gain enough competence to succeed in further composition courses.

We all want to have our opinions heard, our thoughts understood, our input respected. Carefully crafting our messages according to universally accepted rules of grammar, spelling, and usage encourages readers to pay attention to what we have to say. In fact, in decoding our messages, members of our reading audience assume that we have followed the rules.

This textbook offers an upbeat yet comprehensive study of how to express your ideas well. If you have unhappy memories of "dangling participles" and "subordinate clauses," you will be delighted that *The Least You Should Know about English* guides readers through the maze of correct grammar and usage without the use of fancy terminology. As a result, the book's lessons are accessible and user-friendly. If you are willing to make an honest commitment to learning, you will feel a new sense of self-confidence in tackling writing tasks.

This book also uses refreshing approaches to upgrade language skills that have gotten a bit rusty over the years. If you once felt in control of your writing but are now less sure of your abilities, reading this book and completing its exercises will dust out the cobwebs caused by informal language use. You'll discover that recalling basic principles is not as difficult as you may have feared.

Qualified individuals in any career field know how to use the right tools to get a job done. Naturally, you will place a high importance on learning the tools of the trade for the career field you have chosen.

But regardless of where you see yourself headed in life, regardless of which occupation attracts you, the ability to communicate correctly and effectively will make a significant contribution to your professional and personal success.

For that reason, fine-tuning your language skills is just as important to your future as learning about the tools and procedures specific to your chosen career path.

Because words are the fundamental building blocks of communication, you need to understand how words work—what jobs they do—before you can comfortably and confidently build sentences, paragraphs, and longer written messages.

Think of this book as a language toolbox. It contains the word and communication tools you will need to build effective pieces of communication. Just as a carpenter carefully selects the right techniques to construct fine furniture, you should carefully apply the principles explained in this book to compose fine written messages.

Simple explanations, no complicated rules to memorize, plenty of opportunities for hands-on application of the principles, and even an answer key to check your work—it just doesn't get any better than this!

The Least You Should Know about English makes it easy to learn exactly what you need to know to avoid the most common writing mistakes. Turn the page and allow this book to be your tour guide on the road to effective communication.

Best wishes on your journey!

Kathleen A. Wagner
Sudbury, Ontario, Canada

ACKNOWLEDGEMENTS

For their thoughtful commentary on the book, we would like to thank the following reviewers: Irene Badaracco, Fordham University; Cheryl Delk, Western Michigan University; Nancy Dessommes, Georgia Southern University; Donna Ross Hooley, Georgia Southern University; Sandra Jensen, Lane Community College; Anastasia Lankford, Eastfield College; Ben Larson, York College; Sue McKee, California State University at Sacramento; Karen McGuire, Pasadena City College; Kevin Nebergall, Krikwood Community College; Peggy Porter, Houston Community College; and Anne Simmons, Olean Business Institute.

In addition, we would like to thank our publishing team for their expertise and hard work: Steve Dalphin, Acquisitions Editor; Michell Phifer, Developmental Editor; Kathryn Stewart, Project Editor; James McDonald, Production Manager; and Garry Harman, Art Director.

We would also like to thank the following people for their specific contributions: Roman Dodson, Roberta Hales, Paul Miller, Pat Rose, Joseph Sierra, and Lillian Woodward.

Finally, we are indebted to Herb and Moss Rabbin, Kenneth Glazier, and the rest of our families and friends for their support and encouragement.

Teresa Ferster Glazier

Paige Wilson

The thoughtful contributions of others ensure that this edition fairly represents perspectives and topics of interest to Canadian readers. In particular, I am grateful to Kate Christie of Humber College (Toronto, Ontario) and Peter Smith, now retired from the North York Board of Education (Toronto, Ontario), for their reviews.

Also, the long-overdue Canadian edition was made possible through the support of a very special group of professionals in the Harcourt Canada Division: Anne Williams, Acquisitions Editor (who determinedly worked to acquire Canadian rights); Eliza Marciniak, Developmental Editor (who patiently encouraged the process throughout); Laurie Thomas, Production Editor; Trish Letient, Copy Editor; and Cheri Westra, Production Co-ordinator.

Finally, Deane L. Jensen deserves my personal thanks for his faith in this writing project.

Kathleen A. Wagner
Sudbury, Ontario

A **Test Packet** with additional exercises and ready-to-photocopy tests accompanies this text and is available to instructors.

Thank you for selecting *The Least You Should Know About English, Form A*, by Teresa Ferster Glazier, Paige Wilson, and Canadian Editor, Kathleen A. Wagner. The authors and publisher have devoted considerable time and care to the development of this book. We appreciate your recognition of this effort and accomplishment.

We want to hear what you think about *The Least You Should Know About English, Form A*. Please take a few minutes to fill in the stamped reply card at the back of the book. Or, if you prefer, e-mail your comments to us at **english_harcourt canada@harcourt.com**. Your comments and suggestions will be valuable to us as we prepare new editions and other books.

CONTENTS

What Is the Least You Should Know?

Most English textbooks try to teach you more than you need to know. This one will teach you the least you need to know — and still help you learn to write acceptably. You won't have to bother with grammatical terms like gerunds and modal auxiliary verbs and demonstrative pronouns and all those others you've been hearing about for years. You can get along without knowing these terms if you learn a few basic concepts thoroughly. You *do* have to know how to spell common words; you *do* have to recognize subjects and verbs to avoid writing fragments; you *do* have to know a few rules of sentence structure and punctuation — but rules will be kept to a minimum.

The English you'll learn in this book is sometimes called Standard Written English, and it may differ slightly or greatly from the spoken English you use. Standard Written English is the accepted form of writing in business and the professions. So no matter how you speak, you will communicate better in writing when you use Standard Written English. You might *say* something like "That's a whole nother problem," and everyone will understand, but you would probably want to *write*, "That's a completely different problem." Knowing the difference between spoken English and Standard Written English is essential in college and university, in business, and in life.

Unless you learn the least you should know, you'll have difficulty communicating in writing. Take this sentence for example:

I hope my application will be excepted by the hiring committee.

We assume the writer will not actually be happy to be overlooked by the committee but merely failed to use the right word. If the sentence had read

I hope my application will be *accepted* by the hiring committee.

then the writer would convey the intended meaning. Or take this sentence.

The manager fired Lee and Dave and I received a $100 raise.

The sentence needs a comma.

The manager fired Lee and Dave, and I received a $100 raise.

But perhaps the writer meant

The manager fired Lee, and Dave and I received a $100 raise.

Punctuation makes all the difference, especially if you are Dave. What you'll learn from this text is simply to make your writing so clear that no one will misunderstand it.

As you make your way through the book, it's important to master every rule as you come to it because many rules depend on previous ones. For example, unless you learn to pick out subjects and verbs, you'll have trouble with fragments, with subject-verb agreement, and with punctuation. The rules are brief and clear, and it won't be difficult to master all of them — *if you want to*. But you do have to want to!

How to Master the Least You Should Know

1. Study the explanation of each rule carefully.

2. Do the first exercise. Correct your answers using the answer section at the back of the book. If you miss even one answer, study the explanation again to find out why.

3. Do the second exercise and correct it. If you miss a single answer, go back once more and study the explanation. You must have missed something. Be tough on yourself. Don't just think, "Maybe I'll get it right next time." Go back and master the rules, and *then* try the next exercise. It's important to correct each group of ten sentences before going on so that you'll discover your mistakes while you still have sentences to practise on.

4. You may be tempted to quit after you do one or two exercises perfectly. Don't! Make yourself finish another exercise. It's not enough to *understand* a rule. You have to *practise* it.

If you're positive, however, after doing several exercises, that you've mastered the rule, take the next exercise as a test. If you miss even one answer, you should do all the rest of the questions. But if you again make no mistakes, move on to the proofreading and sentence writing exercises so that your understanding of the rule carries over into your writing.

Mastering the essentials of spelling, sentence structure, and punctuation will take time. Generally, community college and university students spend a couple of hours outside of class for each hour in class. You may need more. Undoubtedly, the more time you spend, the more your writing will improve.

Spelling

Anyone can learn to spell better. You can eliminate most of your spelling errors if you want to. It's just a matter of deciding you're going to do it. If you really intend to learn to spell, study each of the seven parts of this section until you make no more mistakes in the exercises.

Your Own List of Misspelled Words

Words Often Confused (Sets 1 and 2)

Contractions

Possessives

Words That Can Be Broken into Parts

Rule for Doubling a Final Letter

Using a Dictionary

Study these seven parts, and you'll be a better speller.

Your Own List of Misspelled Words

On the inside cover of your English notebook or in some other obvious place, write correctly all the misspelled words in the papers handed back to you. Review them until you're sure of them.

Words Often Confused (Set 1)

Learning the differences between these often-confused words will help you overcome many of your spelling problems. Study the words carefully, with their examples, before trying the exercises.

a, an Use *an* before a word that begins with a vowel *sound* (*a, e, i,* and *o,* plus *u* when it sounds like *uh*) or silent *h*.

Note that it's not the letter but the *sound* of the letter that matters.

> an apple, an essay, an inch, an onion
>
> an umpire, an ugly design (the *u*'s sound like *uh*)
>
> an hour, an honest person (silent *h*)

Use *a* before a word that begins with a consonant sound (all the sounds except the vowels, plus *u* or *eu* when they sound like *you*).

> a chart, a pie, a history book (the *h* is not silent in *history*)
>
> a union, a uniform, a unit (the *u*'s sound like *you*)
>
> a European vacation, a euphemism (*eu* sounds like *you*)

accept, except   *Accept* means "to receive willingly."

> I *accept* your apology.

Except means "excluding" or "but."

> Everyone arrived on time *except* him.

advise, advice   *Advise* is a verb (pronounce the *s* like a *z*).

> I *advise* you to take your time finding the right job.

Advice is a noun (it rhymes with *rice*).

> My counsellor gave me good *advice*.

affect, effect   *Affect* is a verb and means "to alter or influence."

> All quizzes will *affect* the final grade.
>
> The happy ending *affected* the mood of the audience.

Effect is most commonly used as a noun and means "a result." If *a, an,* or *the* is in front of the word, then you'll know it isn't a verb and will use *effect*.

> The strong coffee had a powerful *effect* on me.
>
> We studied the *effects* of sleep deprivation in my psychology class.

all ready, already   If you can leave out the *all* and the sentence still makes sense, then *all ready* is the form to use. (In that form, *all* is a separate word and could be left out.)

We're *all ready* for the trip. (*We're ready for the trip* makes sense.)

The banquet is *all ready*. (*The banquet is ready* makes sense.)

But if you can't leave out the *all* and still have the sentence make sense, then use *already* (the form in which the *al* has to stay in the word).

They've *already* eaten. (*They've ready eaten* doesn't make sense.)

We have seen that movie *already*.

are, our   *Are* is a verb.

We *are* going to Saskatoon.

Our shows we possess something.

We painted *our* fence to match the house.

brake, break   *Brake* used as a verb means "to slow or stop motion." It's also the name of the device that slows or stops motion.

I had to *brake* quickly to avoid an accident.

Luckily I just had my *brakes* fixed.

Break used as a verb means "to shatter" or "to split." It's also the name of an interruption, as in "a coffee break."

She never thought she would *break* a world record.

Enjoy your spring *break*.

choose, chose   The difference here is one of time. Use *choose* for present and future; use *chose* for past.

I will *choose* a new area of study this semester.

We *chose* the wrong time of year to get married.

clothes, cloths   *Clothes* are something you wear; *cloths* are pieces of material you might clean or polish something with.

I love the *clothes* that characters wear in movies.

The car wash workers use special *cloths* to dry the cars.

coarse, course   *Coarse* describes a rough texture, or something crude or vulgar.

I used *coarse* sandpaper to smooth the surface of the board.

His *coarse* language offended some listeners.

Course is used for all other meanings.

Of *course* we saw the golf *course* when we went to Wasaga Beach.

complement, compliment
The one spelled with an *e* means to complete something or bring it to perfection.

Use a colour wheel to find a *complement* for purple.

Juliet's personality *complements* Romeo's; she is practical, and he is a dreamer.

The one spelled with an *i* has to do with praise. Remember "*I* like compliments," and you'll remember to use the *i* spelling when you mean praise.

My evaluation included a really nice *compliment* from my co-workers.

We *complimented* them on their new home.

conscious, conscience
Conscious means "aware."

They weren't *conscious* of any problems before the accident.

Conscience means that inner voice of right and wrong. The extra *n* in *conscience* should remind you of *No*, which is what your conscience often says to you.

My *conscience* told me to turn in the expensive watch I found.

dessert, desert
Dessert is the sweet one, the one you like two helpings of. So give it two helpings of *s*.

We had a whole chocolate cheesecake for *dessert*.

The other one, *desert*, is used for all other meanings and has two pronunciations.

I promise that I won't *desert* you.

The snake slithered slowly across the *desert*.

do, due
Do is a verb, an action. You *do* something.

I always *do* my best work at night.

But a payment or an assignment is *due*; it is scheduled for a certain time.

Our first essay is *due* tomorrow.

Due can also be used before *to* in a phrase that means *because of.*

The outdoor concert was cancelled *due to* rain.

feel, fill   *Feel* describes *feel*ings.

Whenever I stay up late, I *feel* sleepy in class.

Fill describes what you do to a cup or a gas tank.

Did they *fill* the pitcher to the top?

fourth, forth   The word *fourth* has *four* in it. (But note that *forty* does not. Remember the word *forty-fourth*.)

This is our *fourth* quiz in two weeks.

My grandparents celebrated their *forty-fourth* anniversary.

If you don't mean a number, use *forth*.

We wrote back and *forth* many times during my trip.

have, of   *Have* is a verb. Sometimes, in a contraction, it sounds like *of.* When you say *could've*, the *have* may sound like *of*, but it is not written that way. Always write *could have, would have, should have, might have.*

We should *have* planned our vacation sooner.

Then we could *have* used our coupon for a free one-way ticket.

Use *of* only in a prepositional phrase (see p. 55).

She sent me a box *of* chocolates for my birthday.

hear, here   The last three letters of *hear* spell "ear." You *hear* with your ear.

When I listen to a sea shell, I *hear* ocean sounds.

The other spelling *here* tells "where." Note that the three words indicating a place or pointing out something all have *here* in them: *here, there, where.*

I'll be *here* for three more weeks.

it's, its   *It's* is a contraction and means "it is" or "it has."

It's hot. (*It is* hot.)

It's been hot all week. (*It has* been hot. …)

Its is a possessive. (Possessives such as *its, yours, hers, ours, theirs, whose* are already possessive and never need an apostrophe. See p. 31.)

> The jury had made *its* decision.

> The dog pulled at *its* leash.

knew, new   *Knew* has to do with knowledge (both start with *k*).

New means "not old."

> They *knew* that she wanted a *new* bike.

know, no   *Know* has to do with knowledge (both start with *k*).

> By Friday, I must *know* the names of all the past prime ministers.

No means "not any" or the opposite of "yes."

> My boss has *no* patience. *No*, I need to work late.

E X E R C I S E S

Underline the correct word. Don't guess! If you aren't sure, turn back to the explanatory pages. When you've finished ten sentences, compare your answers with those at the back of the book. Correct each group of ten sentences before continuing so you'll catch your mistakes while you still have sentences to practise on.

Exercise 1

1. (Hear, Here) are some tips on how to stay healthy by eating well, based on (a, an) pamphlet entitled "Canada's Food Guide to Healthy Eating."

2. The Food Guide (advices, advises) you to eat several servings each day from the four basic food groups: grains, vegetables and fruit, milk products, and meats and alternatives.

3. (Its, It's) important to remember that fish, eggs, beans, tofu, and peanut butter can be meat substitutes.

4. Be (conscious, conscience) of the fact that different people need different amounts of food, depending on age, body size, activity level, and gender.

5. Male teenagers, for example, (do, due) eat more because (their, there) bodies require it.

6. You may (all ready, already) (no, know) this, but (its, it's) hard to (accept, except) that most (desserts, deserts) are not good for you.

7. (Choose, Chose) low-fat dairy products, lean meat, and healthy foods when you go to the grocery store, and don't feel you should (of, have) purchased that box of cookies.

8. What you eat will (affect, effect) how you feel, as well as how well your (clothes, cloths) fit.

9. Eat in moderation; you will (feel, fill) better, if you do not (fill, feel) yourself with too many (courses, coarses).

10. Also, (complimenting, complementing) your diet with lots of fresh air and exercise can have (a, an) excellent (affect, effect) on your eating habits.

Source: Health Canada, "Canada's Food Guide to Healthy Eating," 1997.

Exercise 2

1. I've been reading that (are, our) individual dreams say (a, an) awful lot about us, but that some dreams (are, our) common to us all.

2. (It's, Its) strange, for example, that many people (feel, fill) as though they are falling or flying in a dream.

3. In another common dream experience, we realize suddenly that we are not wearing any (clothes, cloths), and we don't (know, no) how we got that way.

4. Or we dream that we have missed a deadline when a test or an essay was (do, due), but we have forgotten to (do, due) it.

5. Whether we are (conscious, conscience) of it or not, our dream lives can have (a, an) (affect, effect) on (are, our) real lives.

6. If in a dream we (brake, break) the heart of someone we love, we might wake up the next morning with a guilty (conscious, conscience).

7. Of (coarse, course), we may dream of eating (a, an) entire container of chocolate ice cream for (dessert, desert) and (feel, fill) another kind of guilt.

8. Dream experts give the following (advise, advice) to those who want to call (fourth, forth) the dreams that slip away from the (conscious, conscience) mind once we are awake.

9. They suggest that dreamers put paper and a pencil by the bed before going to sleep in order to write down a dream as soon as (it's, its) over.

10. We all (know, no) that (know, no) amount of coaxing will bring back a dream that our brain (all ready, already) (choose, chose) to forget.

Exercise 3

1. The T-shirt had (it's, its) modern beginnings when the U.S. Navy (choose, chose) it as (a, an) official undergarment in the early 1900s.

2. The first printed T-shirt was used during the 1948 U.S. presidential campaign as (a, an) ad for one of the candidates.

3. (It's, Its) message read "Dew it with Dewey," and (it's, its) now on display at the Smithsonian Institution in Washington, D.C.

4. Whether he was (conscious, conscience) of it or not, Marlon Brando started a fashion trend by wearing (a, an) white T-shirt in the movie *A Streetcar Named Desire*.

5. James Dean's T-shirt and blue jeans also had an (affect, effect) on the look of the 1950s (do, due) to the popularity of his film *Rebel without a Cause*.

6. After that, people began to (accept, except) T-shirts as regular (clothes, cloths).

7. Advertisers started to use the fronts and backs of T-shirts as spaces to (feel, fill) with slogans, brand names, and pictures of products.

8. In the 1960s, the (knew, new) look was colourful tie-dyed T-shirts used to (complement, compliment) bell-bottomed pants and sandals.

9. Of (coarse, course), an old T-shirt can be cut up into (clothes, cloths) that are the perfect texture to wax a car or to polish silver. The material is not too smooth and not too (coarse, course); (it's, its) just right.

10. Over the (coarse, course) of the twentieth century, we have seen the T-shirt (feel, fill) many of (are, our) needs as comfortable and stylish (clothes, cloths) to wear and as useful (clothes, cloths) to clean with.

Exercise 4

1. Before I went to Japan, my friend said, "I (advise, advice) you not to pack your video camera."

2. However, I wanted to make (a, an) Japanese vacation video to (complement, compliment) the one I (all ready, already) had of our trip to China.

3. Consequently, I (choose, chose) not to take my friend's (advise, advice).

4. That decision had (a, an) unfortunate (affect, effect) on my trip.

5. I could (of, have) enjoyed myself everywhere I went, but instead I (choose, chose) to capture the moment on video.

6. At the hotel, when a woman dressed in traditional Japanese (clothes, cloths) greeted us with refreshments, I couldn't even (accept, except) any because I was too busy recording.

7. I filmed a tea ceremony, though I didn't (do, due) any tea drinking myself.

8. Now as I watch my Japanese video back home, I am (conscious, conscience) of the discussions that I (hear, here) going on in the background.

9. At the airport, one friend says, "I've got to (complement, compliment) Jack on his persistence. He's going to have a great memento of this trip after we've (all ready, already) forgotten it."

10. Next time I go to Japan or anywhere else on vacation, I'll pack everything I need — (accept, except) my video camera.

Exercise 5

1. You have probably (all ready, already) heard the expression "peeping Tom" used to describe a person who peers into neighbours' windows.

2. But you might not (know, no) (it's, its) origins.

3. (It's, Its) (a, an) old story that involves someone else you might (have, of) heard of — Lady Godiva — who lived in Coventry, England, in the eleventh century.

4. Lady Godiva's husband, Leofric, was (a, an) powerful man, the Earl of Coventry, but her (conscious, conscience) was bothered by his treatment of the townspeople.

5. Leofric forced the people to pay heavy taxes, but Lady Godiva couldn't (accept, except) his unfairness, so she asked him to reduce the tax.

6. Leofric made his wife (a, an) unusual offer: he would get rid of the tax if she would ride naked through the streets of Coventry on a horse with only her hair to cover her.

7. Lady Godiva (choose, chose) to (accept, except) her husband's challenge, for she believed that the townspeople would not (dessert, desert) her and would not look at her.

8. So Lady Godiva rode through Coventry without wearing any (clothes, cloths).

9. The townspeople promised to stay indoors with the shutters closed, and they did — (accept, except) one man, the tailor named Tom.

10. Tom magically was struck blind (do, due) to his decision to (brake, break) his promise to Lady Godiva, and (it's, its) from this story that we get (are, our) expression "peeping Tom."

Source: A Hog on Ice & Other Curious Expressions (New York: Harper & Row, 1948).

PROOFREADING EXERCISE

Find and correct the ten errors contained in the following student paragraph. All of the errors involve Words Often Confused (Set 1).

My dog had six puppies last night, and they were all strong and active accept the littlest one born last — it was the runt. It's head and body were much smaller than those of it's brother and sisters. We named him first and called him Pee-Wee because we were all ready starting to fill that he was special. At first, the other puppies wouldn't let Pee-Wee eat, and we could here him cry for milk. It's almost as if the others were trying to get rid of him. We didn't know what to do, so we called the animal hospital to get some advise. They told us that we could make sure he got enough milk by taking the others out of the box after they seemed full and that eventually Pee-Wee would be excepted by the others. The plan worked. By the second day, Pee-Wee was part of the family. We could of lost are favourite puppy if we hadn't received such good advice.

SENTENCE WRITING

The surest way to learn these Words Often Confused is to use them immediately in your own writing. Choose the five pairs or groups of words that you most often confuse from Set 1. Then use each of them correctly in a new sentence. No answers are provided at the back of the book, but you can see if you are using the words correctly by comparing your sentences to the examples in the explanations.

Words Often Confused (Set 2)

Study this second set of words carefully, with their examples, before attempting the exercises. Knowing all of the word groups in these two sets will take care of many of your spelling problems.

lead, led   *Lead* is the metal that rhymes with *bead*.

Old paint is dangerous because it often contains *lead*.

The past form of the verb "to lead" is *led*.

What factors *led* to your decision?

I *led* our school's debating team to victory last year.

If you don't mean past time, use *lead*, which rhymes with *bead*.

I will *lead* the debating team again this year.

loose, lose   *Loose* means "not tight." Note how *l o o s e* that word is. It has plenty of room for two *o*'s.

> My dog's tooth is *loose*.

Lose is the opposite of win.

> If we *lose* this game, we will be out for the season.

passed, past   The past form of the verb "to pass" is *passed*.

> She easily *passed* her math class.

> The runner *passed* the baton to her teammate.

> We *passed* your house twice before we saw the address.

Use *past* when it's not a verb.

> We drove *past* your house. (the same as "We drove *by* your house")

> I always use my *past* experiences to help me solve problems.

> In the *past*, he had to borrow his brother's car.

personal, personnel   Pronounce these two correctly, and you won't confuse them — *pérsonal, personnél*.

> She shared her *personal* views as a parent.

Personnel means "a group of employees."

> I had an appointment in the *personnel* office.

piece, peace   Remember "piece of pie." The one meaning "a *piece* of something" always begins with *pie*.

> One child asked for an extra *piece* of candy.

The other one, *peace*, is the opposite of war.

> The two gangs discussed the possibility of a *peace* treaty.

principal, principle   *Principal* means "main." Both words have *a* in them: princip*a*l, m*a*in.

> The *principal* concern is safety. (main concern)

> He lost both *principal* and interest. (main amount of money)

Also, think of a school's "princi*pal*" as your "*pal*."

An elementary school *principal* must be kind. (main administrator)

A *principle* is a "rule." Both words end in *le*: princip*le*, ru*le*

I am proud of my high *principles*. (rules of conduct)

We value the *principle* of truth in advertising. (rule)

quiet, quite
Pronounce these two correctly, and you won't confuse them. *Quiet* means "free from noise" and rhymes with *diet*.

Tennis players need *quiet* in order to concentrate.

Quite means "very" and rhymes with *bite*.

It was *quite* hot in the auditorium.

right, write
Right means "correct" or "proper."

You will find your keys if you look in the *right* place.

It also means in the exact location, position, or moment.

Your keys are *right* where you left them.

Let's go *right* now.

Write means to compose sentences, poems, essays, and so forth.

I asked my teacher to *write* a letter of recommendation for me.

than, then
Than compares two things.

I am taller *than* my sister.

Then tells when (*then* and *when* rhyme, and both have *e* in them).

I always write a rough draft of an essay first; *then* I revise it.

their, there, they're
Their is a possessive, meaning belonging to them.

Their cars have always been red.

There points out something. (Remember that the three words indicating a place or pointing out something all have *here* in them: *here, there, where*.)

I know that I haven't been *there* before.

There was a rainbow in the sky.

They're is a contraction and means "they are."

>*They're* living in Halifax. (*They are* living in Halifax now.)

threw, through   *Threw* is the past form of "to throw."

>We *threw* snowballs at each other.

>I *threw* away my chance at a scholarship.

If you don't mean "to throw something," use *through*.

>We could see our beautiful view *through* the new curtains.

>They worked *through* their differences.

two, too, to   *Two* is a number.

>We have written *two* papers so far in my English class.

Too means "extra" or "also," and so it has an extra *o*.

>The movie was *too* long and *too* violent. (extra)

>They are enrolled in that biology class *too*. (also)

Use *to* for all other meanings.

>They like *to* ski. They're going *to* the mountains.

weather, whether   *Weather* refers to conditions of the atmosphere.

>Snowy *weather* is too cold for me.

Whether means "if."

>I don't know *whether* it is snowing there or not.

>*Whether* I travel with you or not depends on the weather.

were, wear, where   These words are pronounced differently but are often confused in writing.

Were is the past form of the verb "to be."

>We *were* interns at the time.

Wear means to have on, as in wearing clothes.

>I always *wear* a scarf in winter.

Where refers to a place. (Remember that the three words indicating a place or pointing out something all have *here* in them: *here, there, where*.)

>*Where* is the mailbox? There it is.

Where are the closing papers? Here they are.

who's, whose   *Who's* is a contraction and means "who is" or "who has."

Who's responsible for signing the cheques? (*Who is* responsible?)

Who's been reading my journal? (*Who has* been ... ?)

Whose is a possessive. (Possessives such as *whose, its, yours, hers, ours, theirs* are already possessive and never take an apostrophe. See p. 31.)

Whose keys are these?

woman,   The difference here is one of number: wo*man* refers to
women   one female; wo*men* refers to two or more females.

I know a *woman* who won $8000 on a single horse race.

I bowl with a group of *women* from my work.

you're, your   *You're* is a contraction and means "you are."

You're as smart as I am. (*You are* as smart as I am.)

Your is a possessive meaning belonging to you.

I borrowed *your* lab book.

E X E R C I S E S

Underline the correct word. When you've finished ten sentences, compare your answers with those at the back of the book. Do only ten sentences at a time so you can teach yourself while you still have sentences to practise on.

Exercise 1

1. Living a longer and healthier life is the (personal, personnel) goal of many men and (woman, women).

2. According to ongoing research, (their, there, they're) are a number of factors that have (lead, led) to the probability that we will live much longer (than, then) our ancestors.

3. In the (passed, past), people rarely reached the age of 100, but currently the number of 100-year-olds is increasing more rapidly (than, then) any other group.

4. One (woman, women) who is still healthy at 104 stresses that she leaves her window open every night in all kinds of (weather, whether).

5. (Through, Threw) extensive studies, scientists have proven that eating (right, write) is the (principal, principle) difference found in the lifestyles of those who live long and healthy lives.

6. And researchers can point (two, too, to) one food that seems to produce the most negative results; in fact, (their, there, they're) (quiet, quite) sure that eating (two, too, to) much salt can have disastrous effects on a person's health.

7. Most North Americans get (their, there, they're) high levels of salt (through, threw) (their, there, they're) love of processed foods.

8. One (piece, peace) of fruit or a small tomato, for instance, contains fewer than 10 mg of salt, whereas the equivalent amount of processed tomato sauce might have more than 500 mg.

9. Of course, getting regular exercise is also a factor, (weather, whether) people want to be healthier, live longer, or (loose, lose) weight.

10. Companionship seems to help, (two, too, to); studies have shown that aging people with (two, too, to) or more good friends do much better (than, then) those who are alone.

Source: Newsweek, 30 June 1997.

Exercise 2

1. Test (you're, your) knowledge of animal history by answering the following question: which came first, sharks or dinosaurs?

2. (You're, Your) (right, write) if you answered sharks; they have been around for millions of years, and (their, there, they're) really (quiet, quite) amazing creatures.

3. Most sharks travel (through, threw) the water constantly without stopping, but some appear (two, too, to) sleep (right, write) on the bottom of the ocean.

4. (Their, There, They're) teeth never have a chance to (were, wear, where) down because each tooth is designed to come (loose, lose) easily, and (their, there, they're) is always another tooth waiting to take its place.

5. Sharks range in size from the fifteen-centimetre cigar shark (two, too, to) the eighteen-metre whale shark, and most of them are (quiet, quite) harmless (two, too, to) humans if they are left in (piece, peace).

6. More people die each year from being stung by bees (than, then) from being attacked by sharks, so (their, there, they're) reputation as killers is perhaps exaggerated.

7. Sharks can sense the movements of a fish in trouble or a swimmer (who's, whose) bleeding, and that's when (their, there, they're) likely to attack.

8. A shark doesn't chew its food, but bites off and swallows one big (piece, peace) at a time.

9. Baby sharks are called pups, and different species of sharks have different numbers of pups at a time — from (two, too, to) to close to a hundred.

10. A few sharks lay (their, there, they're) eggs in pouches with descriptive names like "mermaid's purses" and "devil's wheelbarrows"; these pouches are then laid on the ocean floor, and they stay (their, there, they're) until the shark pups hatch.

Source: 1996 Aqua Facts (Vancouver Aquarium).

Exercise 3

1. Last week, I went on a field trip with the children from the preschool (were, wear, where) I work; we took them to see a production of *The Wizard of Oz.*

2. The children (were, wear, where) told to (were, wear, where) their nicest clothes for our outing and to (right, write) their names on (their, there, they're) lunch bags.

3. On the bus (were, wear, where) twenty-five children and six (woman, women) — five teachers and one bus driver.

4. We weren't sure (weather, whether) the (principal, principle), Ms. Martyniuk, would be able to come with us.

5. As it turned out, she had to interview someone in the (personal, personnel) office at the same time, so she could not attend.

6. I (lead, led) my own small group of children (through, threw) the lobby of the theatre, (passed, past) the ushers checking tickets, and down the aisle to our seats.

7. My children were on (their, there, they're) best behaviour; they sat still and remained (quiet, quite) (through, threw) the whole performance.

8. At intermission, one of the children in the row ahead of ours (through, threw) a program out like a paper airplane and had to (loose, lose) the privilege of seeing the end of the show.

9. (Than, Then) as we boarded the bus back to school, we learned that another child's (loose, lose) tooth had come out in a (piece, peace) of chewing gum.

10. Once we figured out (who's, whose) tooth it was and once we (were, wear, where) all back on the bus, we headed for home.

Exercise 4

1. If you live (were, wear, where) there are pine trees, you can make (you're, your) own bird feeder very easily.

2. All you need is a pine cone or (two, too, to), a jar of peanut butter, some birdseed, and a long (piece, peace) of string.

3. The first step is (two, too, to) tie the string to the top of the pine cone securely.

4. Use a string that's long enough to allow the feeder to hang (were, wear, where) you will be able to see it later.

5. Try to use a pine cone that has a (loose, lose) rather (than, then) a tight shape.

6. Step (two, too, to) involves spreading the peanut butter in the spaces all around the outside of the pine cone.

7. This process can be (quiet, quite) messy, so you may want to (were, wear, where) rubber gloves and cover (you're, your) work surface with a (piece, peace) of newspaper.

8. Once (you're, your) finished with the second step, roll the peanut butter-covered pine cone in birdseed.

9. Hang the results from a tree branch, and sit back and watch the birds enjoy (their, there, they're) special treat in (piece, peace) and (quiet, quite).

10. And you can take (personal, personnel) pleasure in the fact that (you're, your) not adding more plastic to the environment since the pine cone bird feeder is made of all-natural ingredients.

Exercise 5

1. Many people take (their, there, they're) feet for granted.

2. Yet a person (who's, whose) (lead, led) a normal life will eventually walk more than 400 000 km on these (two, too, to) wonders of design.

3. (Their, There, They're) are 26 bones and nearly 40 muscles in a single foot, (who's, whose) job it is to log those kilometres without causing pain.

4. (Two, Too, To) many times, however, people have problems with their feet.

5. Doctors point out that the condition of a person's feet depends on (weather, whether) he or she treats them the (right, write) way or abuses them, rather (than, then) on heredity.

6. Many (woman, women) suffer from foot problems because they (were, wear, where) heels that are (two, too, to) high or shoes that are (two, too, to) small.

7. Hormones during pregnancy can cause the foot of a (woman, women) (two, too, to) increase by one whole shoe size.

8. The (principal, principle) result of foot pain for men and (woman, women) is often back trouble as they change (their, there, they're) normal posture and movements to avoid the pain in their feet.

9. Some foot problems can be eased (through, threw) massage, exercise, and something as simple as putting the feet up after a hard day.

10. Perhaps it's no surprise that nine out of ten patients who require foot surgery are (woman, women).

Source: Ladies' Home Journal, June 1998.

PROOFREADING EXERCISE

See if you can correct the ten errors in this student paragraph. All errors involve Words Often Confused (Set 2).

When I was in high school, the principle was always complaining about our homework record. The teachers had told him that about half the students didn't do there homework on time, and some never did any at all. So one September he started the first-day assembly by saying, "This year your all going to do you're homework every night for at least the first month of school. And if there is a school-wide perfect homework record during September, I will where a swimsuit to school on the first of October and dive off the high diving board into the school pool in front of everyone no matter what the whether is like that day." We students were not about to loose a bet like that. September past, and on the first of October, the principal lead us to the school pool; then he through off his heavy coat and climbed to the top of the diving board.

SENTENCE WRITING

Write several sentences using any words you missed in doing the exercises for Words Often Confused (Set 2).

Sentence writing is a good idea not only because it will help you remember these words often confused but also because it will be a storehouse for ideas you can later use in writing papers. Here are some topics you might consider writing your sentences about:

— Your career goals
— Your favourite movie or TV show at the moment
— A lesson you've learned the hard way
— Where you see yourself in ten years
— How your values are changing

Contractions

When two words are condensed into one, the result is called a contraction:

is not ········▶ isn't   you have ········▶ you've

The letter or letters that are left out are replaced with an apostrophe. For example, if the two words *do not* are condensed into one, an apostrophe is put where the *o* is left out.

do not   don't

Note how the apostrophe goes in the exact place where the letter or letters are left out in these contractions:

I am	I'm
I have	I've
I shall, I will	I'll
I would	I'd
you are	you're
you have	you've
you will	you'll
she is, she has	she's
he is, he has	he's
it is, it has	it's

we are	we're
we have	we've
we will, we shall	we'll
they are	they're
they have	they've
are not	aren't
cannot	can't
do not	don't
does not	doesn't
have not	haven't
let us	let's
who is, who has	who's
where is	where's
were not	weren't
would not	wouldn't
could not	couldn't
should not	shouldn't
would have	would've
could have	could've
should have	should've
that is	that's
there is	there's
what is	what's

One contraction does not follow this rule: *will not* becomes *won't*.

In all other contractions that you're likely to use, the apostrophe goes exactly where the letter or letters are left out. Note especially *it's, they're, who's,* and *you're*. Use them when you mean two words. (See pp. 31–32 for the possessive forms — *its, their, whose,* and *your* — which don't have an apostrophe.)

E X E R C I S E S

Put an apostrophe in each contraction. Then compare your answers with those at the back of the book. Be sure to correct each group of ten sentences before going on so you'll catch your mistakes while you still have sentences to practise on.

Exercise 1

1. Whats the story behind crying?

2. Ive been reading about the process of crying in my physiology class, and its more complicated than Id originally thought.

3. All tears arent the same; there are tears used to moisten the eyes and wash away irritating substances, and there are tears shed because were feeling a particular emotion.

4. Lets look at some statistics about emotional tears: first of all, crying doesnt have to result from sadness, but thats often the reason.

5. A person in sorrow sobs for an average of seven minutes, but a person whos extremely happy cries for only about two minutes.

6. It shouldnt come as a surprise to know that babies do a lot of crying, perhaps because they cant communicate their needs verbally.

7. Theres one interesting thing Ive learned about crying, and thats the fact that a good cry seems to have a positive effect on the brain.

8. Researchers showed emotional movie scenes to two groups of people (including both men and women); they told one group not to cry and the other to cry if they felt like it.

9. After theyd seen the movies, the two groups were asked to solve word puzzles.

10. Those who werent allowed to cry didnt do nearly as well on the test as those who let their tears flow freely.

Source: Ladies' Home Journal, June 1998.

Exercise 2

1. Grizzly bears dont live in Canada's prairies any more; theyve disappeared because they were hunted to extermination.

2. Youll find that once-plentiful species, such as the whooping crane, the burrowing owl, the bowhead whale, and the wolverine are now hard to locate in Canada.

3. Even sea otters cant easily be found; theyve become vulnerable because of pollution — especially oil spills.

4. Theyre all on a list of species at risk thats put out by the Committee on the Status of Endangered Wildlife in Canada (COSEWIC).

5. COSEWIC members, made up of scientists, cant actually protect these endangered species; they can only state that theyre threatened and suggest a plan of action.

6. At the COSEWIC annual meeting, each species is discussed and its decided whos on the endangered species list.

7. Sometimes theres a change in an animal's circumstance and its status is downlisted to a less serious category or its even removed from the endangered list; thats good news.

8. Youll be happy to know that other jurisdictions and organizations take over the duties of protecting the animals and their habitats.

9. COSEWIC members are telling industry that corporations cant continue to clear land and pollute as they have in the past and theyre alerting citizens to these issues.

10. Im sure that air and water pollution, as well as pesticides, arent any better for animals than they are for us.

Source: Adapted from the Web site http://www.cosewic.gc.ca/COSEWIC/Procedures.cfm.

Exercise 3

1. Ive just discovered that for most of this century, Yellowstone National Park in the United States hasnt had any wolves in it.

2. With the help of an act of U.S. Congress in 1914, theyd been killed off in an effort to get rid of predators in Yellowstone and on other public lands.

3. Now its obvious that the policy was a mistake; people realized that Yellowstone wouldnt be complete without its wolves.

4. The U.S. Endangered Species Act in 1973 helped to start the plan of putting wolves back into Yellowstone, but its taken twenty years to get to the point where theyre actually being released.

5. The first wolves to be moved were from Alberta; thats where the land is similar to Yellowstone's and where theres no disease among the wolf population.

6. Once transplanted to Yellowstone, the Canadian wolves were kept in pens so that they wouldnt just try to go back home once released into the park.

7. But feeding the wolves in their half-hectare-sized pens wasnt easy; its illegal to use motor vehicles in the wild part of Yellowstone, so the wolves' food had to be brought in on sleds pulled by mules.

8. Other animals dont like wolves, so as soon as a mule saw the hungry wolves circling for dinner, the mule wouldnt go any further; thats a problem which was eventually solved.

9. In March of 1995, the gate was opened on one of the pens to release the first group of wolves back into their natural habitat, but the wolves wouldnt use the gate.

10. Scientists realized that they shouldve known that the wolves wouldnt trust the opening that the humans used, so a hole was made in the fence near the spot where the wolves felt most comfortable, and thats where the wolves made their escape to freedom in Yellowstone.

Source: The Wolves of Yellowstone (San Diego: Voyageur Press, 1996).

Exercise 4

1. Im sure youve heard of Barbie and Ken, the famous toy couple.

2. These two may be boyfriend and girlfriend in their doll lives, but they werent that way to begin with.

3. In real life, shes his sister, hes her brother, and theyre both the children of Ruth Handler, whos the inventor of the Barbie doll.

4. Handler named the dolls after her own daughter and son, but thats where the similarity ends.

5. The Barbie doll was an idea that came when Handler noticed that her young daughter, Barbie, wanted to play with realistic, grown-up looking dolls instead of baby or little girl dolls.

6. Thats where the Barbie weve all seen got her start, and shes got lots of accessories and outfits that wouldnt fit any other doll.

7. When Barbie was first introduced at a toy show in 1959, the reaction wasnt positive at all.

8. Handler's idea didnt need any help in the stores, however; Barbie made $500 million by the late 1960s, and shes been extremely popular ever since.

9. Handler's husband, Elliot, co-founded the Mattel company before Barbie came along, and hes responsible for the success of its toy furniture and musical instruments.

10. Ruth Handler doesnt take anything for granted; shes used her life experiences in another positive way by helping design a more natural-looking artificial breast after her own bout with breast cancer.

Source: Mothers of Invention (New York: Morrow, 1988).

Exercise 5

1. Wouldnt it be nice not to worry about what we should or shouldnt eat to stay healthy?

2. Im definitely suspicious of some of the news stories about food.

3. For instance, one study supposedly showed that feeding sugar to children doesnt raise their activity levels or make them hard to control.

4. Lets just say that anyone whos got children isnt going to believe that study for a minute.

5. Weve seen the effects of a candy bar eaten right before its time for a child to go to bed.

6. Wheres that group of scientists when youre carpooling the kids to a soccer game and theyve all had two cans of pop and a bag of jelly beans?

7. No, I wont believe those findings until Ive seen every experiment with my own eyes.

8. Most of us havent followed all the rules of good eating because as soon as we cut out one oil or seasoning, another study says its okay after all.

9. Im sure well never hear the end of these suggestions, however.

10. Theyre part of whats called "news," and lets face it, we all want to know whats best for us.

PROOFREADING EXERCISE

Can you correct the ten errors in this student paragraph? They could be from any of the areas studied so far.

Iv'e had trouble excepting the fact that I cant learn to speak German. I have taken first- and second-year German, but their was'nt much speaking in either of those too classes. My mouth doesn't make the write sounds when I try to say German words. I think that my teeth get in the way. I have decided to ask my teacher for advise but cant bring myself to go see her because I know that shes going to ask me to tell her about my problem — in German.

SENTENCE WRITING

Doing exercises helps you learn a rule, but even more helpful is using the rule in writing. Write ten sentences using contractions. You might write about your reaction to the week's big news story, or you can choose your own subject.

Possessives

The trick in writing possessives is to ask yourself the question, "Who (or what) does it belong to?" (Modern usage has made *who* acceptable when it comes first in a sentence, but some people still say, "*Whom* does it belong to?" or even "*To whom* does it belong?") If the answer to your question doesn't end in *s,* then add an apostrophe and *s*. If the answer to your question ends in *s*, add an apostrophe. Then you must see if you need another sound to make the possessive clear. If you need another *s* sound, add the apostrophe and another *s* (as in the last of the following examples).

one girl (uniform)	Who does it belong to?	girl	Add *'s*	girl's uniform
two girls (uniforms)	Who do they belong to?	girls	Add *'*	girls' uniforms
a man (coat)	Who does it belong to?	man	Add *'s*	man's coat
men (hats)	Who do they belong to?	men	Add *'s*	men's hats
children (game)	Who does it belong to?	children	Add *'s*	children's game
a month (pay)	What does it belong to?	month	Add *'s*	month's pay
Brahms (Lullaby)	Who does it belong to?	Brahms	Add *'*	Brahms' Lullaby
my boss (office)	Who does it belong to?	boss	Add *'s*	boss's office

This trick will always work, but you must ask the question every time. Remember that the key word is *belong*. Who (or what) does it belong to? If you ask the question another way, you may get an answer that won't help you. Also, if you just look at a word without asking the question, you may think the name of the owner ends in *s* when it really doesn't.

TO MAKE A POSSESSIVE

   1. Ask "Who (or what) does it belong to?"
   2. If the answer doesn't end in *s*, add an apostrophe and *s*.
   3. If the answer ends in *s*, add just an apostrophe *or* an apostrophe and *s* if you need the extra sound to show a possessive (as in *boss's office*).

E X E R C I S E S

Follow the directions carefully for each of the following exercises. Because possessives can be tricky, explanations follow some exercises to help you understand them better.

Exercise 1

Cover the right column and see if you can write the following possessives correctly. Ask the question "Who (or what) does it belong to?" each time. Don't look at the answer before you try!

1. an employee (qualifications)	_____	an employee's qualifications
2. the women (gym)	_____	the women's gym
3. Davorka (degree)	_____	Davorka's degree
4. James (major)	_____	James' or James's major
5. the Johnsons (house)	_____	the Johnsons' house
6. Ms. Yamamoto (trees)	_____	Ms. Yamamoto's trees
7. Russ (computer)	_____	Russ's computer
8. the baby (feet)	_____	the baby's feet
9. the babies (feet)	_____	the babies' feet
10. a country (laws)	_____	a country's laws

(Sometimes you may see a couple of choices when the word ends in s. *James' major* may be written *James's major*. That is also correct, depending on how you want your reader to say it. Be consistent when given such choices.)

> **NOTE:** Don't assume that any word that ends in s is a possessive. The s may indicate more than one of something, a plural noun. Make sure the word actually possesses something before you add an apostrophe.

A few commonly used words are already possessive and don't need an apostrophe added to them. Memorize this list:

our, ours	its
your, yours	their, theirs
his, her, hers	whose

Note particularly *its, their, whose,* and *your.* They are already possessive and don't take an apostrophe. (These words sound like *it's, they're, who's,* and *you're,* which are *contractions* that use an apostrophe in place of their missing letters.)

Exercise 2

Cover the right column below and see if you can write the correct form. The answer might be a *contraction* or a *possessive.* If you miss any, go back and review the explanations.

1. (It) been raining.	It's
2. (You) car needs washing.	Your
3. (Who) keys are these?	Whose
4. The hurricane lost (it) force.	its
5. I don't know (who) been invited.	who's
6. (They) shopping for a television.	They're
7. (It) time to turn in the quizzes.	It's
8. (They) minivan seats seven.	Their
9. These are my books; are those (her)?	hers
10. (You) a real friend to me.	You're

Exercise 3

Here's another chance to check your progress with possessives. Cover the right column again as you did in Exercises 1 and 2, and add apostrophes to the possessives. Each answer is followed by an explanation.

1. Our neighbours went to their grandparents house.	grandparents' (You didn't add an apostrophe to *neighbours,* did you? The neighbours don't possess anything.)
2. The students bus broke down during their field trip.	students' (Who does the bus belong to?)
3. I invited Kyoko to my friends party.	friend's (if it belongs to one friend), friends' (two or more friends)
4. Two of my sisters went to my dads alma mater.	dad's (The sisters don't possess anything in the sentence.)
5. Sandeeps apartment is similar to yours.	Sandeep's (*Yours* is already possessive and doesn't take an apostrophe.)

6. Last months tips were the best yet.	month's (The tips belonged to last month.)
7. The Rogers farm house is just a house outside of town.	The Rogers' (Who does the farm belong to?)
8. The womens team played the mens team.	women's, men's (Did you ask who each team belongs to?)
9. The jurors handed the judge their verdict.	No apostrophe. *Their* is already possessive, and the jurors don't possess anything in the sentence.
10. The sign by the gate said, "The Lams."	Lams (meaning that the Lams live there) or Lams' (meaning that it's the Lams' house)

Exercises 4 and 5

Now you're ready to put the apostrophe in each possessive that follows. But be careful. *First*, make sure the word really possesses something; not every word ending in *s* is a possessive. *Second*, remember that certain words are already possessive and don't take an apostrophe. *Third*, remember that even though a word ends in *s*, you can't tell where the apostrophe goes until you ask the question, "Who (or what) does it belong to?" Check your answers at the back of the book after the first set.

Exercise 4

1. The snowmobiles history goes back just 50 years.

2. What began as an idea to help transport people and cargo through Canadas deep snow has developed into one of winters most popular recreational activities.

3. Until the snowmobile was manufactured, people, especially those in the far North, relied on the power and stamina of dogsled teams to haul cargo and family.

4. In 1922, when he was only 15 years old, J. Armand Bombardier of Valcourt, Quebec, developed the first snowmobile. The snowmobiles earliest design consisted of a sleigh with an attached car engine. In 1937, Bombardiers application for a patent was granted.

5. The inventions initial use was applied to the military, but the market was very small. By 1959, he created a new model, which consisted of a steering wheel and propulsion on a single track. It later became known as the "Ski-Doo®."

6. By the late 1960s, the Ski-Doos fame spread throughout the Canadian North and transformed the social life of Inuit and arctic communities.

7. From sales of 225 in 1959, this recreational vehicles sales soared to such an extent that there were about 700 000 households in Canada with at least one snowmobile.

8. Despite the rapid growth of snowmobile manufacturers in North America, Bombardier never yielded its lead and remained the worlds largest.

9. The publics use of snowmobiles for recreation created a new set of safety concerns.

10. By 1972, most provinces legislation restricted the use of snowmobiles, but the provision of extensive trails promoted the sport in many regions.

Sources: 1) *The Canadian Encyclopedia,* s. v. "Bombardier."
2) http://www.Bombardier.com/htmen/10_0.htm
3) http://www.capcan.ca/english/canadiana/inventions/bombardier3.html

Exercise 5

1. I was stunned by a 1998 news report of a young mans accomplishment in Costa Rica: Geovanny Escalante had broken a world record previously held by Kenny G.

2. Specifically, Escalante surpassed the famous saxaphonists record for continually blowing one musical note on a saxophone.

3. Kenny Gs record-setting note had lasted for longer than 45 minutes.

4. But Escalante was able to maintain his musical note for more than an hour and a half.

5. While it may seem unbelievable for someone to blow for that long, musicians have developed a way of blowing and breathing at the same time that makes it possible.

6. To be sure that Escalantes record would be accepted by Guinness, the young mans performance was videotaped.

7. And a couple of lawyers, notary publics, and even Escalantes parents were on hand to witness the event.

8. Guinnesss research staff should be satisfied with such documentation.

9. In the meantime, the bar in which the record-breaking note was played is cashing in on Escalantes success.

10. I imagine a world record holders biggest fear is that someone like Geovanny Escalante will come along and take it away.

PROOFREADING EXERCISE

Find the five errors in this student paragraph. All of the errors involve possessives.

The Labelles are a family that has lived next door to me for twenty years. I have grown up with the Labelle's daughter, Nicole. My family is bigger than her's. When I go to her house, Nicoles favourite pastime is doing jigsaw puzzles. We always start off by separating a puzzles pieces into different categories. She makes piles of edge pieces, sky pieces, flower pieces, and so on. Then I start putting the edge piece's together to form the border. The Labelles' son is named Marc, and he usually shows up just in time to put the last piece in the puzzle.

SENTENCE WRITING

Write ten sentences using the possessive forms of the names of members of your family or the names of your friends. You could write about a recent event where your family or friends got together. Just tell the story of what happened that day.

REVIEW OF CONTRACTIONS AND POSSESSIVES

Here are two review exercises. First, add the necessary apostrophes to the following sentences. Try to get all the correct answers. Don't excuse an error by saying, "Oh, that was just a careless mistake." A mistake is a mistake. Be tough on yourself.

1. Ive never looked forward to anything on TV as much as I did *Seinfeld*s last episode.

2. The shows premise wasnt hard to understand — it was about nothing.

3. Im sure that many viewers waited anxiously to see what would become of televisions favourite group of misfits — Jerry, George, Elaine, and Kramer — in the series final moments.

4. Although there wasnt any way to know in advance what would or wouldnt happen, part of the last shows script was leaked to the press.

5. There would be a plane crash, and while the plane was going down, Elaine was supposedly going to confess her love for Jerry.

6. There actually was plane trouble in the last show, but the plane recovered its power just before a crash.

7. Most of the final shows scenes took place in court, where the four friends were on trial for not trying to stop a mugging that theyd all witnessed.

8. The four main characters earlier despicable actions were shown in the form of flashbacks while the witnesses testimonies were being given.

9. The jurys verdict was "guilty," but I wouldve liked to see them acquitted since theyre really no worse than many of the rest of us.

10. Jerry, George, Elaine, and Kramer are off to prison in the end, yet theres no doubt that its a show that will be seen in reruns for a long time to come.

Second, add the necessary apostrophes to the following short student essay.

Going to the Globe

I was very fortunate to attend a high school where theres an English teacher, Ms. Evans, who absolutely loves Shakespeare. Ever since shed heard that a new Globe Theatre was being built in London, England, shed been saying, "Im going to see it as soon as its finished, and Ill take a group of students with me."

Shakespeares original Globe Theatre had been destroyed by a fire in 1613 during a performance of one of his plays, and it hadnt been rebuilt since then. Im one of the lucky students who accompanied Ms. Evans on her first trip to the new Globe.

When we arrived in London, Ms. Evans excitement rubbed off on all of us. We found the Globes location just across the Thames River from another of Londons most famous landmarks — Big Ben.

The theatres outside was just as beautiful as its inside, and it smelled like freshly cut lumber. In fact, thats what its almost entirely made of. Theres not a nail used in the whole outer frame structure. The huge wooden beams visible from the outside are held in place with more than 6000 wooden pegs, just as they wouldve been in Shakespeares time.

We didnt get to see a performance at the Globe, but the tour guides description of one of them made it possible to imagine an audiences excitement, an actors challenges, and a playwrights satisfaction at the rebuilding of his Globe Theatre.

Words That Can Be Broken into Parts

Breaking words into their parts will often help you spell them correctly. Each of the following words is made up of two shorter words. Note that the word then contains all the letters of the two shorter words.

chalk board	... chalkboard	room mate	... roommate
over due	... overdue	home work	... homework
super market	... supermarket	under line	... underline

Becoming aware of prefixes such as *dis, inter, mis,* and *un* is also helpful. When you add a prefix to a word, note that no letters are dropped, either from the prefix or from the word.

dis appear	... disappear	mis represent	... misrepresent
dis appoint	... disappoint	mis spell	... misspell
dis approve	... disapprove	mis understood	... misunderstood
dis satisfy	... dissatisfy	un aware	... unaware

inter act	...	interact	un involved	...	uninvolved
inter active	...	interactive	un necessary	...	unnecessary
inter related	...	interrelated	un sure	...	unsure

Have someone dictate the above list for you to write, and then mark any words you miss. Memorize the correct spellings by noting how each word is made up of a prefix and a word.

Rule for Doubling a Final Letter

Most spelling rules have so many exceptions that they aren't much help. But here's one worth learning because it has only a few exceptions.

Double a final letter [consonants only] when adding an ending that begins with a vowel (such as *ing, ed, er*) if all three of the following are true:

1. the word ends in a single consonant,

2. which is preceded by a single vowel (the vowels are *a, e, i, o, u*),

3. and the accent is on the last syllable (or the word only has one syllable).

This is not, however, always the Canadian preference. Sometimes the final letters *l, p, s, t* are doubled when the accent in a word with more than one syllable is *not* on the last syllable (travelled, focussed). When in doubt, look up the first choice in a Canadian dictionary. The main rule here is to be consistent, whichever choice you make.

We'll try the rule on a few words to which we'll add *ing, ed,* or *er.*

begin   **1.** It ends in a single consonant — *n,*
 2. is preceded by a single vowel — *i,*
 3. and the accent is on the last syllable — *be gin´.*
 Therefore we double the final consonant and write *beginning, beginner.*

stop   **1.** It ends in a single consonant —*p,*
 2. is preceded by a single vowel — *o,*
 3. and the accent is on the last syllable (there is only one).
 Therefore we double the final consonant and write *stopping, stopped, stopper.*

filter   **1.** It ends in a single consonant — *r,*
 2. is preceded by a single vowel — *e,*
 3. but the accent isn't on the last syllable. It's on the first —*fil´ter.*
 Therefore we don't double the final consonant. We write *filtering, filtered.*

keep   **1.** It ends in a single consonant —*p,*
 2. but it isn't preceded by a single vowel. There are two *e*'s.
 Therefore we don't double the final consonant. We write *keeping, keeper.*

> **NOTE:** Be aware that *qu* is treated as a consonant because *q* is almost never written without *u*. Think of it as *kw*. In words like *equip* and *quit*, the *qu* acts as a consonant. Therefore *equip* and *quit* both end in a single consonant preceded by a single vowel, and the final consonant is doubled in *equipped* and *quitting*.

E X E R C I S E S

Add *ing* to these words. Correct each group of ten before continuing so you'll catch any errors while you still have words to practise on.

Exercise 1

1. get	**6.** miss
2. trust	**7.** read
3. trip	**8.** occur
4. plan	**9.** skim
5. benefit	**10.** scream

Exercise 2

1. shop	**6.** omit
2. offer	**7.** honour
3. wrap	**8.** brag
4. nail	**9.** mark
5. knit	**10.** hop

Exercise 3

1. steam	**6.** wed
2. expel	**7.** stress
3. sip	**8.** flop
4. suffer	**9.** spin
5. war	**10.** differ

Exercise 4

1. creep	**6.** weed
2. subtract	**7.** fog
3. abandon	**8.** drop
4. droop	**9.** refer
5. happen	**10.** submit

Exercise 5

1. interpret	**6.** infer
2. prefer	**7.** guess
3. bet	**8.** bug
4. stoop	**9.** jog
5. flip	**10.** build

Progress Test

This test covers everything you've studied so far. One sentence in each pair is correct. The other is incorrect. Read both sentences carefully before you decide. Then write the letter of the incorrect sentence in the blank. Try to isolate and correct the error if you can.

1. ___ **A.** The Powell's house is the one next to ours.

       B. Their children's voices are too soft to hear.

2. ___ **A.** I don't know whether I'll go on the field trip or not.

       B. I'm sure it won't have any affect on our grade.

3. ___ **A.** It's important to chose your friends carefully.

       B. After I lied, my conscience bothered me for days.

4. ___ **A.** My father lost his voice but refused to stay quite.

       B. He should have listened to our advice.

5. ___ **A.** His neat printing complemented her organization skills.

       B. They submited their scholarship applications together.

6. ___ **A.** Whose going to plan our vacation this year?

       B. Equipping ourselves for a camping trip can take weeks.

7. ___ **A.** Last month, Liz led the class in quiz scores and extra credit.

       B. She should of worked that hard all semester.

8. ___ **A.** Let me know when we've past 100 000 km on the odometer.

       B. That's the point when an engine might choose to break down.

9. ___ **A.** My supervisor complimented me on a good day's work.

       B. I took a coffee brake in the employees' lounge.

10. ___ **A.** Their dog dragged it's favourite toy across the floor.

       B. I couldn't tell whether they thought it was cute or not.

Using a Dictionary

Some dictionaries are more helpful than others. A tiny pocket-sized dictionary or one that fits on a single sheet in your notebook might help you find the spelling of very common words, but for all other uses, you will need a complete, recently published dictionary. For Canadian preferences in spelling and usage, use an up-to-date Canadian dictionary, such as the *Gage Canadian Dictionary, The Oxford Canadian Dictionary, or the ITP Nelson Canadian Dictionary*. A good Canadian dictionary will also include Canadian idioms, proper names, and geographic designations. Note that dictionaries may not always agree on the Canadian standard.

Work through the following thirteen exercises using a good dictionary. Then you will understand what a valuable resource it is.

1. Pronunciation

Look up the word *hyperbole* and copy the pronunciation here.

_____

_____

_____

_____

Now under each letter with a pronunciation mark over it, write the key word having the same mark. You'll find the key words at the bottom or top of one of the two dictionary pages open before you. Note especially that the upside-down *e* (ə) always has the sound of *uh* like the *a* in *ago* or *about*. Remember that sound because it's found in many words.

Next, pronounce the key words you have written, and then slowly pronounce *hyperbole*, giving each syllable the same sound as its key word.

Finally, note which syllable has the heavy accent mark. (In most dictionaries the accent mark points to the stressed syllable, but in one dictionary it is in front of the stressed syllable.) The stressed syllable is *per*. Now say the word, letting the full force of your voice fall on that syllable.

When more than one pronunciation is given, the first is more common. If the complete pronunciation of a word isn't given, look at the word above it to find the pronunciation.

Look up the pronunciation of these words, using the key words at the bottom of the dictionary page to help you pronounce each syllable. Then note which syllable has the heavy accent mark, and say the word aloud.

aubade   malign   longitude   piquant

2. Definitions

The dictionary may give more than one meaning for a word. Read all the meanings for each italicized word, and then write a definition appropriate to the sentence.

1. Parsa and Isabella have an M.A. and a Ph.D., *respectively.* _____

_____

2. She was chosen to be the *penultimate* speaker at the conference. _____

_____

3. They took their *biennial* trip to Banff. _____

_____

4. As a lifeguard, he suffered from a *sporadic* fear of water. _____

_____

3. Spelling

By making yourself look up each word you aren't sure how to spell, you'll soon become a better speller. When two spellings are given in the dictionary, the first one (or the one with the definition) is preferred. In a Canadian dictionary, the first one is the Canadian preference.

Use a dictionary to find the preferred spelling for each of these words. Canadian and American dictionaries may differ in their preference.

cancelled, canceled   dialog, dialogue

judgment, judgement   gray, grey

4. Compound Words

If you want to find out whether two words are written separately, written with a hyphen between them, or written as one word, consult your dictionary. For example:

second cousin   is written as two words

sister-in-law   is hyphenated

stepchild   is written as one word

Write each of the following correctly:

mix up   _____   left handed _____

on going _____   week day   _____

5. Capitalization

If a word is capitalized in the dictionary, that means it should always be capitalized. If it is not capitalized in the dictionary, then it may or may not be capitalized, depending on how it is used (see p. 184). For example, *Asian* is always capitalized, but *school* is capitalized or not, according to how it is used.

Last year, I graduated from high school.

Last year, I graduated from Laura Secord Secondary School.

Write the following words as they're given in the dictionary (with or without a capital) to show whether they must always be capitalized or not. Take a guess before looking them up.

democracy   _____   maple leaf _____

thanksgiving _____   french   _____

6. Usage

Just because a word is in the dictionary doesn't mean that it's in standard use. The following labels indicate whether a word is used today and, if so, where and by whom.

obsolete	no longer used
archaic	not now used in ordinary language but still found in some biblical, literary, and legal expressions
colloquial, informal	used in informal conversation but not in formal writing
dialectal, regional	used in some localities but not everywhere
slang	popular but nonstandard expression
nonstandard, substandard	not used in Standard Written English

Look up each italicized word and write the label indicating its usage for the meaning used in the sentence. Dictionaries differ. One may list a word as slang whereas another will call it colloquial. Still another may give no designation, thus indicating that that particular dictionary considers the word in standard use.

1. The hula hoop was a *fad* that began in the 1950s. _____

2. You *guys* don't know how to have fun anymore. _____

3. That *tidbit* of gossip made my day. _____

4. I got a *cool* new pair of boots._____

5. We would like to *bum* around with you all summer. _____

7. Derivations

The derivations or stories behind words will often help you remember the current meanings. For example, if you read that someone is *narcissistic* and you consult your dictionary, you'll find that *narcissism* is a condition named after Narcissus, who was a handsome young man in Greek mythology. One day Narcissus fell in love with his own reflection in a pool, but when he tried to get closer to it, he fell in the water and drowned. A flower that grew nearby is now named for Narcissus. And *narcissistic* has come to mean "in love with oneself."

Look up the derivation of each of these words. You'll find it in square brackets either just before or just after the definition.

Procrustean _____

rigmarole (or rigamarole) _____

malapropism_____

Gordian _____

8. Synonyms

At the end of a definition, a group of synonyms is sometimes given. For example, at the end of the definition of *injure*, you'll find several synonyms, such as *damage* or *harm*. And if you look up *damage* or *harm*, you'll be referred to the same synonyms listed under *injure*.

List the synonyms given for the following words.

native _____

plan _____

summit_____

9. Abbreviations

Find the meaning of the following abbreviations.

R.S.V.P. _____   e.g. _____

P.S. _____   R.N. _____

10. Names of People

The names of famous people will sometimes be found either in the main part of your dictionary or in a separate biographical names section at the back.

Identify the following famous people.

Mohammed _____

M. Montessori _____

A. Kurosawa _____

N. Mandela _____

11. Names of Places

The names of places will sometimes be found either in the main part of your dictionary or in a separate geographical names section at the back.

Identify the following places.

Liverpool _____

Quanzhou _____

Mount Ossa _____

Ka Lae _____

12. Foreign Words and Phrases

Find the language and the meaning of the italicized expressions.

1. A child's mind seems like much more than a *tabula rasa.* _____

2. We were given *carte blanche* to gamble at the casino. _____

3. I met my *doppelgänger* in a Montreal airport. _____

13. Miscellaneous Information

See if you can find these miscellaneous bits of information in a dictionary.

1. What part of its body does a *gastropod* walk on? _____

2. How many zeroes does a *googol* have? _____

3. Who named the *googol*? _____

4. In what year did *virtual reality* become an expression? _____

5. What sound does *tintinnabulation* refer to? _____

Sentence Structure

Sentence structure refers to the way sentences are built using words, phrases, and clauses. Words are single units, and words link up in sentences to form clauses and phrases. Clauses are word groups *with* subjects and verbs, and phrases are word groups *without* subjects and verbs. Clauses are the most important because they make statements — they tell who did what (or what something is) in a sentence. Look at the following sentence for example:

We bought oranges at the farmer's market on Queen Street.

It contains ten words, each playing its own part in the meaning of the sentence. But which of the words together tell who did what? *We bought oranges* is correct. That word group is a clause. Notice that *at the farmer's market* and *on Queen Street* also link up as word groups but don't have somebody (subject) doing something (verb). Instead, they are phrases to clarify *where* we bought the oranges.

Importantly, you could leave out one or both of the phrases and still have a sentence — *We bought oranges*. However, you cannot leave the clause out. Then you would just have *At the farmer's market on Queen Street*. Remember, every sentence needs at least one clause that can stand by itself.

Learning about the structure of sentences helps you control your own. Once you know more about sentence structure, then you can understand writing errors and learn how to correct them.

Among the most common errors in writing are fragments, run-ons, and awkward phrasing.

Here are some fragments:

Wandering around the mall all afternoon.

Because I tried to do too many things at once.

By interviewing the applicants in groups.

They don't make complete statements — not one has a clause that can stand by itself. Who was *wandering*? What happened *because you tried to do too many things at once*? What was the result of *interviewing the applicants in groups*? These incomplete sentence structures fail to communicate a complete thought.

In contrast, here are some run-ons:

Computer prices are dropping they're still beyond my budget.

The forecast calls for rain I'll wait to wash my car.

A truck parked in front of my driveway I couldn't get to school.

Unlike fragments, run-ons make complete statements, but the trouble is they make *two* complete statements; the first *runs on* to the second without correct punctuation. The reader has to go back to see where there should have been a break.

So fragments don't include enough information, and run-ons include too much. Another problem occurs when the information in a sentence just doesn't make sense.

Here are a few sentences with awkward phrasing:

The problem from my grades started to end.

It was a time at the picnic.

She won me at chess.

Try to find the word groups that show who did what, that is, the clauses. Once you find them, then try to put the clauses and phrases together to form a precise meaning. It's difficult, isn't it? You'll see that many of the words themselves are misused or unclear, such as *from*, *it*, and *won*. These sentences don't communicate clearly because the clauses, phrases, and even words don't work together. They suffer from awkward phrasing.

Fragments, run-ons, awkward phrasing, and other sentence structure errors confuse the reader. Not until you get rid of them will your writing be clearer and easier to read. Unfortunately there is no quick, effortless way to learn to avoid errors in sentence structure. First, you need to understand how clear sentences are built. Then you will be able to avoid common errors in your own writing.

This section will describe areas of sentence structure one at a time and then explain how to correct errors associated with the different areas. For instance, we start by helping you find subjects and verbs and understand dependent clauses; then we show you how to avoid fragments. You can go through the whole section yourself to master all of the areas. Or your teacher may assign only parts based on errors the class is making.

Finding Subjects and Verbs

The most important words in a sentence are those that make up its independent clause, the subject and the verb. When you write a sentence, you write about *something* or *someone*. That's the subject. Then you write what the subject *does* or *is*. That's the verb.

Lightning strikes.

The word *Lightning* is the something you are writing about. It's the subject, and we'll underline it once. *Strikes* tells what the subject does. It shows the action in the sentence. It's the verb, and we'll underline it twice. But most sentences do not include only two words — the subject and the verb. However, these two words still make up the core of the sentence even if other words and phrases are included with them.

Lightning strikes back and forth from the clouds to the ground very quickly.

Often lightning strikes people on golf courses or in boats.

When many words appear in sentences, the subject and verb can be hard to find. Because the verb often shows action, it's easier to spot than the subject. Therefore, always look for it first. For example, in the sentence

The neighbourhood cat folded its paws under its chest.

which word shows the action? Folded. It's the verb. Underline it twice. Now ask yourself who or what folded? Cat. It's the subject. Underline it once.

Study the following sentences until you understand how to pick out subjects and verbs.

Tomorrow our school celebrates its fiftieth anniversary. (Which word shows the action? Celebrates. It's the verb. Underline it twice. Who or what celebrates? School. It's the subject. Underline it once.)

The team members ate several boxes of chocolates. (Which word shows the action? Ate. Who or what ate? Members ate.)

Internet users crowd the popular services. (Which word shows the action? Crowd. Who or what crowd? Users crowd.)

Often the verb doesn't show action but merely tells what the subject *is* or *was*. Learn to spot such verbs — *is, am, are, was, were, seems, feels, appears, becomes, looks* ... (For more information on these verbs, see the discussion of sentence patterns on pp. 122–24).

Sasha is a neon artist. (First spot the verb is. Then ask who or what is? Sasha is.)

The bread appears mouldy. (First spot the verb appears. Then ask who or what appears? Bread appears.)

Sometimes the subject comes after the verb.

In the audience were two reviewers from *The Globe and Mail.* (Who or what were in the audience? Reviewers were.)

There was a fortune-teller at the carnival. (Who or what was there? Fortune-teller was there.)

There were name tags for all the participants. (Who or what were there? Name tags were there.)

Here are the worksheets. (Who or what are here? Worksheets are here.)

NOTE: Remember that *there* and *here* (as in the last three sentences) are not subjects. They simply point to something.

In commands, often the subject is not expressed. It is *you* (understood).

Sit down. (You sit down.)

Place flap A into slot B. (You place flap A into slot B.)

Meet me at 7:00. (You meet me at 7:00.)

There may be more than one subject in a sentence.

Toys and memorabilia from the 1950s are high-priced collectables.

Celebrity dolls, board games, and even cereal boxes from that decade line the shelves of antique stores.

There may also be more than one verb.

Water boils at a consistent temperature and freezes at another.

The ice tray fell out of my hand, skidded across the floor, and landed under the table.

As you pick out subjects in the following exercises, you may wonder whether you should say the subject is, for example, *forecasts* or *weather forecasts*. It makes no difference so long as you get the main subject, *forecasts*, right. In the answers at the back of the book, usually — but not always — the single word is used. Don't waste your time worrying whether to include an extra word with the subject. Just make sure you get the main subjects right.

E X E R C I S E S

Underline the subjects once and the verbs twice. When you've finished ten sentences, compare your answers carefully with those at the back of the book.

Exercise 1

1. Weather forecasts affect many people.

2. But they are not always correct.

3. Sometimes rain and wind arrive instead of sunny skies.

4. Travellers need accurate weather predictions.

5. There are many possible dangers in travelling.

6. A hurricane is never a welcome event on a vacation.

7. At times, the weather seems more enemy than friend.

8. Often the skies cooperate with people's travel plans.

9. At times like this, the sun shines as if by special request.

10. Then the weather is perfect and feels like a friend again.

Exercise 2

1. There is a long-standing tradition in aviation.

2. Passengers get peanuts and a drink as a mid-flight snack.

3. Any drink tastes better with peanuts.

4. And the tiny foil packages please people.

5. But peanuts are dangerous to passengers with peanut allergies.

6. Most people eat peanuts and feel fine.

7. A mildly allergic person gets watery eyes and hives.

8. In extreme cases, people with peanut allergies die.

9. So, many airlines propose peanut-free zones on airplanes.

10. Needless to say, peanut companies are not happy about the proposal.

Exercise 3

1. I never knew much about curses and magic spells.

2. According to a magazine article, the Greeks and Romans used them all the time.

3. There were magicians for hire back then.

4. These magicians made money through their knowledge of the art of cursing.

5. Some people took revenge on their enemies with special curses for failure.

6. Others wanted only love and placed spells on the objects of their desires.

7. The magicians wrote the commissioned curses or love spells on lead tablets.

8. Then they positioned these curse tablets near their intended victims.

9. Archeologists found one 1700-year-old curse tablet over the starting gate of an ancient race course.

10. It named the horses and drivers of specific chariots and itemized the specifics of the curse.

Source: Smithsonian, Apr. 1996.

Exercise 4

1. Plastic snow domes are popular souvenir items.

2. They are clear domes usually on white oval bases.

3. People display these water-filled objects or use them as paperweights.

4. Inside are tiny replicas of famous tourist attractions like the Eiffel Tower or Big Ben.

5. Snow or glitter mixes with the water for a snowstorm effect.

6. These souvenirs often hold startling combinations.

7. In a snow dome, even the Bahamas has blizzards.

8. There is also a dome with smog instead of snow.

9. Some people consider snow domes valuable collectables.

10. Others just buy them as inexpensive mementos.

Exercise 5

1. In Canada, there is a widespread concern about endangered species.

2. Habitat loss causes about 80 percent of animal extinction.

3. The International Fund for Animal Welfare designed a survey to test the public response to plans for a new federal bill to protect the environment.

4. The proposed federal bill protects swamps, wetlands, and forests, and safeguards the animals that live there.

5. It regulates both public and private land.

6. In addition, it guarantees the right to government compensation to landowners who encounter financial hardship as a result of habitat protection measures.

7. Provincial governments, however, argue that land management is their jurisdiction.

8. Environmental groups criticize provincial governments for not doing enough to protect endangered species.

9. Sometimes habitat protection requires complete banning of industrial activity in a given area, but some species have less extensive requirements.

10. A skylark, for example, needs an open-field nesting site for only six weeks a year.

Source: "Report finds eighty percent of Canadians..." *The Globe and Mail,* 21 Sept. 1999.

PARAGRAPH EXERCISE

Underline the subjects once and the verbs twice in the following student paragraph.

My friend Maria spends every weekday afternoon in the school library. She does her homework, finishes her reading assignments, and organizes her notes and handouts. I envy her good study skills. She is always ready for the next day of class. I, however, go back to my apartment in the afternoon. There are so many distractions at home. The television blares, and my roommates invite their friends over. I am usually too tired to do school work. Maybe the library is a better place for me too.

SENTENCE WRITING

Write ten sentences about any subject — your favourite colour, for instance. Keeping your subject matter simple in these sentence writing exercises will make it easier to find your sentence structures later. After you have written your sentences, go back and underline your subjects once and your verbs twice.

Locating Prepositional Phrases

Prepositional phrases are among the easiest structures in English to learn. Remember that a phrase is just a group of words (at least two) without a subject and a verb. And don't let a term like *prepositional* scare you. If you look in the middle of that long word, you'll find a familiar one — *position*. In English, we tell the *positions* of people and things in sentences using prepositional phrases. Look at the following sentence with its prepositional phrases in parentheses:

Our field trip (to the mountain) begins (at 6:00) (in the morning) (on Friday).

One phrase tells where the field trip is going (*to the mountain*), and three phrases tell when the trip begins (*at 6:00*, *in the morning*, and *on Friday*). As you can see, prepositional phrases show the position of someone or something in space or in time.

Here is a list of prepositions that can show positions in space:

above	behind	in	past
across	below	inside	through
against	between	near	to
among	beyond	on	under
around	by	outside	without
at	from	over	

Here are prepositions that can show positions in time:

after	by	in	throughout
at	during	past	until
before	for	since	within

These lists include only individual words, *not phrases*. Remember, a preposition must be followed by an object — someone or something — to create a prepositional phrase. Notice that in the added prepositional phrases that follow, the position of the plane in relation to the object, *the clouds*, changes completely.

The passenger plane flew *above the clouds.*
below the clouds.
within the clouds.
between the clouds.
past the clouds.
around the clouds.

Now notice the different positions in time:

The plane landed *at 3:30.*
by 3:30.
past 3:30.
before the thunderstorm.
during the thunderstorm.
after the thunderstorm.

NOTE: A few words — such as *of, as, like,* and *except* — are prepositions that do not fit neatly into either the space or time category, yet they are very common prepositions (box *of candy*, note *of apology*, type *of bicycle;* act *as a substitute*, use *as an example*, as happy *as my little brother;* vitamins *like A, C, and E*, shaped *like a watermelon*, moved *like a snake*, everyone *except Gilbert*, the whole house *except the upstairs washroom*, all knobs *except the red one*).

By locating prepositional phrases, you will be able to find subjects and verbs more easily. For example, you might have difficulty finding the subject and verb in a long sentence like this:

> After the rainy season, one of the windows in the attic leaked at the corners of its moulding.

But if you put parentheses around all the prepositional phrases like this

> (After the rainy season), one (of the windows) (in the attic) leaked (at the corners) (of its moulding).

then you have only two words left — the subject and the verb. Even in short sentences like the following, you might pick the wrong word as the subject if you don't put parentheses around the prepositional phrases first.

> Many (of the characters) survived (in that movie).

> The waves (around the ship) looked real.

NOTE: Don't mistake *to* plus a verb for a prepositional phrase. For example, *to quit* is not a prepositional phrase because *quit* is not the name of something. It's a form of verb.

E X E R C I S E S

Locate and put parentheses around the prepositional phrases in the following sentences. Be sure to start with the preposition itself (*in, on, to, at, of* ...) and include the word or words that go with it (*in the morning, on our sidewalk, to Halifax* ...). Then underline the subjects once and the verbs twice. Remember that subjects and verbs are never inside prepositional phrases. Review the answers given at the back for each group of ten sentences before continuing.

Exercise 1

1. Tornadoes are the fiercest of all weather patterns.
2. They begin during thunderstorms and bring with them rain, hail, and lightning.
3. The circling winds of a tornado often achieve speeds of 320 km per hour.
4. Most of the damage and many of the injuries come from flying debris.
5. Tornadoes normally travel across the land at about 48 km per hour.

6. But they sometimes move as quickly as a speeding car.

7. The part like a vacuum cleaner hose at the centre of the tornado pulls up anything in its path — automobiles, buildings, livestock.

8. Among their amazing tricks, tornadoes suck the fish and frogs out of small lakes and drop them on land in another location.

9. I like watching movies about tornadoes, like *The Wizard of Oz* and *Twister*.

10. But professional "storm chasers" like to watch the real ones.

Source: Weather (New York: Golden Press, 1987).

Exercise 2

1. The many cases of food poisoning in North America in the past few years alarm people.

2. Some food scientists point to food irradiation as one possible solution.

3. The irradiation of food kills bacteria through exposure to gamma rays.

4. With irradiation, farmers would need to spray fewer pesticides on their crops.

5. And irradiated food lasts longer on the shelf or in the refrigerator.

6. However, many scientists worry about the risks of food irradiation.

7. Irradiation reduces vitamins and alters nutrients in the food.

8. The radioactive materials at the irradiation plants are also potentially dangerous.

9. Critics predict accidents in the transportation and use of these radioactive substances.

10. In North America, the controversy about food irradiation continues.

Source: Popular Science, Jan. 1994.

Exercise 3

1. *Romeo and Juliet* is my favourite play by William Shakespeare.

2. It is one of the most famous love stories in the world.

3. Many movies use this story as part of their plots.

   4. One thing about the story surprised me.

   5. Both Romeo and Juliet have other love interests at some point in the play.

   6. Romeo has his eyes on another woman before Juliet.

   7. And after Tybalt's death, Juliet promises against her will to marry Paris.

   8. But before that, Juliet marries Romeo in secret.

   9. Friar Lawrence helps the newlyweds with a plan for them to escape without anyone's notice.

   10. However, the complicated timing of the plan has tragic results in the lives of Romeo and Juliet.

Exercise 4

   1. For a change of pace, I shopped for my Mother's Day gift at an antique mall.

   2. I found old jewellery in every shade of yellow, red, blue, and green.

   3. There were even linens from all the way back to pre-Confederation.

   4. One booth sold only drinking glasses with advertising slogans and cartoon characters on them.

   5. Another stocked old metal banks with elaborate mechanisms for children's pennies.

   6. In the back corner of the mall, I found a light blue pitcher with a dark blue design.

   7. My mother had had one like it in the early years of my childhood.

   8. My sisters and I drank punch from it on hot days in the summer.

   9. I checked the price on the tag underneath the pitcher's handle.

   10. But at a moment like that, money didn't matter.

Exercise 5

   1. Over the weekend, I watched a hilarious old movie, *Genevieve,* on late-night television.

   2. The whole story takes place in the countryside of England.

   3. It is a black-and-white movie from the 1930s or 1940s.

4. The clothes and manners of the characters in *Genevieve* are very proper and old-fashioned.

5. Two young couples enter their cars in a road rally for fun.

6. They participate in the race strictly for adventure.

7. Genevieve is the name of the main couple's car.

8. During the road rally, the two couples' polite manners disappear in the rush for the finish line.

9. Predictably, they begin to fight with each other and try to sabotage each other's cars.

10. But like all good comedies, *Genevieve* and its ending hold a surprise for everyone.

PARAGRAPH EXERCISE

Put parentheses around the prepositional phrases in this paragraph from *Vampires* by Daniel C. Scavone.

Folklore from all over the world reveals that people in many cultures throughout history have believed in some type of vampire. Many of the ancient vampires, however, do not resemble the ones we are familiar with from movies and books. ... [A]ncient vampires do not possess prominent canine teeth or fear garlic, the cross, and the dawn. These are modern touches, added by the writers of horror novels and films to intrigue and scare us.

SENTENCE WRITING

Write ten sentences on the topic of your favourite snack — or choose any topic you like. When you go back over your sentences, put parentheses around your prepositional phrases and underline your subjects once and your verbs twice.

Understanding Dependent Clauses

All clauses contain a subject and a verb; however, there are two kinds of clauses: independent and dependent. An independent clause has a subject and a verb and can stand alone as a sentence. A dependent clause has a subject and a verb but can't stand alone because it begins with a dependent word (or words) such as

after	since	where
although	so that	whereas
as	than	wherever
as if	that	whether
because	though	which
before	unless	whichever
even if	until	while
even though	what	who
ever since	whatever	whom
how	when	whose
if	whenever	why

Whenever a clause begins with one of these dependent words, it is a dependent clause (unless it's a question, which would be followed by a question mark). If we take an independent clause such as

<u>We ate</u> dinner together.

and put one of the dependent words in front of it, it becomes a dependent clause and can no longer stand alone:

After we ate dinner together ...

Although we ate dinner together ...

As we ate dinner together ...

Before we ate dinner together ...

Since we ate dinner together ...

That we ate dinner together ...

When we ate dinner together ...

While we ate dinner together ...

With the added dependent words, these do not make complete statements. They leave the reader expecting something more. Therefore, these clauses can no longer stand alone. Each would depend on another clause — an independent clause — to make a sentence. We'll place a broken line beneath the dependent clauses.

After we ate dinner together, we went to the evening seminar.

We went to the evening seminar *after* we ate dinner together.

The speaker didn't know *that* we ate dinner together.

While we ate dinner together, the restaurant became crowded.

Note that in the examples above, *when a dependent clause comes at the beginning of a sentence, it is followed by a comma.* Often the comma prevents misreading, as in the following sentence:

When he returned, the video was almost over.

Without a comma after *returned*, the reader would read *When he returned the video* before realizing that this was not what the author meant. The comma prevents misreading. Sometimes if the dependent clause is short and there is no danger of misreading, the comma can be left off, but it's safer simply to follow the rule that a dependent clause at the beginning of a sentence is followed by a comma.

You'll learn more about the punctuation of dependent clauses on page 165, but right now just remember this rule.

Note that sometimes the dependent word is the subject of the dependent clause:

Theirs is the house that was remodelled last month.

The children understood what was happening.

Sometimes the dependent clause is in the middle of the independent clause:

The house that was remodelled last month is theirs.

The events that followed were confusing.

And sometimes the dependent clause is the subject of the entire sentence:

> What you do also affects me.

> Whichever they choose will be best for them.

> How it looks doesn't mean anything.

Also note that sometimes the *that* of a dependent clause is omitted.

> I know *that* you can tell the difference between red and green.

> I know you can tell the difference between red and green.

> Did everyone get the classes *that* they wanted?

> Did everyone get the classes they wanted?

The word *that* doesn't always introduce a dependent clause. It may be a pronoun and serve as the subject of the sentence.

> That was a big mistake.

> That is my book.

That can also be a descriptive word.

> That movie makes me cry every time.

> I will take him to that restaurant tomorrow.

E X E R C I S E S

Underline the subjects once and the verbs twice in both the independent and the dependent clauses. Then put a broken line under the dependent clauses. Some sentences may have no dependent clauses, and others may have more than one.

Exercise 1

> **1.** I am not a big talker in school.

> **2.** Whenever a teacher asks me a question in class, I get nervous.

3. When I know the answer, I usually find the courage to speak.

4. If I don't know the answer, I look up at the ceiling as if I am thinking about it.

5. Usually, the teacher calls on someone else before I finish "thinking."

6. Obviously, when I take a public speaking class, I must talk sometimes.

7. In my last public speaking class, the assignment was to give a speech that demonstrated some sort of process.

8. The speech that I gave explained how crêpes are made.

9. Since I work at a French restaurant, I borrowed a crêpe pan to use in my demonstration.

10. The crêpes cooked quickly, and the teacher and students were so busy eating them that I didn't have to say much at all.

Exercise 2

1. Many of us remember when microwave ovens were first sold to the public.

2. People worried about whether they were safe or not.

3. Before we had the microwave oven, we cooked all of our food over direct heat.

4. At first, it was strange that only the food heated up in a microwave.

5. And microwave ovens cooked food so much faster than ordinary ovens did.

6. We had to get used to the possibilities that the microwave offered.

7. Since they are fast and don't heat up themselves, microwave ovens work well in offices, in restaurants, and on school campuses.

8. People who are on a budget can bring a lunch from home and heat it up at work.

9. Now that the microwave oven is here, we can even make popcorn without a pan.

10. As each new technology arrives, we wonder how we ever lived without it.

Exercise 3

1. When Canadians gather at sporting events, everyone sings "O Canada," while the Canadian flag proudly flies overhead.

2. "O Canada" is the song that Canada has chosen as its national anthem.

3. After Calixa Lavallée composed the music, the song was first performed at a banquet for skaters in Quebec City on June 24, 1880.

4. Adolphe-Basile Routhier wrote the French version, which he called "Chant national."

5. It was translated into English by Stanley Weir, who was a schoolteacher in Toronto.

6. Though French Canadians sang the anthem widely, English Canadians did not use it until the end of the nineteenth century.

7. When it gathered in 1967, the Parliament approved "O Canada" as the Canadian national anthem.

8. The words, which were altered somewhat after parliamentary debate, became official through the National Anthem Act, which was passed on June 27, 1980.

9. Canada's flag was hotly debated from Confederation to 1964, when the flag with the single red maple leaf became official.

10. Before that time, the United Kingdom's Union Jack was used for Canadian ceremonies, whether Canadian nationalists liked it or not.

Source: The Canadian Encyclopedia, s.v. "O Canada."

Exercise 4

1. Since we all want our documents to look perfect, we have probably used a bottle of white correction fluid at some time in our lives.

2. Liquid Paper or, as it was first known, "Mistake Out" was invented by Bette Nesmith (later Graham).

3. After the young bank secretary noticed that sign painters always painted over their errors instead of erasing them, she had an idea.

4. Nesmith started filling up small bottles with white paint, which she used to cover her typing mistakes.

5. As soon as her friends saw how well Nesmith's paint worked, they all wanted their own bottles.

6. Once she realized that the idea was a success, she developed a liquid that was more than just paint.

7. She patented her formula and called it Liquid Paper.

8. She decided to sell the product to a big corporation.

9. After IBM turned down Nesmith's invention, she formed The Liquid Paper Company herself and earned a large fortune.

10. Michael Nesmith, who is Bette Nesmith's son, helped his mother in her business even after he became a member of the famous singing group called The Monkees.

Source: Mothers of Invention (New York: Morrow, 1988).

Exercise 5

1. When I first heard the expression "white elephant," I didn't know what it meant.

2. Yesterday I finally learned what "white elephant" means.

3. A white elephant is an unwanted object that may be difficult to get rid of.

4. Most white elephants are gifts that friends or relatives give us.

5. As I read the story behind the expression, I understood it better.

6. The ruler of an ancient land received any white elephants born in his country; it was a custom that sometimes came in handy.

7. The ruler then gave the white elephants as presents to people who had angered him.

8. The elephants would eat so much and become so difficult to keep that they ruined the lives of the people who received them as "gifts."

9. That is why we now use the term to describe objects that cause us to feel responsible and burdened.

10. Whenever I give a present, I choose it carefully so that it will not become a white elephant.

Source: A Hog on Ice & Other Curious Expressions (New York: Harper & Row, 1948).

PARAGRAPH EXERCISE

Underline the subjects once, the verbs twice, and put a broken line under the dependent clauses in these paragraphs from *The Moon* by Isaac Asimov.

We can think about an eclipse of the Sun in another way. Since sunlight cannot pass through the Moon, the Moon casts a shadow. The shadow is cone-shaped. It usually does not touch the Earth. But sometimes it moves across the Earth. When that happens, there is an eclipse. Inside of the small place where the shadow touches, people can see a total eclipse. There is darkness. In places that are near the shadow, people can see only a partial eclipse. Farther away from the shadow, people can see no eclipse at all.

The Moon's shadow makes a circle when it touches the Earth. The circle moves as the Moon does. So an eclipse of the Sun can be seen in one place for only a few minutes.

SENTENCE WRITING

Write ten sentences about your morning routine (getting up, getting ready for school or work, eating breakfast, etc.). Try to write sentences that contain both independent and dependent clauses. Then underline your subjects once and your verbs twice, and put a broken line under your dependent clauses.

Correcting Fragments

Sometimes a group of words looks like a sentence — with a capital letter at the beginning and a period at the end — but it is missing a subject or a verb or both. Such incomplete sentence structures are called fragments. Here are a few examples:

> Just ran around hugging everyone in sight. (no subject)

> Paul and his sister with the twins. (no verb)

> Nothing to do but wait. (no subject and no verb)

To change these fragments into sentences, we must make sure each has a subject and an adequate verb:

> The sweepstakes <u>winner</u> just <u>ran</u> around hugging everyone in sight. (We added a subject.)

> <u>Paul</u> and his <u>sister</u> <u>reconciled</u> with the twins. (We added a verb.)

> <u>We</u> <u>had</u> nothing to do but wait. (We added a subject and a verb.)

Sometimes we can simply attach such a fragment to the sentence before or after it.

> <u>I</u> <u>want</u> to find a fulfilling job. A career like teaching, for example.

> <u>I</u> <u>want</u> to find a fulfilling job, a career like teaching, for example.

Or we can change a word or two in the fragment and make it into a sentence.

> A teaching <u>career</u> <u>is</u> one example.

PHRASES

Phrases by definition are word groups without subjects and verbs, so whenever a phrase is punctuated as a sentence, it is a fragment. Look at this example of a sentence followed by a phrase fragment beginning with *hoping* (see pp. 112–13 for more about verbal phrases).

> <u>I</u> <u>waited</u> outside the director's office. Hoping to have a chance for an audition.

We can correct this fragment by attaching it to the previous sentence.

> <u>I</u> <u>waited</u> outside the director's office, hoping to have a chance for an audition.

Or we can change it to include a subject and a real verb.

I waited outside the director's office. I hoped to have a chance for an audition.

Here's another example of a sentence followed by a phrase fragment:

The actor's profile was striking. Sketched on an envelope by a famous artist.

Here the two have been combined into one complete sentence:

The actor's striking profile was sketched on an envelope by a famous artist.

Or a better revision might be

A famous artist sketched the actor's striking profile on an envelope.

Sometimes, prepositional phrases are also incorrectly punctuated as sentences. Here a prepositional phrase follows a sentence, but the word group is a fragment — it has no subject and verb of its own. Therefore, it needs to be corrected.

I have lived a simple life so far. With my family on our farm in Saskatchewan.

Here is one possible correction:

I have lived a simple life so far with my family on our farm in Saskatchewan.

Or it could be corrected this way:

My family and I have lived a simple life on our farm in Saskatchewan.

DEPENDENT CLAUSES

Dependent clauses punctuated as sentences are still another kind of fragment. A sentence needs a subject, a verb, *and* a complete thought. As discussed in the previous section, a dependent clause has a subject and a verb, but it begins with a word that makes its meaning incomplete, such as *after, while, because, since, although, when, if, where, who, which,* and *that* (see p. 60 for a full list). To correct such fragments, you need to take off the word that makes the clause dependent *or* add an independent clause.

FRAGMENT
While some of us worked on our journals.

CORRECTED

Some of us worked on our journals.

or

While some of us worked on our journals, the fire alarm rang.

FRAGMENT

Which kept me from finishing my journal entry.

CORRECTED

The fire alarm kept me from finishing my journal entry.

or

We responded to the fire alarm, *which* kept me from finishing my journal entry.

Are fragments ever permissible? Fragments are sometimes used in advertising and in other kinds of writing. But such fragments are used by professional writers who know what they're doing. These fragments are used intentionally, not in error. Until you're an experienced writer, stick with complete sentences. Especially in college and university writing, fragments should not be used.

E X E R C I S E S

Some — but not all — of the following word groups are sentences. The others suffer from incomplete sentence structure. Put a period after each of the sentences. Make any fragments into sentences by assuring that each has a subject and an adequate verb.

Exercise 1

1. My car's compact disc player is difficult to use while driving

2. The discs reflecting the sunlight and shining in my eyes

3. The old CD ejects from the slot with a hissing sound

4. Nowhere to put it while getting the new one

5. Then inserting the new CD without touching its underside

6. Fumbling with those flat plastic cases can be really frustrating

7. One case for the old one and one case for the new one

8. Meanwhile I am driving along

9. Not paying any attention to the road

10. I hope I don't hit anything

Exercise 2

1. The largest of the dinosaurs were vegetarians

2. Tyrannosaurus rex, a meat-eater or carnivore

3. Supposed to be the biggest of the carnivorous dinosaurs

4. In 1995 scientists discovered the remains of a carnivore bigger than T. Rex

5. In Africa living around 90 million years ago

6. Named for having sharklike teeth and living in the Sahara Desert

7. It's called Carcharodontosaurus saharicus

8. Over fifteen metres long and weighing eight tonnes

9. Just its skull measured over one and a half metres in length

10. T. Rex being an easier name to remember

Source: Newsweek, 27 May 1996.

Exercise 3

Correct each phrase fragment by changing or adding words or by attaching the phrase to the complete sentence nearby.

1. We shopped all day at the mall. Looking for the perfect suitcases to take on our cruise this summer.

2. We were sure that one of the specialty stores would carry a good selection. With hard and soft luggage, large and small sizes, and lots of accessories to choose from.

3. Walking from store to store and getting tired. We gave up after a while and ate lunch.

4. We could not believe how crowded the mall was on a weekday. In every shop and at the food court, too.

5. Everywhere we looked people stood around. Crowding the walkways and window shopping.

6. Many teenagers gathered in groups. Laughing at each other and ignoring the shoppers.

7. Pairs of older people walked briskly around the balconies. Using the mall as an exercise track.

8. Actually, we did enjoy ourselves as we ate. Watching all the curious people around us.

9. We finally found the luggage we were looking for in a tiny shop. Near the elevators at the end of the mall.

10. Without the crowds and the poor selection. Our shopping trip would have been a complete success.

Exercise 4

Correct each dependent clause fragment by eliminating its dependent word or by attaching the dependent clause to the independent clause before or after it.

1. Thrift stores, yard sales, and flea markets have become very popular places to shop. Because they sell items that are not available anywhere else as cheaply.

2. Most thrift stores benefit charities. Which use the profits to help people in need.

3. Although the styles of clothing and furniture found in thrift stores are often outdated. Many people prefer the old styles over the new.

4. Modern shelving units are made of particle board or plastic, but thrift store shoppers can find more substantial ones. Which are made of solid wood or thick metal.

5. There are also famous stories of people becoming rich. Because they visited yard sales and flea markets.

6. One man bought a framed picture for a few dollars at a flea market. Since he liked the frame itself but not the picture.

7. When he removed the picture from the frame at home. He found the signature of a famous artist.

8. At a yard sale, a woman bought a small table. Which she later discovered was worth half a million dollars.

9. Of course, collectors always shop at these places. Where they hope to find treasures like rare cookie jars, pens, paintings, records, toys, and others objects of value.

10. In a way, shopping at thrift stores, yard sales, and flea markets is a kind of recycling. Which is something that benefits everyone.

Exercise 5

All of the following word groups are clauses. If the clause has a subject and a verb and *does not* begin with a dependent word (such as *when, while, after, because, since, although, where, if, who, which,* or *that*), put a period after it. If the clause has a subject and a verb and *does* begin with a dependent word (making it a dependent clause fragment), add an independent clause either before or after it to make it a sentence. Remember that if the dependent clause comes first, a comma should follow it. These ten clauses are not about the same topic.

1. Because the car cost too much

2. Then I asked him for directions to the museum

3. Since the government protects endangered species

4. Where I'll be in ten years

5. While the spectators left the stadium and the players left the field

6. She was a tough comic with a painful past

7. Mozart did not live a very long life

8. A Canadian family saw her story on the news

9. If cars could fly

10. Although we had no insurance at the time

PROOFREADING EXERCISE

Correct the five fragments in the following paragraph.

The information superhighway, or the Internet as it's called, was quick to arrive in our homes and businesses. Bringing with it access to merchandise, movies, services, and much more. Although it is not clear yet exactly where this "highway" is going. Holding up the process are legal questions and software and hardware limitations. And whether everyone will have equal access to the benefits the Internet provides. Because fees for these services can be high. Also, people worry about credit card security. If and when these problems are solved. We will be ready for the future.

SENTENCE WRITING

Write ten fragments and then revise them so that they are complete sentences. Or exchange papers with another student, and turn your classmate's ten fragments into sentences.

Correcting Run-On Sentences

Any word group having a subject and a verb is a clause. As we have seen, the clause may be independent (able to stand alone) or dependent (unable to stand alone). If two independent clauses are written together without proper punctuation between them, the result is called a run-on sentence. Here are some examples.

> Classical music is soothing I listen to it in the evenings.

> I love the sound of piano therefore, Chopin is one of my favourites.

Run-on sentences can be corrected in one of four ways:

1. Make the two independent clauses into two sentences.

> Classical music is soothing. I listen to it in the evenings.

> I love the sound of piano. Therefore, Chopin is one of my favourites.

2. Connect the two independent clauses with a semicolon.

> Classical music is soothing; I listen to it in the evenings.

> I love the sound of piano; therefore, Chopin is one of my favourites.

When a connecting word such as

also	however	otherwise
consequently	likewise	then
finally	moreover	therefore
furthermore	nevertheless	thus

is used to join two independent clauses, the semicolon comes before the connecting word, and a comma usually comes after it.

> Cellular phones are convenient; however, they can be intrusive.

> Earthquakes scare me; therefore, I don't live in Los Angeles.

> We travelled to London; then we took the "Chunnel" to Paris.

> The college recently built a large new library; thus students have more quiet study areas.

NOTE: The use of the comma after the connecting word depends on how long the connecting word is. If it is only a short word, like *then* or *thus*, no comma is needed.

---

3. Connect the two independent clauses with a comma and one of the following seven words (the first letters of which create the word *fanboys***):** *for, and, nor, but, or, yet, so.*

Classical music is soothing, *so* I listen to it in the evenings.

Chopin is one of my favourites, *for* I love the sound of piano.

Each of the *fanboys* has its own meaning (for example, *so* means "as a result," and *for* means "because").

Swans are beautiful birds, *and* they mate for life.

Students may register for classes by phone, *or* they may do so in person.

I applied for financial aid, *but* (or *yet*) I was still working at the time.

Beth doesn't know how to use a computer, *nor* does she plan to learn.

But before you put a comma before a *fanboys*, be sure there are two independent clauses. The first sentence that follows has two independent clauses. The second sentence is merely one independent clause with two verbs, so no comma should be used.

The snow began falling at dusk, and it continued to fall through the night.

The snow began falling at dusk and continued to fall through the night.

4. Make one of the clauses dependent by adding a dependent word (such as *since, when, as, after, while,* **or** *because* **— see p. 60 for a full list).**

Since classical music is soothing, I listen to it in the evenings.

Chopin is one of my favourites *because* I love the sound of piano.

WAYS TO CORRECT RUN-ON SENTENCES

They learned a new routine. They needed to practise it. (two sentences)

They learned a new routine; they needed to practise it. (semicolon)

They learned a new routine; therefore, they needed to practise it. (semicolon + transition)

They learned a new routine, so they needed to practise it. (comma + *fanboys*)

Because they learned a new routine, they needed to practise it. (dependent clause first)

They needed to practise because they learned a new routine. (dependent clause last)

Learn these ways to join two clauses, and you'll avoid run-on sentences.

E X E R C I S E S

Exercises 1 and 2

CORRECTING RUN-ONS WITH PUNCTUATION

Most — but not all — of the following sentences are run-ons. If the sentence has two independent clauses, separate them with correct punctuation. For the first two exercises, *don't create any dependent clauses*; use only a period, a semicolon, or a comma to separate the two independent clauses. Your answers may differ from those at the back of the book depending on how you choose to separate the clauses. Remember that a comma may be used only before the words *for, and, nor, but, or, yet, so.*

Exercise 1

1. I planned a surprise party for my sister Nina's birthday it was a disaster.

2. All of her friends arrived at our house on time however, no one could find Nina.

3. Many people had left work early to be there for the big "Surprise!"

4. We waited in the heavily decorated living room with presents and cake for the party.

5. An hour passed but there was no sign of the birthday girl.

6. After two hours, we began to worry about Nina she was usually home by dinnertime.

7. By nine o'clock the cake had almost disappeared and most of Nina's friends had gone home.

8. Nina finally drove up at 10:30 so the remaining guests hid behind the furniture.

9. "Happy Birthday!" we all yelled she looked more confused than surprised.

10. She had treated herself to a movie for her birthday I treated myself to the last piece of her cake.

Exercise 2

1. I am writing a research paper on Margaret Laurence she was one of Canada's most celebrated novelists and a pioneer in the world of Canadian literature.

2. She was born in Neepawa, Manitoba in her novels *The Stone Angel, A Jest of God, The Fire-Dwellers,* and *The Diviners,* the town was called "Manawaka."

3. Laurence was encouraged to write by Jack McClelland he also published the works of other Canadian writers such as Mordecai Richler and Farley Mowat.

4. Margaret and her husband, Jack, briefly lived in England then they moved to Africa.

5. She became very interested in European/African relations as a result her early books, *This Side Jordan* and *The Tomorrow-Tamer,* deal with this issue.

6. Her husband wanted her to be a traditional wife and mother but Margaret wanted to be a full-time writer.

7. When they divorced, she had to support herself and her children with her writing.

8. Laurence received her first Governor General's Award for her masterpiece *The Stone Angel.*

9. Twice her books were condemned or banned in schools yet today they are taught as Canadian classics.

10. In 1986, she was diagnosed with inoperable and fatal lung cancer several months later she took her own life.

Source: James King, *Margaret Laurence* (Toronto: Alfred A. Knopf, 1997).

Exercises 3 and 4

CORRECTING RUN-ONS WITH DEPENDENT CLAUSES

Most — but not all — of the following sentences are run-ons. Correct any run-on sentences by making one of the clauses dependent. You may change the words. Use a dependent word (such as *since, when, as, after, while, because,* or the others listed on p. 60) to begin the dependent clause. In some sentences you will want to put the dependent clause first; in others you may want to put it last (or in the middle of the sentence). Since various words can be used to start a dependent clause, your answers may differ from those suggested at the back of the book.

Exercise 3

1. My family and I get a lot of annoying phone calls in the early evening.

2. The calls are made by companies their salespeople try to interest us in the newest calling plan or credit card offer.

3. They don't call during the day then nobody is home.

4. I feel sorry for some of the salespeople they're just doing their job.

5. My father tells them to call during business hours they hang up right away.

6. I pick up the receiver sometimes and hear a computerized voice trying to sell me a subscription to a magazine.

7. My mother answers she is too polite, so they just keep talking.

8. We try to ignore the ringing it drives us all crazy.

9. One time my brother pretended to be my father and almost ordered a new roof for the house.

10. We never buy anything over the phone maybe these companies will all get the message and leave us alone.

Exercise 4

1. Glenn Gould died and Canada lost a great musician.

2. Gould was a sublime pianist he was also a composer of international fame.

3. If you are interested in classical piano music, you will know Glenn Gould's name.

4. He was a child prodigy he was put on the stage at a very young age.

5. He was 14 years old and he became a soloist with the Toronto Symphony.

6. Gould began touring across Canada at age 19 in later years he stopped performing in public.

7. While he is best known for his interpretations of Bach, he also played with great mastery the music of many other composers.

8. He was an eccentric and a loner few people knew much about his personal life.

9. The day after he turned 50, he had a severe stroke and died.

10. Gould's music continues to live on he is no longer alive.

Source: Adapted from *The Toronto Star,* 16 Nov. 1999, D4.

Exercise 5

Correct the following run-on sentences using any of the methods studied in this section: adding a period, a semicolon, a semicolon + a transition word, or a comma + a *fanboys*, or using a dependent word to create a dependent clause.

1. There is a new way to find a date in Japan singles use vending machines to sell information about themselves to others.

2. Men provide personal details in packets to be sold in the machines first the men swear they are not married.

3. A woman chooses to purchase a packet for a couple of dollars in it she will find a picture of the man, his age, and his employment status.

4. The packets also include the men's phone numbers the women can use the numbers to contact only the men they like.

5. The system seems to be working many of the couples are dating more than once.

6. A lot of Japanese businesspeople use the machines they do not have time to meet people in other ways.

7. Employees have little opportunity to socialize in Japan it is normal to stay at work until late into the evening.

8. A man might pay almost $50 to put many of his packets into the machines that doesn't mean that women will call him.

9. Japan is famous for its vending machines they are even used to sell meat and clothes.

10. Other countries might find it unusual to sell personal information in vending machines they seem to be working well as matchmakers in Japan.

Source: Fortune, 6 April 1992.

REVIEW OF FRAGMENTS AND RUN-ON SENTENCES

If you remember that all clauses include a subject and a verb, but only independent clauses can be punctuated as sentences (since only they can stand alone), then you will avoid fragments in your writing. And if you memorize these six rules for the punctuation of clauses, you will be able to avoid most punctuation errors.

PUNCTUATING CLAUSES	
I am a student. I am still learning.	(two sentences)
I am a student; I am still learning.	(two independent clauses)
I am a student; therefore, I am still learning.	(two independent clauses connected by a word such as *also, consequently, finally, furthermore, however, likewise, moreover, nevertheless, otherwise, then, therefore, thus*)
I am a student, so I am still learning.	(two independent clauses connected by *for, and, nor, but, or, yet, so*)
Because I am a student, I am still learning.	(dependent clause at beginning of sentence)
I am still learning because I am a student.	(dependent clause at end of sentence) The dependent words are *after, although, as, as if, because, before, even if, even though, ever since, how, if, in order that, since, so that, than, that, though, unless, until, what, whatever, when, whenever, where, whereas, wherever, whether, which, whichever, while, who, whom, whose, why.*

It is essential that you learn the italicized words in this table — which ones come between independent clauses and which ones introduce dependent clauses.

PROOFREADING EXERCISE

Rewrite the following paragraph, making the necessary changes so there will be no fragments or run-on sentences.

Unlike the one-way communication of the mass media. Personal interaction isn't something we do *to* others rather it is an activity we do *with* them. In this sense, person-to-person communication. Is rather like dancing — at least the kind of dancing we do with partners. Like dancing, communication depends on the involvement of a partner. And like good dancing, successful communication doesn't depend only on the person who takes the lead a great dancer who forgets to consider and adapt to the skill level of his or her partner can make both people look bad. In communication and dancing. Even two talented partners don't guarantee success. When two skilled dancers perform without coordinating their movements. The results feel bad to the dancers and look foolish to the audience finally, relational communication — like dancing — is a unique creation. That arises out of the way in which the partners interact. The way you dance probably varies from one partner to another likewise the way you communicate almost certainly varies with different partners.

Source: Ronald B. Adler, Neil Towne, and Judith A. Rolls, *Looking Out, Looking In: Interpersonal Communication* 1st Canadian edition (Fort Worth: Harcourt College Publishers, 2001), 14.

SENTENCE WRITING

Write a sample sentence of your own to demonstrate each of the six ways a writer can use to punctuate two clauses. You may model your sentences on the examples used in the preceding review chart.

Identifying Verb Phrases

Sometimes a verb is one word, but often the whole verb includes more than one word. These are called verb phrases. Look at several of the many forms of the verb *speak*, for example. Most of them are verb phrases, made up of the main verb (*speak*) and one or more helping verbs.

speak	is speaking	had been speaking
speaks	am speaking	will have been speaking
spoke	are speaking	is spoken
will speak	was speaking	was spoken
has spoken	were speaking	will be spoken
have spoken	will be speaking	can speak
had spoken	has been speaking	must speak
will have spoken	have been speaking	should have spoken

Note that words like the following are never verbs even though they may be near a verb or in the middle of a verb phrase:

already	ever	not	really
also	finally	now	sometimes
always	just	often	usually
probably	never	only	possibly

Jason has *never* spoken to his instructor before. She *always* talks with other students.

Two verb forms — *speaking* and *to speak* — look like verbs, but neither can ever be the verb of a sentence. No *ing* word by itself can ever be the verb of a sentence; it must be helped by another verb in a verb phrase. (See the discussion of verbal phrases on pp. 112–13.)

Natalie speaking French. (not a sentence because there is no complete verb phrase)

Natalie is speaking French. (a sentence with a verb phrase)

And no verb with *to* in front of it can ever be the verb of a sentence.

Ted to speak in front of groups. (not a sentence because there is no real verb)

Ted hates to speak in front of groups. (a sentence with *hates* as the verb)

These two forms, *speaking* and *to speak*, may be used as subjects, or they may have other uses in the sentence.

Speaking on stage is scary. To speak on stage is scary. Ted had a *speaking* part in that play.

But neither of them alone can ever be the verb of a sentence.

E X E R C I S E S

Underline the subjects once and the verbs or verb phrases twice. It's a good idea to put parentheses around prepositional phrases first. (See pp. 54–55 if you need help in locating prepositional phrases.) The sentences may contain independent *and* dependent clauses, so there could be several verbs and verb phrases.

Exercise 1

1. John Harrison has been tasting ice cream for nearly twenty years.

2. He has recently hired an insurance company to protect his very valuable taste buds.

3. The new policy will pay $1 million in the event of damage to his tongue.

4. Harrison knows that the ice cream's taste would be altered by a metal or a wooden spoon.

5. So he always samples the different flavours from a spoon plated with gold.

6. This professional taster does not smoke, drink caffeinated beverages, or eat hot chilis.

7. He never even gets to swallow the ice cream itself.

8. He just swishes it briefly around his mouth.

9. Harrison may have inherited his special tasting talents.

10. Many of his family members have also worked in the ice cream business.

Source: Los Angeles Times, 23 April 1998.

Exercise 2

1. I have just discovered "The Farnsworth Chronicles," an Internet site that is devoted to the life of Philo T. Farnsworth.
2. Thirteen-year-old Philo T. Farnsworth was ploughing a field in 1922 when he visualized the concept that led to television as we know it.
3. Others were working on the idea of sending images through the air, but Farnsworth actually solved the problem in that open field.
4. He looked at the rows that the plough had made in the earth.
5. And he reasoned that images could be broken down into rows, and each row could be sent through the air and onto a screen.
6. Farnsworth's idea made television a reality, but historically he has not been fully recognized for this and his other accomplishments.
7. In 1957, he was featured as a guest on *I've Got a Secret,* a television show that presented mystery contestants.
8. The panelists on the show were supposed to guess the guest's secret, which the audience was shown so that everyone knew the answer except the people asking the questions.
9. They asked if he had invented something painful, and he replied that he had; the panelists never guessed that he was the inventor of television.
10. Farnsworth did receive a box of cigarettes and $80 for being on the show.

Exercise 3

1. The theatre is known for its excesses — take, for example, a 1998 stage production of *Beauty and the Beast* in London, England.
2. The set alone contained 64 automated props, including the Beast's castle, which weighed nearly thirteen tonnes.
3. Many of the main characters' wigs were fashioned from human hair.
4. Nine kilograms of hair — some real and some artificial — were used to make the Beast's original costume, which took over 400 hours to complete.
5. Each of the eight different wigs Belle's character wore for every performance required human hair that had grown to a length of 75 cm or more.

6. An entirely new pyrotechnic device was invented for this show; experts in stage explosives worked for a year and a half to perfect it.

7. They designed a hand-held fireball that could be thrown by the enchantress character when she turned the prince into a beast.

8. The candelabra character wore a costume that included huge lighted candles at the end of each hand.

9. Some people enjoy watching a play; others would rather watch a football game.

10. Coincidentally, the energy that one performance of *Beauty and the Beast* used was equivalent to the amount needed to light an entire sports stadium.

Source: London Theatre News, 1 Feb. 1998.

Exercise 4

1. Aspirin has recently turned 100 years old; Felix Hoffmann, a chemist, was trying to ease his own father's pain when he discovered aspirin in 1897.

2. Although aspirin can cause side effects, each year people around the world give themselves 50 billion doses of the popular painkiller.

3. But people in different countries take this medicine in different ways.

4. The British like to dissolve aspirin powder in water.

5. The French have insisted that slow-release methods work best.

6. Italians prefer aspirin drinks with a little fizz.

7. And North Americans have always chosen to take their aspirin in pill form.

8. However it is taken, aspirin continues to surprise researchers with benefits to human health.

9. It has been found to benefit people susceptible to heart attack, colon cancer, and Alzheimer's disease.

10. Where would we be without aspirin?

Source: Newsweek, 18 Aug. 1997.

Exercise 5

1. I like to walk around the park with my two little poodles in the early evening.

2. The three of us have enjoyed this ritual for several years now.

3. On Friday evening, we were just passing the duck pond, and a big dog with no owner ran over to us.

4. It was obviously looking for other dogs to play with.

5. Yip and Yap have never barked so loudly before.

6. I had originally named them for their distinct barking noises.

7. But lately I had not heard these short, ear-splitting sounds very often.

8. The big dog was shocked by the fierceness of my little dogs' reply and quickly ran to find other friends.

9. Even I could not believe it.

10. I will never worry about their safety around big dogs again.

REVIEW EXERCISE

To practise finding all of the sentence structures we have studied so far, mark the following article about Canada's governor general. First, put parentheses around prepositional phrases, then underline subjects once and verbs or verb phrases twice. Finally put a broken line beneath dependent clauses. Begin by marking the first paragraph, then check your answers at the back of the book before going on to the next paragraph. (Remember that *ing* verbs alone and the *to*____ forms of verbs are never real verbs in sentences. You will learn more about them on pp. 112–13.)

In October 1999, Adrienne Clarkson was appointed Canada's newest governor general. Most people do not know that the governor general outranks even the prime minister. The person who holds this office is, in fact, the Queen's representative to Canada. The governor general's responsibility entails signing bills passed by Parliament, which is the final step a bill takes before becoming a law. Today, however, this office is really a ceremonial post and symbolizes Canada's traditional ties with the British Crown. Nevertheless, the position of governor general still comes with a lot of responsibility. The person who fills this office must attend many functions and, among other things, deliver countless speeches. This is definitely not a job for somebody who is afraid of public attention.

When the prime minister introduced the new governor general, many were pleased with his decision. Ms. Clarkson is the first Canadian of Chinese descent to hold such a position. Although she may now call the luxurious surroundings of Rideau Hall — the governor general's official residence — her home, her story is similar to that of many other families who have immigrated to Canada.

Her mother and father, William and Ethel Poy, escaped from Hong Kong during World War II with their two young children. When they arrived in Ottawa, they had all their worldly possessions in just a few suitcases. Her high school teachers and fellow students remember Adrienne as being especially bright and hard-working. While her brother, Neville, went on to become a successful surgeon, Adrienne devoted herself to studying English literature and art. She was fascinated by culture and learned to speak French and Italian fluently.

Soon, others began to recognize her talents. She was asked to review books on CBC radio, and eventually she began a career as a TV journalist on *the fifth estate*, a news program. Here, she showed herself to be a strong-willed person who stood up for her beliefs. The long hours and busy schedule of a television career, however, were very demanding.

In 1982, Clarkson left the world of TV journalism and began working as a Canadian diplomat in France. Even when she performed her official duties there, she continued to show her fondness for the arts. Clarkson was a hit in Paris, where she managed to turn what was once a dreary diplomatic residence into an exciting cultural centre. After completing her duties in Paris, Clarkson moved back to Canada and began working on a new TV program. For her new show, she produced and directed hour-long documentaries that examined such subjects as film, music, and modern dance.

Her appointment to the post of governor general is the pinnacle of a life filled with hard work. In her nationally televised speech, she made clear her devotion to the arts and her commitment to Canada. Clarkson compared Canada to a work in progress. According to her, Canada is a three-legged stool built of French, English, and Aboriginal cultures that has expanded to include all colours and religions. She said that Canada is made up of many immigrant parents like her own, "dreaming their children into being Canadians."

© Lazaros Simeon

Sources: 1) *Maclean's: Canada's Weekly Newsmagazine,* 18 Oct. 99, Vol. 112, No. 42: 36. 2) http://www.thestar.ca/thestar/back_issues/ED19991006/news/991006NEW01b_NA-GOV6.html

Using Standard English Verbs

The next two discussions are for those who need practice in using Standard English verbs. Many of us grew up doing more speaking than writing. But in college and university, and in the business and professional world, the use of Standard Written English is essential.

The following charts show the forms of four verbs as they are used in Standard Written English. These forms might differ from the way you use these verbs when you speak. Memorize the Standard English forms of these important verbs. The first verb (*talk*) is one of the regular verbs (verbs that all end the same way according to a pattern); most verbs in English are regular. The other three verbs charted here (*have, be,* and *do*) are irregular and are important because they are used not only as main verbs but also as helping verbs in verb phrases.

Don't go on to the exercises until you have memorized the forms of these Standard English verbs.

REGULAR VERB: TALK

PRESENT TIME		PAST TIME	
I		I	
you	talk	you	talked
we		we	
they		they	
he, she, it	talks	he, she, it	

IRREGULAR VERB: HAVE

PRESENT TIME		PAST TIME	
I		I	
you		you	
we	have	we	had
they		they	
he, she, it	has	he, she, it	

IRREGULAR VERB: BE

PRESENT TIME		PAST TIME	
I	am	I	was
you		we	
we	are	you	were
they		they	
he, she, it	is	he, she, it	was

IRREGULAR VERB: DO

PRESENT TIME		PAST TIME	
I		I	
you		you	
we	do	we	did
they		they	
he, she, it	does	he, she, it	

Sometimes you may have difficulty with the correct endings of verbs because you don't hear the words correctly. Note carefully the *s* sound and the *ed* sound at the end of words. Occasionally the *ed* is not clearly pronounced, as in *They tried to help*, but most of the time you can hear it if you listen.

Read the following sentences aloud, making sure that you say every sound.

1. He seems satisfied with his new job.

2. She likes saving money for the future.

3. It takes strength of character to control spending.

4. Todd makes salad for every potluck he attends.

5. I used to know all their names.

6. They supposed that they were right.

7. He recognized the suspect and excused himself from the jury.

8. Susan sponsored Reina in the school's charity event.

Now read some other sentences aloud from this text, making sure that you sound all the s's and ed's. Reading aloud and listening to others will help you use the correct verb endings automatically.

E X E R C I S E S

In these pairs of sentences, use the present form of the verb in the first sentence and the past form in the second. All the verbs follow the pattern of the regular verb *talk* except the irregular verbs *have*, *be*, and *do*. Keep referring to the tables if you're not sure which form to use. Correct your answers for each exercise before going to the next.

Exercise 1

1. (walk) I often _____ my dog to the store. I _____ him to the store yesterday.

2. (be) She _____ glad to be graduating. She _____ unsure about her future just two years ago.

3. (have) They _____ a minivan now. They _____ a station wagon before.

4. (do) I _____ my homework in the afternoons. I _____ my homework in the evenings in high school.

5. (need) He _____ a new pair of skis. He _____ new boots last season.

6. (be) Now I _____ a part-time employee. I _____ a full-time employee last year.

7. (have) I bought an antique ring; it _____ a large green stone in its setting. It _____ another stone in it before, but it was chipped.

8. (be) They _____ the hosts of their family reunion this year. They _____ not the hosts of last year's reunion.

9. (do) He _____ the dishes when I cook. He _____ the dishes yesterday.

10. (work)   She _____ several hours of overtime a week. She _____ twelve hours of overtime last week.

Exercise 2

1. (be)   She _____ an employee now. She _____ an intern last year.

2. (do)   They _____ their best work at home. They _____ an especially good job on their homework last night.

3. (have)   I _____ two weeks left to prepare for my trip. I originally _____ six weeks, but I procrastinated.

4. (ask)   He never _____ his friends for help anymore. He _____ them for help before without results.

5. (have)   I always _____ a cold at this time of year. I _____ one last year right on schedule.

6. (learn)   We _____ a new technique each day in my ceramics class. Yesterday we _____ how to throw pots on a wheel.

7. (be)   Most of us _____ beginners. We _____ not particularly interested in art before we took this class, but now we love it.

8. (do)   He _____ well on all of his tests. He _____ very well on the final exam.

9. (play)   She _____ the guitar now. She _____ the piano as her first instrument.

10. (be)   I _____ a collector by nature. However, last month I _____ too busy to go shopping.

In Exercises 3 and 4, underline the Standard English verb forms. All the verbs follow the pattern of the regular verb *talk* except the three irregular verbs *have, be,* and *do.* Keep referring to the tables if you are not sure which form to use.

Exercise 3

1. I (start, started) a new job last month, and so far I really (like, likes) it.

2. The company (create, creates) special effect devices for television and movies.

3. My co-workers (is, are) all nice, so we (has, have) a good work environment.

4. Yesterday, we (finish, finished) a movie project that (need, needed) lots of explosives.

5. The boss, who (own, owns) the company, always (do, does) his best to explain the safety procedures to us.

6. And he (watch, watches) us to make sure we (follow, follows) them.

7. I can tell that the boss (enjoy, enjoys) his work; he (was, were) happy to see us safely mixing and loading the inventory for the movie.

8. We (complete, completed) the movie project in just one week even though the boss (expect, expected) it to take us two weeks.

9. We (has, have) our boss to thank for a smooth-running company.

10. And I (has, have) my co-workers to thank for being my friends.

Exercise 4

1. My sister and I (do, does) our homework together every night so that we (don't, doesn't) fall behind.

2. I (is, am) better in math, and my sister Aileen (is, am) better in English.

3. When I (need, needs) help with grammar, Aileen (explain, explains) the rule to me.

4. And if she gets stuck on a math problem, I (help, helps) her understand it; then she (do, does) it herself.

5. This system (work, works) very well for us, and I (hope, hopes) we will always use it.

6. Before we (do, did) it this way, I (drop, dropped) an English class.

7. It (was, were) too hard for me, but now I (do, does) as well as the other students.

8. Aileen and I both (work, works) hard, and we (check, checks) each other's progress.

9. When I (learn, learns) more English skills and Aileen (learn, learns) more math skills, we will be equal.

10. Our parents (expect, expects) a lot from both of us, and we (don't, doesn't) want to let them down.

Exercise 5

Correct any of following sentences that do not use Standard English verb forms.

1. Last year our high school drama class travel to London, England.

2. Twenty of us and one teacher boarded the plane.

3. We was all very excited about the trip.

4. Before the trip, we learn to read the London subway map.

5. We discover that the people in London call the subway "the tube."

6. Once we was there, we understood why.

7. The underground walls is round just like a tube.

8. We liked the Tower of London and Big Ben and the boats on the Thames.

9. We even walk right past the Crown Jewels.

10. They were close enough to touch.

PROOFREADING EXERCISE

Correct any sentences in the following paragraph that do not use Standard English verb forms.

Everyday as we drive though our neighbourhoods on the way to school or to work, we see things that needs to be fixed. Many of them cause us only a little bit of trouble, so we forget them until we face them again. Every morning, I has to deal with a truck that someone park right at the corner of my street. It block my view as I try to turn onto the main avenue. I need to move out past the truck into the oncoming lane of traffic just to make my left turn. One day last week, I turn too soon, and a car almost hit me. This truck don't need to be parked in such a dangerous place.

SENTENCE WRITING

Write ten sentences about a problem in your neighbourhood. Check your sentences to be sure that they use Standard English verb forms. Try exchanging papers with another student if possible.

Using Regular and Irregular Verbs

All regular verbs end the same way in the past form and when used with helping verbs. Here is a table showing all the forms of some regular verbs and the various helping verbs they are used with.

REGULAR VERBS				
BASE FORM	**PRESENT**	**PAST**	**PAST PARTICIPLE**	***ING* FORM**
(Use after can, may, shall, will, could, might, should, would, must, do, does, did.*)*			*(Use after* have, has, had. *Some can be used after forms of* be.*)*	*(Use after forms of* be.*)*
ask	ask *(s)*	asked	asked	asking
bake	bake *(s)*	baked	baked	baking
count	count *(s)*	counted	counted	counting
dance	dance *(s)*	danced	danced	dancing
decide	decide *(s)*	decided	decided	deciding
enjoy	enjoy *(s)*	enjoyed	enjoyed	enjoying
finish	finish *(es)*	finished	finished	finishing
happen	happen *(s)*	happened	happened	happening
learn	learn *(s)*	learned	learned	learning
like	like *(s)*	liked	liked	liking
look	look *(s)*	looked	looked	looking
mend	mend *(s)*	mended	mended	mending
need	need *(s)*	needed	needed	needing
open	open *(s)*	opened	opened	opening
start	start *(s)*	started	started	starting
suppose	suppose *(s)*	supposed	supposed	supposing
tap	tap *(s)*	tapped	tapped	tapping
walk	walk *(s)*	walked	walked	walking
want	want *(s)*	wanted	wanted	wanting

NOTE: When there are several helping verbs, the last one determines which form of the main verb should be used: they *should* finish soon; they should *have* finished an hour ago.

When do you write *ask, finish, suppose, use*? And when do you write *asked, finished, supposed, used*? Here are some rules that will help you decide.

Write *ask, finish, suppose, use* (or their *s* forms) when writing about the present time, repeated actions, or facts:

He *asks* questions whenever he is confused.

They always *finish* their projects on time.

I *suppose* you want me to help you move.

Birds *use* leaves, twigs, and feathers to build their nests.

Write *asked, finished, supposed, used*

1. When writing about the past:

He *asked* the teacher for another explanation.

She *finished* her internship last year.

They *supposed* that there were others bidding on that house.

I *used* to study piano.

2. When some form of *be* (other than the word *be* itself) comes before the word:

He was *asked* the most difficult questions.

She is *finished* with her training now.

They were *supposed* to sign at the bottom of the form.

My essay was *used* as a sample of clear narration.

3. When some form of *have* comes before the word:

The teacher has *asked* us that question before.

She will have *finished* all of her exams by the end of May.

I had *supposed* too much without any proof.

We have *used* many models in my drawing class this year.

All the verbs in the chart on page 94 are regular. That is, they're all formed in the same way — with an *ed* ending on the past form and on the past participle. But many verbs are irregular. Their past and past participle forms change spelling instead of just adding an *ed*. Here's a chart of some irregular verbs. Notice that the base, present, and *ing* forms end the same as regular verbs. Refer to this list when you aren't sure which verb form to use. Memorize all the forms you don't know.

IRREGULAR VERBS				
BASE FORM	**PRESENT**	**PAST**	**PAST PARTICIPLE**	***ING* FORM**
(Use after can, may, shall, will, could, might, should, would, must, do, does, did.*)*			*(Use after* have, has, had. *Some can be used after forms of* be.*)*	*(Use after forms of* be.*)*
be	am, is, are	was, were	been	being
become	become *(s)*	became	become	becoming
begin	begin *(s)*	began	begun	beginning
break	break *(s)*	broke	broken	breaking
bring	bring *(s)*	brought	brought	bringing
buy	buy *(s)*	bought	bought	buying
build	build *(s)*	built	built	building
catch	catch *(es)*	caught	caught	catching
choose	choose *(s)*	chose	chosen	choosing
come	come *(s)*	came	come	coming
do	do *(es)*	did	done	doing
draw	draw *(s)*	drew	drawn	drawing
drink	drink *(s)*	drank	drunk	drinking
drive	drive *(s)*	drove	driven	driving
eat	eat *(s)*	ate	eaten	eating
fall	fall *(s)*	fell	fallen	falling
feel	feel *(s)*	felt	felt	feeling
fight	fight *(s)*	fought	fought	fighting
find	find *(s)*	found	found	finding
forget	forget *(s)*	forgot	forgotten	forgetting
forgive	forgive *(s)*	forgave	forgiven	forgiving
freeze	freeze *(s)*	froze	frozen	freezing
get	get *(s)*	got	got *or* gotten	getting
give	give *(s)*	gave	given	giving
go	go *(es)*	went	gone	going
grow	grow *(s)*	grew	grown	growing
have	have *or* has	had	had	having
hang	hang *(s)*	hanged	hung	hanging
hear	hear *(s)*	heard	heard	hearing
hold	hold *(s)*	held	held	holding
keep	keep *(s)*	kept	kept	keeping

BASE FORM	PRESENT	PAST	PAST PARTICIPLE	*ING* FORM
know	know *(s)*	knew	known	knowing
lay (to put)	lay *(s)*	laid	laid	laying
lead (like "bead")	lead *(s)*	led	led	leading
leave	leave *(s)*	left	left	leaving
lie (to rest)	lie *(s)*	lay	lain	lying
lose	lose *(s)*	lost	lost	losing
make	make *(s)*	made	made	making
meet	meet *(s)*	met	met	meeting
pay	pay *(s)*	paid	paid	paying
read (pron. "reed")	read *(s)*	read (pron. "red")	read (pron."red")	reading
ride	ride *(s)*	rode	ridden	riding
ring	ring *(s)*	rang	rung	ringing
rise	rise *(s)*	rose	risen	rising
run	run *(s)*	ran	run	running
say	say *(s)*	said	said	saying
see	see *(s)*	saw	seen	seeing
sell	sell *(s)*	sold	sold	selling
shake	shake *(s)*	shook	shaken	shaking
shine (give light)	shine *(s)*	shone	shone	shining
shine (polish)	shine *(s)*	shined	shined	shining
sing	sing *(s)*	sang	sung	singing
sleep	sleep *(s)*	slept	slept	sleeping
sneak	sneak *(s)*	sneaked *or* snuck	sneaked *or* snuck	sneaking
speak	speak *(s)*	spoke	spoken	speaking
spend	spend *(s)*	spent	spent	spending
stand	stand *(s)*	stood	stood	standing
steal	steal *(s)*	stole	stolen	stealing
strike	strike *(s)*	struck	struck	striking
swim	swim *(s)*	swam	swum	swimming
swing	swing *(s)*	swung	swung	swinging
take	take *(s)*	took	taken	taking
teach	teach *(es)*	taught	taught	teaching
tear	tear *(s)*	tore	torn	tearing
tell	tell *(s)*	told	told	telling
think	think *(s)*	thought	thought	thinking
throw	throw *(s)*	threw	thrown	throwing
wear	wear *(s)*	wore	worn	wearing
win	win *(s)*	won	won	winning
write	write *(s)*	wrote	written	writing

Sometimes verbs from the past participle column are used after some form of the verb *be* (or verbs that take the place of *be* like *appear, seem, look, feel, get, act, become*) to describe the subject or to say something in a passive, rather than active, way.

She is contented.

You appear pleased. (You are pleased.)

He seems delighted. (He is delighted.)

She looked surprised. (She was surprised.)

I feel shaken. (I am shaken.)

They get bored easily. (They are bored easily.)

You acted concerned. (You were concerned.)

He was thrown out of the game. (Active: *The referee threw him out of the game.*)

They were disappointed by the news. (Active: *The news disappointed them.*)

Often these verb forms become words that describe the subject; other times they still act as part of the verb of the sentence. What you call them doesn't matter. The only important thing is to be sure you use the correct form from the past participle column.

E X E R C I S E S

Write the correct form of the verb. Refer to the tables and explanations on the preceding pages if you aren't sure which form to use after a certain helping verb. Check your answers after each exercise.

Exercise 1

1. (look)   Once again, I have _____ everywhere for my keys.

2. (look)   I could _____ in a few more places, but I'm late.

3. (look)   I feel so foolish while I am _____ for them.

4. (look)   I know that if I _____ too hard I won't find them.

5. (look)   Once I _____ for them for over two hours.

6. (look)   I can _____ right past them if I am too frantic.

7. (look)   I have _____ in places where they would never be.

8. (look)   My daughter once caught me while I was _____ for them in the refrigerator.

9. (look)   In fact, my family now _____ at me with scorn whenever I ask, "Has anybody seen my keys?"

10. (look)   From now on I will _____ in the obvious places first and keep my problem to myself.

Exercise 2

1. (drive)   I always _____ my sister to school; in fact, I have _____ her to school for a whole year now.

2. (think)   The other day, I was _____ of new ways to get her there in the morning, but she _____ that they were all bad ideas.

3. (take)   She could _____ a school bus that stops nearby; instead she _____ me for granted.

4. (tell)   It all started when she _____ our mother that some of the other children were _____ her to stay out of their seats.

5. (write)   I _____ a note to the bus driver to see if she could help ease my sister's mind, but so far she hasn't _____ back.

6. (know)   When I was my sister's age, I _____ some tough kids at school, so I _____ how she must feel.

7. (teach)   But experiences like that _____ us how to get along with everyone; they sure _____ me.

8. (tear)   Now I am _____ between wanting to help her avoid the tough kids and _____ my hair out from having to take her to school every day.

9. (ride)   We have _____ together for so long that I might miss her if I _____ alone.

10. (make)   I have _____ up my mind. I will _____ the best of it while she still needs me. What else are big sisters for?

Exercise 3

1. (be, hear)   We _____ surprised when we _____ Uncle Wolf's message on our answering machine yesterday saying that he was in town.

2. (see, begin)   We hadn't _____ him in over a year, and we had _____ to wonder if he would ever visit us again.

3. (fly, eat)   He had _____ in from Vancouver earlier in the day but hadn't _____ dinner yet.

4. (get, do)   We _____ back to him at his hotel and _____ our best to convince him to join us for dinner.

5. (take, eat)   It did not _____ much to convince him, and soon we were _____ roast beef sandwiches at our favourite deli.

6. (write, come, lose)   He said that he had _____ to tell us that he was _____ , and he asked if we had _____ the letter.

7. (swear, feel)   We _____ that we never received it, and he _____ better.

8. (buy, pay)   Just to make sure there were no hard feelings, we _____ his sandwich, and he _____ the tip.

9. (get, think)   It was _____ late, so we _____ that he should go back to his hotel to get some sleep.

10. (see, tell, lie)   When we _____ Wolf the next day, he _____ us that he was so tired the night before that as soon as he _____ down on the hotel pillow, he fell asleep.

Exercise 4

1. (use, suppose)   My brothers and I _____ to stay up all night in our room when we were _____ to be sleeping.

2. (catch, come, hear)   Our parents would _____ us sometimes when they _____ upstairs and _____ us talking.

3. (be, leave)   We _____ not very smart about it; sometimes we even _____ the light on.

4. (read, draw, build)   That way we could _____ or _____ or _____ our secret inventions.

5. (feel, draw)   Those nights _____ really special, and I _____ some of my best pictures then.

6. (do, sleep)   We _____ suffer from fatigue during the day as we _____ through our classes at school.

7. (know, spend)   We _____ that we had to fix the problem, so we _____ several nights withdrawing from our late-night schedule.

8. (go, be)   Gradually we _____ to bed earlier and earlier until we _____ back to a normal sleeping pattern.

9. (wake, stay)   We _____ up on time and _____ awake in our classes.

10. (forget, spend, be)   I will never _____ the quiet, creative, and carefree nights I _____ with my brothers when we _____ just kids.

Exercise 5

1. (lay, lie, feel)   I _____ my towel down on the hot cement next to the pool and was _____ face-down on the towel when I _____ a bee land on the back of my ankle.

2. (know, be)   I _____ that special sensation of a bee's legs on my skin because I have _____ stung before.

3. (break, have)   Last time, I _____ out in hives and _____ to go to the doctor to get an injection of antihistamine.

4. (become, think)   My eyes _____ swollen, and I _____ that I was going to die.

5. (be)   I _____ not going to let that happen again.

6. (read, frighten)   I had _____ that bees only sting when they're _____ .

7. (keep, shake)   So this time I _____ calm and gently _____ my ankle to shoo away the bee without angering it.

8. (work, rise, sneak)   My plan _____ , and as soon as the bee _____ in the air to find a new spot to land, I _____ away.

9. (leave, find)   I _____ my towel by the pool, and I didn't _____ it in the lost-and-found the next day.

10. (lose, sting)   Of course, I would rather _____ a towel than be _____ by a bee again.

Progress Test

This test covers everything you've learned in the Sentence Structure section so far. One sentence in each pair is correct. The other is incorrect. Read both sentences carefully before you decide. Then write the letter of the incorrect sentence in the blank. Try to name the error and correct it if you can.

1. ___ **A.** Mario has ridden Anna's horse before.

   B. Many times if you want to know the truth.

2. ___ **A.** Aboard the boat were the city's mayor and its guest of honour.

   B. They was taking a tour of the harbour.

3. ___ **A.** I will lie down for a nap after lunch.

   B. My keys were laying right where I left them.

4. ___ **A.** Whenever the sun is out and the birds are singing.

   B. Everything looks bright.

5. ___ **A.** He must have forgotten about us.

   B. He was suppose to meet us in the lobby.

6. ___ **A.** I have saved my money, and am finally taking my trip to Europe.

   B. I have bought the tickets and have packed my bags.

7. ___ **A.** The whole restaurant recognized her when she arrived.

   B. And when she left the restaurant became very quiet.

8. ___ **A.** We had already went to the movies by the time you came home.

   B. We saw the new thriller with the incredible car chase.

9. ___ **A.** A raise may be in my future.

   B. I work hard at my job but I enjoy it.

10. ___ **A.** I plan to graduate by the end of the next school year.

    B. Just as soon as I pass my last four classes.

Maintaining Subject/Verb Agreement

As we have seen, the subject and verb in a sentence work together, so they must always agree. Different subjects need different forms of verbs. When the correct verb follows a subject, we call it subject/verb agreement.

The sentences below illustrate the rule that *s* verbs follow most singular subjects but not plural subjects.

One turtle walks.	Three turtles walk.
The baby cries.	The babies cry.
A good leader listens to the people.	Good leaders listen to the people.
One child plays.	Many children play.

And the following sentences show how forms of the verb *be* (*is, am, are, was, were*) and helping verbs (*be, have,* and *do*) are made to agree with their subjects.

This puzzle is difficult.	These puzzles are difficult.
I am amazed.	You are amazed.
He was sleeping.	They were sleeping.
That class has been cancelled.	Those classes have been cancelled.
She does not want to participate.	They do not want to participate.

The following words are always singular and take an *s* verb or the irregular equivalent (*is, was, has, does*):

"ONE" WORDS	"BODY" WORDS	
one	anybody	each
anyone	everybody	either
everyone	nobody	neither
no one	somebody	
someone		

Someone feeds my dog in the morning.

Everybody was at the party.

Each does her own homework.

Remember that prepositional phrases often come between subjects and verbs. You should ignore these interrupting phrases, or you may mistake the wrong word for the subject and use a verb form that doesn't agree.

Someone from the apartments feeds my dog in the morning. (*Someone* is the subject, not *apartments*.)

Everybody on the list of celebrities was at the party. (*Everybody* is the subject, not *celebrities*.)

Each of the twins does her own homework. (*Each* is the subject, not *twins*.)

However, the words *some, any, all, none,* and *most* are exceptions to this rule of ignoring prepositional phrases. These words can be singular or plural, depending on the words that follow them in prepositional phrases.

Some of the *pie* is gone.

Some of the *cookies* are gone.

Is any of the paper still in the supply cabinet?

Are any of the pencils still in the supply cabinet?

All of her work has been published.

All of her poems have been published.

None of the jewellery is missing.

None of the clothes are missing.

On July 1st, most of the country celebrates.

On July 1st, most of the citizens celebrate.

When a sentence has more than one subject joined by *and*, the subject is plural:

The teacher and the tutors eat lunch at noon.

A glazed doughnut and an onion bagel were sitting on the plate.

However, when two subjects are joined by *or*, then the subject closest to the verb determines the verb form:

Either the teacher *or* the tutors eat lunch at noon.

Either the tutors *or* the teacher eats lunch at noon.

A glazed doughnut *or* an onion bagel was sitting on the plate.

In most sentences, the subject comes before the verb. However, in some cases, the subject follows the verb, and subject/verb agreement needs special attention. Study the following examples:

Over the building flies a solitary flag. (flag flies)

Over the building fly several flags. (flags fly)

There is a good reason for my actions. (reason is)

There are good reasons for my actions. (reasons are)

E X E R C I S E S

Underline the verbs that agree with the subjects of the following sentences. Remember to ignore prepositional phrases, unless the subjects are *some, any, all, none,* or *most*. Check your answers ten at a time.

Exercise 1

1. There (is, are) a celebratory sight that occurs around the end of June.

2. From balconies and flagpoles, in windows and doorways (fly, flies) many gaily coloured rainbow flags.

3. Not everyone (know, knows) what these flags (stands, stand) for.

4. No, they (is, are) not flags in preparation for Canada's birthday.

5. A parade with elaborate floats and exquisite costumes (are, is) part of the celebration.

6. Neither the police nor the citizens (seem, seems) to mind the intense crowds that form on the sidewalks to watch the people in the parade (go, goes) by.

7. Certain areas of the city (are, is) cleared of all traffic.

8. Even the mayor and his companions (take, takes) part in the frivolity.

9. Regardless of their sexual orientation, people of all ages (has, have) waited all year to watch this colourful event.

10. Can you guess how many cities in Canada (has, have) Gay Pride Parades?

Exercise 2

1. Banff National Park in the Rockies (is, are) one of Canada's most popular parks.

2. This parkland (was, were) set aside by the federal government in 1885 to preserve the sulphur hot springs for public use.

3. Glaciers from centuries ago (clings, cling) to the upper mountain slopes, creating breathtaking scenery.

4. Cougars, wolves, moose, elk, and two types of bear (makes, make) Banff National Park their home.

5. Forests of evergreens (softens, soften) the slopes of the Banff Rocky Mountains.

6. For visitors on all budgets, there (is, are) campgrounds, resorts, and even a first-class hotel.

7. Either hiking or skiing (is, are) available for most of the months of the year.

8. Hiking trails (radiate, radiates) from the Banff townsite.

9. The Banff Centre School of Fine Arts (overlook, overlooks) the ski resort of Banff and the Banff Springs Hotel.

10. Participants in the program (enjoy, enjoys) the wilderness setting combined with the finest modern facilities in the arts.

Source: The Canadian Encyclopedia, s.v. "Banff."

Exercise 3

1. No one in my film class (has, have) ever seen *2001: A Space Odyssey* before, except me.

2. All of them (has, have) heard of it, but none of them (has, have) watched it.

3. Most of my friends (love, loves) old movies, especially science-fiction ones like *Rollerball* and *Fahrenheit 451*.

4. Each of these sci-fi movies (make, makes) its own point about the human situation.

5. But everybody I know (say, says) *2001: A Space Odyssey* makes the biggest point of all.

6. One of my roommates (think, thinks) that it is the greatest movie ever made.

7. I think that either it or *Fahrenheit 451* (is, are) the best, but I (hasn't, haven't) decided which one yet.

8. George Orwell's famous year 1984 (has, have) passed.

9. Now each of us (is, are) living in the real twenty-first century.

10. No one really (know, knows) yet what new experiences this century will bring.

Exercise 4

1. Some of the world's gems (has, have) been designated as birthstones.

2. Each of these stones (is, are) unique.

3. Either a zodiac sign or a month of the year (is, are) represented by a particular gem.

4. The stone for January (is, are) garnet, and February's (is, are) amethyst.

5. Aquamarine and diamond (is, are) March and April's birthstones.

6. Someone who is born in May (has, have) emerald as a birthstone.

7. The pearl, the ruby, and peridot (represent, represents) those with birthdays in June, July, and August, respectively.

8. And the remaining months — September, October, November, and December — (is, are) associated with sapphire, opal, topaz, and turquoise — in that order.

9. The custom of assigning birthstones to signs of the zodiac (come, comes) from the connection between gems and the stars.

10. Both gemstones and stars (shine, shines).

Source: *Gem Stones* (New York: Dorling Kindersley, 1994).

Exercise 5

1. Everyone in my circle of friends (has, have) plans for the winter break.

2. Each of us (is, are) going to enjoy the break differently.

3. One of my best friends (is, are) flying all the way to Newfoundland.

4. Another of them always (visit, visits) relatives in Vancouver.

5. Most of the students at my school (travel, travels) somewhere to get away.

6. Because of my family's limited travel funds, normally either my sister or I (get, gets) to go on a trip during the break.

7. In the past, my backup plans (has, have) involved driving to the lake nearby and staying with my cousin's family.

8. But this year my parents (has, have) surprised us with news of a family vacation.

9. My sister and I (get, gets) to fly with them to Jamaica.

10. Both of us (is, are) really looking forward to it.

PROOFREADING EXERCISE

Find and correct the ten subject/verb agreement errors in the following paragraph.

My courses for this academic year are really challenging. Each of the classes are difficult in a different way. Some of them requires us to learn on our own in labs. And the others demand that students carefully follows the minute instructions of the professor. The assignments given by my geography instructor, for example, is harder than I expected. Everybody in the class have to prepare a scale model of a mountain range. All of the models so far have looked the same. But one of the models were a little out of scale, and the instructor failed it. The other students and I has decided to work together so none of us makes the same mistake. I guess that all of this hard work are worthwhile. My instructors says it helps prepare us for our future careers.

SENTENCE WRITING

Write ten sentences in which you describe the shoes you are wearing. Use verbs in the present time. Then go back over your sentences — underline your subjects once, underline your verbs twice, and be sure they agree.

Avoiding Shifts in Time

People often worry about using different time frames in writing. Let common sense guide you. If you begin writing a paper in past time, don't shift back and forth to the present unnecessarily; and if you begin in the present, don't shift to the past without good reason. In the following paragraph, the writer starts in the present then shifts to the past, and then shifts again to the present:

> In the novel *Anne of Green Gables,* Anne Shirley is an 11-year-old orphan who is adopted by a couple living in Avonlea, Prince Edward Island. Marilla and Matthew Cuthbert, a rather stern middle-aged couple, expected a boy and were quite surprised to receive a red-haired girl! Initially, the Cuthberts were unsure about keeping her. However, because of her winsome nature, good heart, and spirit, Anne won their love and helped create the family that she has always wanted.

All the verbs should be in the present:

> In the novel *Anne of Green Gables,* Anne Shirley is an 11-year-old orphan who is adopted by a couple living in Avonlea, Prince Edward Island. Marilla and Matthew Cuthbert, a rather stern middle-aged couple, expect a boy and are quite surprised to receive a red-haired girl! Initially, the Cuthberts are unsure about keeping her. However, because of her winsome nature, good heart, and spirit, Anne wins their love and helps create the family that she has always wanted.

This sample paragraph discusses only the events that happen within the novel's plot, so it needs to maintain one time frame — the present, which we use to write about literature and repeated actions.

However, sometimes you will write about the present, the past, and even the future together. Then it may be necessary to use these different time frames within the same paragraph, each for its own reason. For example, if you were to give biographical information about Lucy Maud Montgomery, author of *Anne of Green Gables,* within a discussion of the novel and its influence, you might need to use all three time frames:

> Lucy Maud Montgomery was born in Clifton (now New London), Prince Edward Island, and she based elements in the book on experiences from her childhood. Montgomery was raised by her grandparents in Prince Edward Island after the death of her mother and the departure of her father to Saskatchewan. Like Anne's entry into the Cuthbert household, Montgomery's arrival into her grandparents' home may have been tenuous at first. However, from the story's ending, one can conclude that Montgomery grew to love her grandparents immensely. *Anne of Green Gables* is Montgomery's most famous work and will

be 100 years old in the year 2008. Today it is considered a classic in children's literature.

Sources: 1) http://encarta.msn.com/find/Concise.asp?ti=06DB6000
2) http://w3.one.net/~wilmhoff/ginny/aboutlmm.htm

This paragraph uses past (*was born, based, was raised, may have been, grew*), present (*is*), and future (*will be*) in the same paragraph without committing the error of shifting. Shifting occurs when the writer changes time frames inconsistently or for no reason, confusing the reader (as in the first example given).

PROOFREADING EXERCISES

Which of the following student paragraphs shift *unnecessarily* back and forth between time frames? In those that do, change the verbs to maintain one time frame, thus making the entire paragraph read smoothly. (First, read the paragraphs to determine whether unnecessary shifting takes place. One of the paragraphs is correct.)

1. I loved travelling by train. The rocking motion makes me so calm, and the clackety-clack of the railroad ties as we ride over them sounds like a heartbeat to me. I also enjoy walking down the aisles of all the cars and looking at the different passengers. Whole families sat together, with children facing their parents. I noticed the kids liked to ride backward more than the adults. The food that we ate in the dining car was expensive, but it is always fancy and delicious. My favourite part of the train is the observation car. It is made of glass from the seats up so that we could see everything that we passed along the way.

2. People, especially those who have money, are sometimes wasteful. People exhibited wastefulness in different ways. Restaurants wasted a lot of food every day. Homeowners watered their lawns for too long and let the excess run down the street. People cleaning out their garages threw away their clothes and furniture instead of giving them to charities. I do admit that I am wasteful too, for I am a typical member of my society. I use three sheets of paper for a one-page assignment because I made tiny mistakes, and I order too much food at restaurants. We all needed to start conserving our resources now while there is still time.

3. I recently found out that in Shakespeare's day, all of the characters' parts were played by male actors. That discovery surprised me. The Elizabethans, of course, probably accepted it without question. Now that we are used to realistic action and special effects on stage, I have a hard time imagining a man playing Juliet convincingly. Yet as a drama student, I know how much costume and voice really help to create a believable character. And I was glad to read that, more recently, there have been all-female casts of *Hamlet* and other plays. That seems to balance the scales somehow.

Recognizing Verbal Phrases

We know (from the discussion on p. 82) that a verb phrase is made up of a main verb and at least one helping verb. But sometimes certain forms of verbs are used not as real verbs but as some other part of a sentence. Verbs put to other uses are called *verbals*.

A verbal can be a subject:

Skiing is my favourite Olympic sport. (*Skiing* is the subject, not the verb. The verb is *is*.)

A verbal can be a descriptive word:

His *bruised* ankle healed very quickly. (*Bruised* describes the subject, ankle. *Healed* is the verb.)

A verbal can be an object:

I like *to read* during the summer. (*To read* is the object. *Like* is the verb.)

Verbals link up with other words to form *verbal phrases*. To see the difference between a real verb phrase and a verbal phrase, look at these two sentences:

I was bowling with my best friends. (*Bowling* is the main verb in a verb phrase. Along with the helping verb *was*, it shows the action of the sentence.)

I enjoyed *bowling* with my best friends. (Here the real verb is *enjoyed*. *Bowling* is not the verb; it is part of a verbal phrase — *bowling with my best friends* — which is what I enjoyed.)

THERE ARE THREE KINDS OF VERBALS

1. *ing* verbs used without helping verbs (*running, thinking, baking ...*)

2. verb forms that often end in *ed, en,* or *t* (*tossed, spoken, burnt ...*)

3. verbs that follow *to* _____ (*to walk, to eat, to cause ...*)

Look at the following sentences using the previous examples in verbal phrases:

Running five kilometres a day is great exercise. (real verb = is)

She spent two hours *thinking of a title for her essay.* (real verb = spent)

We had such fun *baking those cherry vanilla cupcakes.* (real verb = had)

Tossed in a salad, artichoke hearts add zesty flavour. (real verb = add)

Sung in Italian, the opera sounds even more beautiful. (real verb = sounds)

The gourmet pizza, *burnt by a careless chef*, shrunk to half its normal size. (real verb = shrunk)

I like *to walk around the zoo by myself.* (real verb = like)

To eat exotic foods takes courage. (real verb = takes)

They actually wanted *to cause an argument.* (real verb = wanted)

EXERCISES

Each of the following sentences contains at least one verbal or verbal phrase. Double underline the real verbs or verb phrases and put brackets around the verbals and verbal phrases. Remember to locate the verbal first (*running, wounded, to sleep ...*) and include any word(s) that go with it (*running a race, wounded in the fight, to sleep all night*). Real verbs will never be inside verbal phrases. Complete the first set before going on to the next.

Exercise 1

1. Choosing a program is one of the most important decisions for students.
2. Many students take a long time to decide about their programs.
3. But they fear wasting time in the wrong courses more than indecision.
4. They spend several semesters as undecided students taking general education classes.
5. Distracted by class work, students can forget to pay attention to their interests.
6. Finally, a particular subject area will attract them to study it further.
7. One student might find happiness in doing a psychology experiment.
8. Writing a poem in an English class may be the assignment to make another decide.
9. Attracted by telescopes, a student might choose to study astronomy.
10. Finding the right program takes time and patience.

Exercise 2

1. I have learned how to manage my time when I am not working.
2. I like to go to the movies on Friday nights.
3. Watching a good film takes me away from the stress of my job.
4. I especially enjoy eating buttery popcorn and drinking a cold pop.
5. It is the perfect way for me to begin the weekend.
6. I get to escape from deadlines and the pressure to succeed.
7. I indulge myself and try to give myself a break — nobody is perfect, and everybody has setbacks.
8. All day Saturday I enjoy lounging around the house in my weekend clothes.
9. I do a little gardening and try to relax my mind.
10. By Sunday evening, after resting for two days, I am ready to start my busy week all over again.

Exercise 3

1. Many people dislike speaking in front of strangers.

2. That is why there is an almost universal fear of giving speeches.

3. Feeling insecure and exposed, people get dry mouths and sweaty hands.

4. Note cards become useless, rearranging themselves in the worst possible order.

5. To combat this problem, people try to memorize a speech, only to forget the whole thing as the audience stares back at them expectantly.

6. And when they do remember parts of it, the microphone decides to quit at the punch line of their best joke.

7. Embarrassed and humiliated, they struggle to regain their composure.

8. Then the audience usually begins to sympathize with and encourage the speaker.

9. Finally used to the spotlight, the speaker relaxes and finds the courage to finish.

10. No one expects giving a speech to get any easier.

Exercise 4

1. Canadian astronaut Roberta Bondar blasted off into space to gather data on how living things function in space.

2. Bondar was aboard the space shuttle *Discovery* in January 1992, setting a record as Canada's first woman in space.

3. After graduating from high school, Bondar assertively pursued her career, obtaining five university degrees in science and medicine.

4. She applied to the new Canadian Space Agency to become a candidate for astronaut.

5. The wait to go into space lasted nine years, but Bondar remained fit and ready.

6. When the astronauts finally left the launch pad on the *Discovery,* Bondar thrust her fists in the air, shouting "Yes, yes, yes."

7. Bondar and her six colleagues spent eight days in space, investigating the effects of weightlessness on the human body.

8. Today Bondar does research at the University of Western Ontario, travelling around the country to encourage young people in the sciences.

9. Bondar was appointed Chair of the Science Advisory Board, a board set up to advise the federal health minister.

10. She believes that protecting the environment is one of the most important responsibilities we have today.

Source: Gale Infobase, August 1997.

Exercise 5

1. We have all seen stage shows where magicians try to hypnotize people beginning with the suggestion, "You are getting very sleepy. ... "

2. Then they order their hypnotized subjects to cluck like chickens or to cry like babies.

3. Hypnotists can even convince subjects to feel very cold even if the room is actually warm.

4. More important, subjects have been able to hallucinate on command and to control pain.

5. Now researchers are studying the brains of supposedly hypnotized people to see if there is such a thing as a real hypnotic state.

6. Measuring the altered blood flow to different locations in the brain allows scientists to visualize the effects of hypnosis.

7. And studies show that these effects can indeed be measured by changes in the brains of hypnotized subjects.

8. To identify people only pretending to be hypnotized, scientists secretly filmed all participants while only an audiotape made suggestions to the subjects.

9. Subjects genuinely able to be hypnotized responded to either the audiotape or the hypnotist himself.

10. Those who did not respond unless a hypnotist was in the room were judged to be faking the effects of hypnosis, and their brain measurements revealed less change than the others.

Source: New Scientist, 4 July 1998.

PARAGRAPH EXERCISE

Double underline the real verbs or verb phrases and put brackets around the verbals and verbal phrases in the following paragraph from the book *Saloons of the Old West* by Richard Erdoes.

In the opinion of most westerners "barkeeps were ... the hardest worked folks in camp. ... " One of these burdens was to act as a human fire alarm. Western saloons never closed, and whenever a fire broke out the saloon owner would dash into the street, running up and down hollering and emptying his six-shooter at the moon. The commotion would send the volunteer firemen pouring into the street in their long johns to put out the fire. Having done so, all and sundry naturally assembled in the saloon to mull over the event while imbibing a tumbler of gut-warming red-eye.

SENTENCE WRITING

Write ten sentences that contain verbal phrases. Use the ten verbals listed here to begin your verbal phrases: *speaking, typing, driving, reading, to eat, to go, to chat, to cook, impressed, taken.* The last two are particularly difficult to use as verbals. There are sample sentences listed in the Answers at the back of the book. But first, try to write your own so that you can compare the two.

Correcting Misplaced or Dangling Modifiers

When we modify something, we often change whatever it is by adding something to it. We might modify a car, for example, by adding special tires. In English we call words, phrases, and clauses *modifiers* when they add information to part of a sentence. To do its job properly, a modifier should be in the right spot — as close to the word it describes as possible. If we put new tires on the roof of the car instead of where they belong, they would be misplaced. In the following sentence, the modifier is too far away from the word it modifies to make sense. It is a misplaced modifier.

> Swinging from tree to tree, we watched the monkeys at the zoo.

Was it *we* who were swinging from tree to tree? That's what the sentence says because the modifying phrase *Swinging from tree to tree* is next to *we*. It should be next to *monkeys*.

> At the zoo, we watched the monkeys swinging from tree to tree.

The next example has no word at all for the modifier to modify:

> At the age of eight, my family finally bought a dog.

Obviously the family was not eight when it bought a dog. Nor was the dog eight. The modifier *At the age of eight* is dangling there with no word to attach itself to, no word for it to modify. We can get rid of the dangling modifier by turning it into a dependent clause. (See p. 60 for a discussion of dependent clauses.)

> When I was eight, my family finally bought a dog.

Here the clause has its own subject and verb — *I was* — and there's no chance of misunderstanding the sentence. Here's another dangling modifier:

> After a ten-minute nap, the plane landed.

Did the plane take a ten-minute nap? Who did?

> After a ten-minute nap, I awoke just as the plane landed.

E X E R C I S E S

Carefully rephrase any of the following sentences that contain misplaced or dangling modifiers. Some sentences are correct.

Exercise 1

1. After ordering pizza for dinner, my cellphone lost its signal.

2. I found a penny jogging around the park.

3. I went to the movies with my mother last week.

4. One year after becoming manager, the store went out of business.

5. The students worked well with their tutors.

6. My sister's smiling face appeared with an armful of flowers for my graduation.

7. The dancer tripped and fell on his shoelace.

8. In an envelope, they sent us several postcards from Bermuda.

9. Trying to open the door with the wrong key, she could not get into the apartment.

10. I bought a new dress with gold buttons.

Exercise 2

1. We stood at the curb and waited for the bus.

2. The students paid attention to each of the speakers taking careful notes.

3. I mailed your invitation in my jogging suit.

4. Giving directions in a booming voice, the recruits listened to their new commander.

5. She helped her sister with the heavy box.

6. The children ate the ice cream sandwiches sitting in their chairs.

7. Full of gas, she drove her new car home from the showroom.

8. After making other plans, the party went on without me.

9. My brother's car pulled into the driveway with a surprised look on his face.

10. We flew to the Bahamas for a week's holiday without sunglasses.

Exercise 3

1. The children saw lions and bears walking around the zoo.

2. As team leaders, many responsibilities fall on your shoulders.

3. Folded neatly, the maid brought in the extra towels we had requested.

4. They noticed an error reading their policy very carefully.

5. She kicked her friend in the auditorium by accident.

6. The teacher handed the tests back to the students with a frown.

7. Talking with the guests, the party finally got underway.

8. We adopted a cat for our mother with a fluffy tail.

9. The farmers planted the new crop in their overalls.

10. At the age of 18, voting rights are accorded to Canadian citizens.

Exercise 4

1. Taking tickets at the Tilt-a-Whirl, the carnival quickly lost its appeal.

2. She asked her manager for a raise and received one.

3. The actors opened the gifts in their costumes.

4. A police car sat in the middle of the intersection.

5. Dragging along the floor, the dog pulled its heavy leash.

6. I sent him a photograph of me in Cape Breton.

7. She found a dollar bill going through her pockets.

8. Promising to return, our guide left us alone in the museum.

9. The Boy Scouts went camping with their fathers.

10. After shouting "Happy New Year!" the room went completely quiet.

Exercise 5

1. One day after turning 40, my new car broke down on the freeway.

2. Liking the rush of fresh air on his face, my brother lets his dog hang out the car window.

3. I ran through the park to try out my new shoes.

4. Studying in the writing lab, my comma problems disappeared.

5. Helping my father gives me great pleasure.

6. Chasing each other up and down a tree, we saw a pair of squirrels.

7. I like to watch television at night.

8. We are proud of our sister for graduating with honours.

9. Lifting the heavy television, her face turned red.

10. I enjoy collecting things from days gone by.

PROOFREADING EXERCISE

Find and correct any misplaced or dangling modifiers in the following paragraphs.

I love parades, so last year my family and I went to Toronto to see the Caribana parade. It turned out to be even more wonderful than I expected.

Arriving one day before the festivities, the city was already crowded with tourists. Early the next morning, people set up lawn chairs on Lakeshore Boulevard. We didn't want to miss one float in the parade, so we found our own spot and made ourselves at home. When the parade began, I had as much fun watching the spectators as the parade itself. I saw children pointing at the breathtaking floats sitting on their parents' shoulders. Decorated extravagantly with feathers and sequins, I couldn't believe how beautiful the costumes were.

The crowd was overwhelmed by the sights and sounds of the parade. Marching and playing their instruments with perfect rhythm, everyone especially enjoyed hearing the steel drum bands. They must have practised the whole year to be that good.

My experience didn't end with the parade, however. After the last float had passed, I found a $20 bill walking up Yonge Street. Now hanging on my wall at home, I framed it as a souvenir of my Caribana experience.

SENTENCE WRITING

Write five sentences that contain misplaced or dangling modifiers; then revise those sentences to put the modifiers where they belong. Use the examples in the explanations as models.

Following Sentence Patterns

Sentences are built according to a few basic patterns. For proof, rearrange each of the following sets of words to form a complete statement (not a question):

apples a ate raccoon the

the crashing beach were waves the on

your in am partner I life

been she school has to walking

you wonderful in look green

There are only one or two possible combinations for each due to English sentence patterns. Either *A raccoon ate the apples*, or *The apples ate a raccoon*, and so on. But in each case, the verb or verb phrase makes its way to the middle of the statement.

To understand sentence patterns, you need to know that verbs can do three things.

1. They can show actions.

The raccoon ate the apples.

The waves were crashing on the beach.

She has been walking to school.

2. They can link subjects with descriptive words.

I am your partner in life.

You look wonderful in green.

3. They can help other verbs form verb phrases.

The waves were crashing on the beach.

She has been walking to school.

Look at these sentences for more examples:

Mel grabbed a slice of pizza. (The verb *grabbed* shows Mel's action.)

His slice was the largest one in the box. (The verb *was* links *slice* with its description as *the largest one.*)

Mel had been craving pizza for a week. (The verbs *had* and *been* help the main verb *craving* in a verb phrase.)

Knowing what a verb does in a clause helps you gain an understanding of the three basic sentence patterns:

SUBJECT + ACTION VERB + OBJECT PATTERN

Some action verbs must be followed by a person or object that receives the action.

S   AV   OBJ.
Sylvia completed the difficult math test. (*Sylvia completed* makes no sense without being followed by the object that she completed — *test.*)

SUBJECT + ACTION VERB (+ NO OBJECT) PATTERN

At other times, the action verb itself finishes the meaning and needs no object after it.

    S   **AV**

She celebrated at home with her family. (*She celebrated* makes sense alone. The two prepositional phrases — *at home* and *with her family* are not needed to understand the meaning of the clause.)

SUBJECT + LINKING VERB + DESCRIPTION PATTERN

A special kind of verb that does not show an action but links a subject with a description is called a *linking verb*. It acts like an equal sign in a clause. Learn to recognize the most common linking verbs: *is, am, are, was, were, seem, feel, appear, become, look.*

    S   **LV**   **DESC.**

Sylvia was always an excellent student. (*Sylvia* equals *an excellent student.*)

    S   **LV**   **DESC.**

Sylvia has become very intelligent. (*Very intelligent* describes *Sylvia.*)

NOTE: We learned on page 82 that a verb phrase includes a main verb and its helping verbs. Helping verbs can be used in any of the sentence patterns.

    S   **AV**

Sylvia is going to Vancouver for a vacation. (Here the verb *is* helps the main verb *going*, which is an action verb with no object followed by two prepositional phrases — *to Vancouver* and *for a vacation.*)

The following chart outlines the patterns using short sentences that you should memorize:

THE THREE BASIC SENTENCE PATTERNS

S + AV + Obj.	S + AV
They hit the ball.	They ran (quickly) (around the bases).
	not objects

S + LV +	Desc.
They are	amateur players.
They look	professional.

These are the three basic patterns of most of the clauses used in English sentences. Knowing them can help writers control their sentences and improve their use of words.

E X E R C I S E S

First, put parentheses around any prepositional phrases. Next, underline the subjects once and the verbs or verb phrases twice. Then mark the sentence patterns above the words. Remember that the patterns never mix together. For example, unlike an action verb, a linking verb will almost never be used alone (for example, "He seems."), nor will an action verb be followed by a description of the subject (for example, "She took tall."). And if there are two independent clauses, each one may have a different pattern. Check your answers after the first set of ten.

Exercise 1

1. I am afraid of flying.
2. The engine sounds scare me.
3. During takeoff, I sit in my seat and close my eyes.
4. With the plane in the air, I can relax and gaze out the window.
5. I use the clouds as a distraction.
6. By the middle of the flight, I am chatting with the passenger next to me.
7. Then I worry about the landing.
8. The plane tilts forward slightly.
9. We bounce in our seats, and I hold my breath.
10. I will always be a nervous flyer.

Exercise 2

1. On November 4, 1922, archeologist Howard Carter discovered the tomb of King Tutankhamen.
2. Carter had been excavating in Egypt for years without success.
3. Then he made his famous discovery.
4. With the help of his workers, Carter found the top step of a stone stairway.
5. They followed the staircase down a total of sixteen steps.

6. At the bottom, Carter and his team encountered a sealed door.

7. They had found a tomb undisturbed for thousands of years.

8. It held the personal belongings of a young Egyptian king.

9. Some of the objects were precious; others were just ordinary household effects.

10. The job of cataloguing and removing the items took ten years.

Source: The Discovery of the Tomb of Tutankhamen (New York: Dover, 1977).

Exercise 3

1. We live in a world with photocopiers, scanners, and fax machines.

2. If we need copies of documents, these machines make them for us.

3. Up until the late 1800s, people copied all documents by hand.

4. As a solution to this problem, Thomas Edison invented an electric pen.

5. Unlike ordinary pens, Edison's electric pen made stencils; the pen itself was inkless.

6. Its sharp tip poked holes in the paper, and later a roller spread ink over the holes.

7. The ink went through the holes onto another sheet of paper underneath.

8. And an exact copy was the result; in fact, one stencil produced many copies.

9. The first documents Edison reproduced with his electric pen were a speech from *Richard III* and the outline of a photograph of Edison's wife, Mary.

10. Although Edison sold many thousands of his electric pens at the time, only six of them have survived.

Source: Smithsonian, July 1998.

Exercise 4

1. People often travel with their dogs, cats, or other pets.

2. Airlines offer some suggestions about flying with pets.

3. First, a pet should be old enough to fly — 9 weeks old at least.

4. All pets must travel in approved carriers with food and water dishes.

5. During the flight, airlines store most pets in the cargo areas.

6. One small pet can ride in the passenger area if the pet's carrier fits under a seat.

7. However, only one pet may travel in the passenger area per flight.

8. Ordinary water in a pet's dish usually spills during loading.

9. But ice cubes in the water dish will melt after loading so that the pet will have water.

10. Sedatives are risky when the pet can't react normally if, for example, its carrier overturns.

Source: Avenues, March–April 1997.

Exercise 5

1. The Hudson's Bay Company was established in 1670 with the development of the fur trade in North America.

2. Originally, the company was controlled by the British overseers until May 1970, when Queen Elizabeth II granted Canadians ownership.

3. The company's first Canadian headquarters were in Winnipeg, but they moved to Toronto in 1987.

4. The Hudson's Bay Company opened its first store in downtown Calgary, Alberta, in 1884.

5. Today, the Hudson's Bay Company is Canada's oldest corporation and largest department store retailer.

6. Many Bay shoppers never contemplate this company's most important historic duty — to supply France and Russia with food and munitions throughout World War I.

7. After the stock market crash of 1929, the company was badly shaken, but it survived the Depression.

8. In 1970, to celebrate the 300th anniversary of the store, the company built a replica of the sailing ship *Nonsuch,* the first ship to explore Hudson Bay. It sailed along the coasts of England, the Great Lakes, and the Pacific Northwest before being placed in a museum in Manitoba.

9. To recognize the Hudson's Bay Company's 325th anniversary, in February 1995, a commemorative silver dollar displaying the co-founders Radisson and des Groseilliers with the *Nonsuch* in the background was produced.

10. In January 1994, the Provincial Archives of Manitoba became the permanent home of the Hudson's Bay Company Archives. They consist of handwritten journals, ships' logs, maps, photos, rare books, and much more.

Source: http://www.hbc.com/hbchistory/hbc_adventures/250th.htm

PARAGRAPH EXERCISE

Label the sentence patterns in the following paragraphs. They are from a book by Robert J. Brym, titled *New Society: Sociology for the 21st Century.* It helps to put parentheses around prepositional phrases first to isolate them from the words that make up the sentence patterns — the subjects, the verbs, and any objects after action verbs or any descriptive words after linking verbs (*is, was, were, seem, appear* ...).

Nature Is a Cultural Phenomenon

Nature is so important to many Canadians that we devote a lot of time and other resources to caring for it. Love of nature flourishes in cultures that have highly developed technologies. With rare exception, we are no longer afraid of the forces of nature. We believe that nature can be controlled, so we see it in a benevolent way, as something to be enjoyed. Nature is a source of fantasies about a way of life different from urban civilization; it is a source of entertainment in nature programs on television; and it provides a retreat from alienating work. We tour through nature, hike, mountain-bike, and cross-country ski.

So many people visit our national parks and other nature reserves in the summer that we must control how we use them. In a period of drought, we may have to accept restrictions on where we light campfires. ... Foreign visitors are sometimes surprised to learn that we voluntarily disarm ourselves before entering places where bears can, and occasionally do, kill us.

In our love of nature, we not only act to conserve it, we also actively manage it. We may have to work hard to restore the "balance of nature" that was disturbed when a park was created. Most provincial parks are too small to support a population of wolves, but, without predators, moose, deer, and elk can multiply to the point where they damage the vegetation. Parks managers may then decide to reduce their numbers by culling the herds, through planned hunting.

Source: Robert J. Brym, *New Society: Sociology for the 21st Century* (Toronto: Harcourt Brace & Company, Canada, 1995), 7-3. Based on A. Wilson, *The Culture of Nature* (Cambridge, MA: Blackwell, 1992).

SENTENCE WRITING

Write ten sentences describing the weather today and your feelings about it — make your sentences short and clear. Then go back and label the sentence patterns you have used.

Avoiding Clichés, Awkward Phrasing, and Wordiness

CLICHÉS

A cliché is an expression that has been used so often it has lost its originality and effectiveness. Whoever first said "light as a feather" had thought of an original way to express lightness, but today that expression is worn out. Most of us use an occasional cliché in speaking, but clichés have no place in writing. The good writer thinks up fresh new ways to express ideas.

Here are a few clichés. Add some more to the list.

the bottom line
older but wiser
last but not least
in this day and age
different as night and day
out of this world
white as a ghost
sick as a dog
tried and true
at the top of their lungs
the thrill of victory
one in a million
busy as a bee
easier said than done
better late than never

Clichés lack freshness because the reader always knows what's coming next. Can you complete these expressions?

the agony of ...
breathe a sigh of ...
lend a helping ...
odds and ...
raining cats and ...
time flies when ...
been there ...
worth its weight ...

Clichés are expressions too many people use. Try to avoid them in your writing.

AWKWARD PHRASING

Another problem — awkward phrasing — comes from writing sentence structures that *no one* else would use because they break basic sentence patterns, omit necessary words, or use words incorrectly. Like clichés, awkward sentences might *sound* acceptable when spoken, but as polished writing, they are usually unacceptable.

AWKWARD

There should be great efforts in terms of the cooperation between coaches and their athletes.

CORRECTED

Coaches and their athletes should cooperate.

AWKWARD

During the experiment, the use of key principles was essential to ensure the success of it.

CORRECTED

The experiment was a success. *or* We did the experiment carefully.

AWKWARD

My favourite was when the guy fell all the way down the ship.

CORRECTED

In my favourite scene, a man fell all the way down the deck of the sinking ship.

WORDINESS

Good writing is concise writing. Don't say something in ten words if you can say it better in five. "In today's society" isn't as effective as "today," and it's a cliché. "At this point in time" could be "presently" or "now."

Another kind of wordiness comes from saying something twice. There's no need to write "in the month of August" or "9 A.M. in the morning" or "my personal opinion." August *is* a month, 9 A.M. *is* morning, and anyone's opinion *is* personal. All you need to write is "in August," "9 A.M.," and "my opinion."

Still another kind of wordiness comes from using expressions that add nothing to the meaning of the sentence. "The point is that we can't afford it" says no more than "We can't afford it."

Here is a sample wordy sentence:

The construction company actually worked on that particular building for a period of six months.

And here it is after eliminating wordiness:

The construction company worked on that building for six months.

WORDY WRITING	**CONCISE WRITING**
advance planning	planning
an unexpected surprise	a surprise
ask a question	ask
at a later date	later
basic fundamentals	fundamentals
green in colour	green
but nevertheless	but (or nevertheless)
combine together	combine
completely empty	empty
down below	below
each and every	each (or every)
end result	result
fewer in number	fewer
free gift	gift
in order to	to
in spite of the fact that	although
just exactly	exactly
large in size	large
new innovation	innovation
on a regular basis	regularly
past history	history
rectangular in shape	rectangular
refer back	refer
repeat again	repeat
serious crisis	crisis
sufficient enough	sufficient (or enough)
there in person	there
two different kinds	two kinds
very unique	unique

E X E R C I S E S

Exercise 1

Rewrite the following sentences to eliminate clichés and awkward phrasing.

1. I like to shop around before I buy something.

2. Three or four different stores is not unusual for me to go to.

3. I always keep my eye on the bottom line.

4. I can save $100 on one item with this foolproof method.

5. Stranger things have happened.

6. Prices may vary significantly on the exact same merchandise.

7. But buying at the right time is easier said than done.

8. Once I waited so long for a sale on a computer that I was left empty-handed.

9. There is a real feeling of satisfaction I get when I do find a bargain though.

10. Looking for good prices is my bottom line.

Exercise 2

Cross out words or rewrite parts of each sentence to eliminate wordiness. Doing these exercises can almost turn into a game to see how few words you can use without changing the meaning of the sentence.

1. I received an unexpected surprise in the mail today.

2. It came in a small little box that was square in size and brown in colour.

3. I discovered as I looked at the mailing label that it had been sent by someone in Cape Dorset.

4. I had a hard time figuring out whether or not I knew anyone in Cape Dorset.

5. After I thought about it for a long period of time, I kind of remembered that one of our old neighbours that used to live next door had moved to Cape Dorset.

6. Due to the fact that I had been good friends with their son Josh, I figured that it must be Josh who was the one who sent the mysterious box.

7. Sure enough, as I saw what it was that was inside the box, I knew for sure that Josh had sent it to me.

8. Josh must have remembered that I collect many different kinds of souvenir snow domes from all the places that I have travelled to in my life.

9. Inside this particular package, there was a large size snow dome with a white polar bear and a man riding on a sled pulled by dogs across the snow and a nameplate that said the words *Cape Dorset* in letters that were red.

10. There was a whole bunch of plastic snow that made the whole thing look like a snowy blizzard was going on when I shook it back and forth.

Exercise 3

Revise the sentences in the remaining exercises to eliminate any clichés, awkward phrasing, or wordiness.

1. The most exciting thing I have ever seen in my life has to be a performance I saw at the Shaw Festival.

2. Each and every spring, the festival begins like clockwork, and the tourists flock like sheep to the very unique town of Niagara-on-the-Lake.

3. On a regular basis, loads of people in cars, vans, and buses in all shapes and sizes come from every town in the world in order to see the tried and true plays.

4. It would be sufficient enough just to see a sublime performance, but nevertheless the enjoyment of travelling through the area comes as an unexpected surprise.

5. It is a perfect time of year in and around town since the surrounding orchards of fruit trees are bursting into bloom with blossoms white as snow, as well as pink and red in colour.

6. Niagara-on-the-Lake has vineyards as far as the eye can see, and zillions of wineries dot the area.

7. Each winery has a wine tasting room, where you can taste absolutely the best wine by the glass for less than nothing.

8. In this day and age, it's hard to get something for nothing.

9. All you have to do is spend an arm and a leg on a bottle or two of a one in a million Canadian wine.

10. Last but not least, the absolute best way to end a visit to the Shaw Festival is to bring along a picnic and enjoy it along the Niagara Escarpment overlooking the river.

Exercise 4

1. In this day and age, it's hard to find a place that is really and truly old-fashioned.

2. Black Creek Pioneer Village is that kind of place; it's near Paramount Canada's Wonderland, but in my personal opinion, these two amusement parks are as different as night and day.

3. First of all, the original Pioneer Village was settled by pioneer families, many of whom were Pennsylvania German farmers who came to Canada in the early nineteenth century.

4. Pioneer Village was a real settlement for the pioneers and has been restored and is shown as it was in the 1860s.

5. The creators of Black Creek Pioneer Village were able to recreate the old village and the past with over 35 carefully restored 1860s' shops and homes.

6. Talk about old fashioned; Pioneer Village also has a blacksmith, a cabinetmaker, and other tradespeople with whom people can talk to about their crafts.

7. There are even an old doctor's house, Roblin's Mill and water wheel, a local schoolhouse, and other authentic homes and shops that people can see during their visit to the past.

8. Pioneer Village is staffed with many hosts dressed as if they were right out of the 1860s who are more than happy to guide guests through a part of Canadian history.

9. And if that's not enough, people can even take a ride on a horse-drawn wagon just as the pioneers did in the olden days.

10. There are a wide variety of activities offered throughout the year includ-
    ing demonstrations of village trades and homecrafts, a Pioneer Festival in
    September, and special Christmas celebrations in December.

Sources: 1) www.trca.on.ca/bcpv.html
2) www.nfb.ca/FMT/E/MSN/15/15338.html

Exercise 5

1. The other day I had to stay home from work because I was as sick as a
   dog with the flu.
2. I told my boss that one day of complete and utter rest would make me
   feel much better, but that was easier said than done.
3. I had forgotten that on Thursdays nearly every house on the block has its
   gardeners come to take care of the plants and trees in the yards.
4. Each and every one of them always uses a power leaf blower and a tree-
   trimming saw to get the work done.
5. The noise around the neighbourhood made my head spin, and I couldn't
   get to sleep for the life of me.
6. I tried watching television in order to drown out the noise and put me to sleep.
7. That was like jumping out of the frying pan into the fire; the shows on
   daytime TV were really hard to take.
8. Once the gardeners finished, I finally got to go to sleep at about 3 p.m.
   in the afternoon.
9. It was better late than never.
10. I got just about sixteen hours of sleep, felt better, and was as happy as a
    clam to be back at work the next day.

PROOFREADING EXERCISE

Revise the sentences in the following paragraph to eliminate any clichés, awkward
phrasing, or wordiness.

Just about everybody in the world loves to collect books and other reading
material, but one woman went overboard. She piled stacks and stacks of books all

around her house. She lived to the ripe old age of 70 years old before her love of books led to her death. It's a sad but true fact that, at the end of the year 1977, the woman's neighbours called the local police station to tell them that she was no longer coming and going from her house and they were worried that something terrible had happened to her. When the police got there in person, they found that the end result of this woman's love of books was that one huge stack had collapsed onto her bed. She was alive when they found her, but she passed away as they took her to the hospital.

Source: A Passion for Books (Eugene, OR: Harvest House, 1998).

SENTENCE WRITING

Go back to the sentences you wrote for the Sentence Writing exercise on p. 59 or p. 93, and revise them to eliminate any clichés, awkward phrasing, or wordiness.

Correcting for Parallel Structure

Your writing will be clearer and more memorable if you use parallel construction. That is, when you make any kind of list, put the items in similar form. If you write

My favourite coffee drinks are lattes, mochas, and the ones with espresso.

the sentence lacks parallel structure. The items don't all have the same form. But if you write

My favourite coffees are lattes, mochas, and espressos.

then the items are parallel. They are all single-word nouns. Or you could write

I like drinks blended with milk, flavoured with chocolate, and made with espresso.

Again the sentence has parallel structure because all three descriptions are verbal phrases. Here are some more examples. Note how much easier it is to read the sentences with parallel construction.

LACKING PARALLEL CONSTRUCTION	**HAVING PARALLEL CONSTRUCTION**
I like to hike, to ski, and going sailing.	I like to hike, to ski, and to sail. (all "to____" verbs)
The office has run out of pens, paper, ink cartridges, and we need more toner, too.	The office needs more pens, paper, ink cartridges, and toner. (all nouns)
They decided that they needed a change, that they could afford a new house, and wanted to move to Calgary.	They decided that they needed a change, that they could afford a new house, and that they wanted to move to Calgary. (all dependent clauses)

The supporting points in an outline should always be parallel. In the following brief outlines, the supporting points in the left-hand column are not parallel in structure. Those in the right-hand column are parallel.

NOT PARALLEL

Food Irradiation
  I. How is it good?
    A. Longer shelf life
    B. Using fewer pesticides
    C. Kills bacteria
  II. Concerns
    A. Nutritional value
    B. Consumers are worried
    C. Workers' safety

PARALLEL

Food Irradiation
  I. Benefits
    A. Extends shelf life
    B. Requires fewer pesticides
    C. Kills bacteria
  II. Concerns
    A. Lowers nutritional value
    B. Alarms consumers
    C. Endangers workers

Using parallel construction will make your writing more effective. Note the effective parallelism in these well-known quotations:

A place for everything and everything in its place.

Isabella Mary Beeton

I have been poor and I have been rich. Rich is better.

Sophie Tucker

The more the data banks record about each of us, the less we exist.

Marshall McLuhan

A Canadian I was born; a Canadian I will die.

John G. Diefenbaker

E X E R C I S E S

Most — but not all — of the following sentences lack parallel structure. In some, you will be able to cross out the part that is not parallel and write the correction above. Other sentences will need complete rephrasing.

Exercise 1

1. Researchers have designed a new kind of robot.

2. It doesn't look like other robots, and what it does is different too.

3. Its "head" contains a microphone for ears, a small screen for a face, and a video camera to act as its eyes.

4. It does not have a body, just a pole to hold up its "head."

5. The pole connects to a box-shaped base with rollers to give it motion.

6. The difference between this and other kinds of robots is that the PRoP, as it's called, becomes an extension of anyone who controls it through the Internet.

7. A person in one city will be able to log on to the PRoP in another city and wander around — seeing what it sees, speaking to people it meets, and the person is able to hear what it hears.

8. The face of the person controlling the PRoP will be displayed on the small screen on its "head," so it will assume the user's identity.

9. The inventors of the PRoP believe that research labs and those in the business world will be most interested in the PRoPs at first.

10. But in the future, PRoPs could make it possible to take a vacation or maybe you could play a game of chess with a faraway friend without ever leaving your desk.

Source: New Scientist, 26 Sept. 1998.

Exercise 2

1. I recently discovered what the word *trivia* means and its history.

2. A Greek goddess named Hecate was famous for frightening travellers.

3. She would do spooky things to them on highways, at crossroads, and when they walked down country paths.

4. Hecate especially liked to haunt three-way intersections.

5. The three roads came together, and a "T" shape was formed.

6. This type of place had two different ancient names: *triodos* in Greek, and in Latin it was *trivium.*

7. So Hecate was also called "Trivia," but the story didn't end there.

8. To please Hecate (Trivia), people placed statues of her with three faces or the same number of bodies wherever three roads met.

9. People began to use these decorated spots as gathering places to talk about daily business, to catch up on gossip, and because these landmarks were so easy to find.

10. That's how the word *trivial* came to mean "commonplace" or unimportant, like the tidbits of information people shared at Hecate's favourite hangout.

Source: By Jove! (New York: HarperCollins, 1992).

Exercise 3

1. There are many coincidences in the lives of the members of my family.

2. My mother and father were both born on July 1, and I was born on Canada's birthday.

3. My mother was named Sarah Louisa at birth; my girlfriend's first name is Louisa and her middle name is Sarah.

4. My mother was 24 when she had her first baby and her sister-in-law was pregnant at the time.

5. Therefore, my cousin and I are the same age.

6. When my father was in high school, he had three jobs: waiter, babysitter, and he delivered newspapers.

7. To earn extra money, I often deliver newspapers, wash dishes in a restaurant, and I get money for babysitting for my neighbour.

8. Sometimes my sister and I will meet accidentally at the movies, and we wore the same shirts.

9. Is this just a coincidence or we have something in common?

10. My sister and I both hope to become veterinarians: I study science at school, and she is doing a volunteer job at an animal shelter this year.

Exercise 4

1. Many students worry that they will not have enough time to complete their assignments before the due date and about writing exams.

2. They feel stressed, both psychologically and in the physical aspect of their lives.

3. On the physical level, they may experience loss of appetite, sleeplessness, having headaches, feeling sweaty, or even ulcers or other illnesses.

4. On the psychological level, stress may involve feeling helpless, anxious, or being afraid of losing control.

5. Although everyone experiences stress from time to time, the level of stress that individuals experience from the same situation varies greatly.

6. For example, when it comes to doing a presentation in class, a student who often speaks in front of groups of people is less likely to be as stressed as a student who has never been in that situation.

7. There are various personal factors that are related to a person's ability to handle stressful events effectively: having a sense of control over one's life, having a network of friends and family, a flexible attitude to unexpected events, and have a hobby or a favourite sport.

8. Nevertheless, most people, at some time or other in their lives, feel stressed and thinking themselves unable to cope.

9. The best way to deal with such a situation is to put in place coping strategies, such as monitoring your responses to everyday demands and expectations, learning relaxation techniques, and to maintain a regular sleep routine.

10. If these strategies fail, talking to another person, such as a counsellor or a person who works in the health profession, is often extremely helpful.

Source: Adapted from Joan Fleet, Fiona Goodchild, and Richard Zajchowski, *Learning for Success: Effective Strategies for Students*, 3rd ed. (Toronto: Harcourt Brace & Company, 1999), 43–46.

Exercise 5

Make the following list parallel.

1. I've made a list of eight basic steps I can follow to improve my writing.

2. First, I need to accept that my writing needs work and I can make it better if I try.

3. Second, a lot of progress can be made by just cutting out wordy expressions.

4. Third, working on my vocabulary will also help a lot.

5. Fourth, I need to proofread my papers more carefully.

6. Fifth, my sentences should be different lengths, some short and others should be longer.

7. Sixth, I've been told that I use the passive voice too much and that I should use the active voice instead.

8. Seventh, budgeting my time will allow a first draft to sit for a while before I revise it.

9. Finally, always look at the overall structure of a paper when I revise, not just the words and sentences.

10. By following these eight steps, I hope to be a better writer.

PROOFREADING EXERCISE

Proofread the following paragraph about Alfred Hitchcock, the famous movie director, and revise it to correct any errors in parallel structure.

Alfred Hitchcock was born in England in 1899, but in 1955 he became a citizen of the United States. He hated his childhood nicknames, "Fred" and another of his nicknames "Cocky." He did not have a close relationship with his brother, his sister, or with any friends. When Hitchcock was only 6 years old, his father gave him a note, and Alfred was supposed to take it to the police station near their house. He delivered the note to one of the officers. The officer followed the directions in the note, put little Alfred in a holding cell for several minutes, telling him that was what happened to bad children. It was his father's way of keeping Alfred on the right track, but it had the opposite effect. Throughout his life, Hitchcock had an intense fear of doing something wrong. He made more than 50 films; the most successful of them was *Psycho*. In the opening credits of his television series, he used to step into a line drawing of his famous profile. Many people don't know that Alfred Hitchcock drew that sketch himself.

Source: Biography Magazine, Oct. 1998.

SENTENCE WRITING

Write ten sentences that use parallel structure in a list or a pair of objects, actions, locations, or ideas. You may choose your own subject or describe a process that you carry out at your job.

Using Pronouns

Nouns name people, places, things, and ideas — such as *students, school, computers,* and *cyberspace*. Pronouns take the place of nouns to avoid repetition and to clarify meaning. Look at the following two sentences. Nouns are needlessly repeated in the first sentence, but the second uses pronouns.

> The boy's mother felt that the children at the party were too loud, so the boy's mother told the children that the party would have to end if the children didn't calm down.

> The boy's mother felt that the children at the party were too loud, so *she* told *them* that *it* would have to end if *they* didn't calm down.

In the second sentence, *she* replaces *mother, they* and *them* replace *children*, and *it* takes the place of *party*.

Of the many kinds of pronouns, the following cause the most difficulty because they include two ways of identifying the same person (or people), but only one form is correct in a given situation:

SUBJECT GROUP	OBJECT GROUP
I	me
he	him
she	her
we	us
they	them

Use a pronoun from the Subject Group in two instances:

1. Before a verb as a subject:

> *He* is my cousin. (*He* is the subject of the verb *is*.)

> *He* is taller than *I*. (The sentence is not written out in full. It means "*He* is taller than *I* am." *I* is the subject of the verb *am*.)

Whenever you see *than* or *as* in a sentence, ask yourself whether a verb is missing at the end of the sentence. Add the verb in both speaking and writing, and then you'll automatically use the correct pronoun. Instead of saying, "She's smarter than (I, me)," say, "She's smarter than I *am*." Also, instead of "She is as tall as (he, him)," say "She is as tall as he *is*."

2. After a linking verb (*is, am, are, was, were*) as a pronoun that renames the subject:

> The one who should apologize is *he*. (*He* is *the one who should apologize*. Therefore the pronoun from the Subject Group is used.)

> The winner of the lottery was *she*. (*She* was *the winner of the lottery*. Therefore the pronoun from the Subject Group is used.)

Modern usage allows some exceptions to this rule, however. For example, *It's me* and *It is her* (instead of the grammatically correct *It is I* and *It is she*) may be common in spoken English.

Use pronouns from the Object Group for all other purposes. In the following sentence, *me* is not the subject, nor does it rename the subject. It follows a preposition; therefore, it comes from the Object Group.

> My boss went to lunch with Rachael and *me*.

A good way to tell whether to use a pronoun from the Subject Group or the Object Group is to leave out any extra name (and the word *and*). By leaving out *Rachel and*, you will say, *My boss went to lunch with me*. You would never say, *My boss went to lunch with I*.

> My father and *I* play chess on Sundays. (*I* play chess on Sundays.)

> *She* and her friends rented a video. (*She* rented a video.)

> We saw Joseph and *them* last night. (We saw *them* last night.)

> The teacher gave *us* students certificates. (Teacher gave *us* certificates.)

> The coach asked Raj and *me* to wash the benches. (The coach asked *me* to wash the benches.)

PRONOUN AGREEMENT

Just as subjects and verbs must agree, pronouns should agree with the words they refer to. If the word referred to is singular, the pronoun should be singular. If the noun referred to is plural, the pronoun should be plural.

> Each classroom has its own chalkboard.

The pronoun *its* refers to the singular noun *classroom* and therefore is singular.

> Both classrooms have their own chalkboards.

The pronoun *their* refers to the plural noun *classrooms* and therefore is plural.

The same rules that we use to maintain the agreement of subjects and verbs also apply to pronoun agreement. For instance, ignore any prepositional phrases that come between the word and the pronoun that takes its place.

The *box* of chocolates has lost *its* label.

Boxes of chocolates often lose *their* labels.

The *player* with the best concentration usually beats *her or his* opponent.

Players with the best concentration usually beat *their* opponents.

When a pronoun refers to more than one word joined by *and*, the pronoun is plural:

The *teacher* and the *tutors* eat *their* lunches at noon.

The *salt* and *pepper* were in *their* usual spots at noon.

However, when a pronoun refers to more than one word joined by *or*, then the word closest to the pronoun determines its form:

Either the *teacher* or the *tutors* eat *their* lunches in the classroom.

Either the *tutors* or the teacher eats *her* lunch in the classroom.

Today many people try to avoid gender bias by writing sentences like the following:

If anyone wants help with the assignment, he or she can visit me in my office.

If anybody calls, tell him or her that I'll be back soon.

Somebody has left his or her pager in the classroom.

But those sentences are wordy and awkward. Therefore some people, especially in conversation, turn them into sentences that are not grammatically correct.

If anyone wants help with the assignment, they can visit me in my office.

If anybody calls, tell them that I'll be back soon.

Somebody has left their pager in the classroom.

Such ungrammatical sentences, however, are not necessary. It just takes a little thought to revise each sentence so that it avoids gender bias and is also grammatically correct:

Anyone who wants help with the assignment can visit me in my office.

Tell anybody who calls that I'll be back soon.

Somebody has left a pager in the classroom.

Probably the best way to avoid the awkward *he or she* and *him or her* is to make the words plural. Instead of writing, "Each actor was in his or her proper place on stage," write, "All the actors were in their proper places on stage," thus avoiding gender bias and still having a grammatically correct sentence.

PRONOUN REFERENCE

A pronoun replaces a noun to avoid repetition, but sometimes the pronoun sounds as if it refers to the wrong word in a sentence, causing confusion. Be aware that when you write a sentence, *you* know what it means, but your reader may not. What does this sentence mean?

The students tried to use the school's computers to access the Internet, but they were too slow, so they decided to go home.

Who or what was too slow, and who or what decided to go home? We don't know whether the two pronouns (both *they*) refer to the students or to the computers. One way to correct such a faulty reference is to use singular and plural nouns:

The students tried to use a school computer to access the Internet, but it was too slow, so they decided to go home.

Here's another sentence with a faulty reference:

Sylvie told her mother that she needed a haircut.

Who needed the haircut — Sylvie or her mother? One way to correct such a faulty reference is to use a direct quotation:

Sylvie told her mother, "You need a haircut."

Sylvie said, "Mom, I need a haircut."

Or you could always rephrase the sentence completely:

Sylvie noticed her mother's hair was sticking out in odd places, so she told her mother to get a haircut.

Another kind of faulty reference is a *which* clause that appears to refer to a specific word, but doesn't really.

I wasn't able to finish all the problems on the exam, which makes me worried.

The word *which* seems to replace exam, but it isn't the exam that makes me worried. The sentence should read

I am worried that I wasn't able to finish all the problems on the exam.

The pronoun *it* causes its own reference problems. Look at this sentence, for example:

When replacing the ink cartridge in my printer, it broke, and I had to call the technician to come and fix it.

Did the printer or the cartridge break? Here is one possible correction:

The new ink cartridge broke when I was putting it in my printer, and I had to call the technician for help.

E X E R C I S E S

Exercise 1

Underline the correct pronoun. Remember the trick of leaving out the extra name to help you decide which pronoun to use. Use the correct grammatical form even though an alternate form may be acceptable in conversation.

1. My father and (I, me) went camping over the long weekend.

2. I usually enjoy these trips to the wilderness more than (he, him).

3. This time, however, both (he and I, him and me) had fun and relaxed.

4. Since my dad is less athletic than (I, me), we didn't hike very much.

5. Every time (he and I, him and me) have gone camping before, I have chosen where to stay and what to do.

6. The one who was in charge on this trip was (he, him).

7. He may like to sit around more than (I, me), but he still knows how to have fun.

8. The fish seemed to come right up to (he and I, him and me) in the boat, as if they thought we were part of the lake.

9. I guess I am a lot less patient than (he, him), but now I have learned how to stay in one spot and enjoy the moment.

10. In the future, I will leave all the big decisions about our camping trips up to (he, him) and Mother Nature.

Exercise 2

Underline the pronoun that agrees with the word the pronoun replaces. If the correct answer is *his or her/her or his,* revise the sentence to eliminate the need for this awkward expression. Check your answers as you go through the exercise.

1. The student awards ceremony was not without (its, their) problems.

2. Each of the three male dolphins knows (his, their) trainer's commands.

3. Many of the other students had not rehearsed (his or her, their) speeches.

4. Each of the prescription drugs has (its, their) own side effects.

5. Either the property owner or the tenants will win (her or his, their) case.

6. We like to hear both of our canaries sing (its, their) beautiful songs.

7. Every one of the women's basketball team members is doing well in (her, their) classes.

8. Everyone in the class turned in (his or her, their) essay.

9. All of the participants at the convention left (her or his, their) business cards on a tray in the lounge.

10. The textbook with the flowers on (its, their) cover is changing editions next year.

Exercise 3

Underline the correct pronoun. Again, if the correct answer is *his or her/her or his,* revise the sentence to eliminate the need for this awkward expression.

1. The coach gave my teammates and (I, me) a few suggestions.

2. (He and she, Him and her) are alike in many ways.

3. Harry Houdini was shorter that (I, me).

4. All of the children finished (his or her, their) homework before the open house.

5. Hotels and motels are not competitive in (its, their) pricing.

6. The one responsible for ordering the food was (I, me).

7. Each of the new teachers has (her or his, their) own set of books.

8. The mixed-doubles tennis teams will continue (his or her, their) tournament.

9. Everyone at the polling place had (her or his, their) own opinion and expressed it with (his or her, their) vote.

10. When it comes to birds, no one that I know is as knowledgeable as (she, her).

Exercise 4

Most — but not all — of the sentences in the next two sets aren't clear because we don't know what word the pronoun refers to. Revise such sentences, making the meaning clear. Since there are more ways than one to rewrite each sentence, yours may be as good as the ones at the back of the book. Just ask yourself whether the meaning is clear.

1. I finished typing my paper, turned off my computer, and put it in my backpack.

2. Elijah told his brother that his car had a new dent in it.

3. They bought their textbooks early, which made them feel better.

4. Lina's mother lets her take her new calculator to school.

5. When I put my jacket in the dryer, it shrunk.

6. Ricardo told his counsellor that he didn't understand him.

7. While we were counting the money from our garage sale, it blew away.

8. Our dog runs away all the time, which makes us angry.

9. Sean asked his friend why he wasn't invited to the party.

10. We shuffled the lottery tickets, and everybody chose one of them.

Exercise 5

1. The MacNeils bought some new trees, but they were too tall for them.

2. We ordered patio furniture, and it arrived the next day.

3. I signed the credit card slip, put my card back in my wallet, and handed it to the cashier.

4. When students work in groups, they get a lot of work done.

5. As he took the lenses out of the frames, they broke.

6. Whenever I put gas in my car, I get a headache from the smell of it.

7. Coupons help people save money on certain items that they buy.

8. Prospectors lived on the hope that they would find enough gold to make them rich.

9. Sheema's teacher asked her to copy her notes for another student.

10. Asked again to consider the rejected applications, the committee made its final decision.

PROOFREADING EXERCISE

The following paragraph contains errors in the use of pronouns. Find and correct the errors.

I told my cousin Miles a secret at our last family reunion, and as soon as I did, I knew it would get out. I forgot that Miles is six years younger than me when I told him that I was taking a job overseas. Right before I told him the secret, I said, "Now this is just between you and I, and you're not going to tell anyone, right?" He assured me that the only person he would talk to about it was me. I made the mistake of believing him. If I had taken out a full-page ad in the newspaper to print my secret and delivered it to my family, it could not have been spread around faster. Miles and I are still cousins, but him and me are no longer friends.

SENTENCE WRITING

Write ten sentences about a misunderstanding between you and someone else. Then check that your pronouns are grammatically correct, that they agree with the words they replace, and that references to specific nouns are clear.

Avoiding Shifts in Person

To understand what "person" means when using pronouns, imagine a conversation between two people about a third person. The first person speaks using "I, me, my ... "; the second person would be called "you"; and when the two of them talked of a third person, they would say "he, she, they... ." You should never forget the idea of "person" if you remember it as a three-part conversation.

First person — *I, me, my, we, us, our*

Second person — *you, your*

Third person — *he, him, his, she, her, hers, they, them, their, one, anyone*

You may use all three of these groups of pronouns in a paper, but don't shift from one group to another without good reason.

Wrong: Few people know how to manage *their* time. *One* need not be an efficiency expert to realize that *one* could get a lot more done if *he* budgeted *his* time. Nor do *you* need to work very hard to get more organized.

Better: *Everyone* should know how to manage *his or her* time. *One* need not be an efficiency expert to realize that *a person* could get a lot more done if *one* budgeted *one's* time. Nor does *one* need to work very hard to get more organized. (Too many *one's* in a paragraph make it sound overly formal, and words such as *everyone* lead to the necessity of avoiding sexism by using *s/he* or *he or she,* etc. Sentences can be revised to avoid using either *you* or *one.*)

Best: Many of *us* don't know how to manage *our* time. *We* need not be efficiency experts to realize that *we* could get a lot more done if *we* budgeted *our* time. Nor do *we* need to work very hard to get more organized.

Often students write *you* in a paper when they don't really mean *you, the reader.*

You wouldn't believe how many times I saw that movie.

Such sentences are always improved by getting rid of the *you.*

I saw that movie many times.

PROOFREADING EXERCISES

Which of the following student paragraphs shift *unnecessarily* between first-, second-, and third-person pronouns? In those that do, revise the sentences to eliminate such shifting, thus making the entire paragraph read smoothly. (First, read the paragraphs to determine whether unnecessary shifting takes place. One of the paragraphs is correct.)

1. People who drive need to be more aware of pedestrians. We can't always gauge what someone walking down the street will do. You might think that all pedestrians will keep walking forward in a crosswalk, but one might decide to turn back if he or she forgot something. You could run into him or her if that happens. A person's life could be affected in an instant. We all should slow down and be more considerate of others.

2. Because Canada is such a large country, it has many different climates. We Canadians experience varied weather, depending on where we reside. Those of us who live in the prairies have an average of about 75 cm of rainfall per year, with the heaviest fall in the summer. Since warm air can hold more moisture than cold, southern parts of Canada have more precipitation than northern areas. If we live in the most northern parts of Canada, the tundra, where the temperatures drop well below zero and the average annual rainfall is less than 25 cm, most of our precipitation comes in the form of snow. Another geographic factor affecting climate is our relative position to the oceans. Those of us who live near the warm Pacific Ocean, for example in Victoria, are used to a more temperate climate, while, for those of us who live in landlocked Winnipeg, winter temperatures can be brutally cold. Our daylight, and therefore the length of our days, is also affected by where we live. If we live in southern Canada, we receive eight hours of daylight in December; however, if we live in Canada's northern tip, we experience no daylight at all.

Source: *The Canadian Encyclopedia,* s.v. "Climate."

3. Scientists and others are working on several inventions that have not been perfected yet. Some of these developments seem like complete science fiction, but they're not. Each of them is in the process of becoming a real new technology. Can you imagine eating meat grown on plants? Scientists will feed the plants artificially made blood. Researchers are also working to produce animals (perhaps even humans) grown in artificial wombs. The development I found most interesting is selective amnesia (memory loss). A patient will be able to ask his or her doctor to erase painful memories as a mental-health tool. And, of course, we all know that computers will gain more and more personality traits to become more like us.

Source: The Futurist, Aug.–Sept. 1998.

REVIEW OF SENTENCE STRUCTURE ERRORS

One sentence in each pair contains an error. Read both sentences carefully before you decide. Then write the letter of the *incorrect* sentence in the blank. Try to name the error and correct it if you can. You may find any of these errors:

awk	awkward phrasing
cliché	overused expression
dm	dangling modifier
frag	fragment
mm	misplaced modifier
pro	incorrect pronoun
pro agr	pronoun agreement error
pro ref	pronoun reference error
ro	run-on sentence
s/v agr	subject/verb agreement error
wordy	wordiness
//	not parallel

1. ___ **A.** I relax in the evenings, on weekends, and the holidays are relaxing too.

   B. The newspaper flew onto the porch and broke a flower pot.

2. ___ **A.** The last one to finish was he.

   B. Each of the puppies are the same size.

3. ___ **A.** Because the guest speaker's presentation was too long.

   B. Last night's debate was not very successful.

4. ___ **A.** We saw dogs wearing sunglasses at the beach; they looked cute.

   B. We ate homemade potato chips and drank fresh lemonade.

5. ___ **A.** He will meet us at the shopping centre after work; and we'll give him a birthday surprise.

   B. I get up at 6 a.m. every morning, and I make a pot of coffee.

6. ___ **A.** Taking tests is like pulling teeth for me.

   B. I will enroll in a study skills class next semester.

7. ___ **A.** On-the-job training can be frustrating.

   B. After a five-minute coffee break, the cash register seemed easier to understand.

8. ___ **A.** The teacher gave my friend and I extra credit for taking such good notes.

   B. I learned to take notes in my English class in high school.

9. ___ **A.** In my opinion, yesterday's weather was perfect.

   B. It was warm and dry I hardly even felt the breeze.

10. ___ **A.** Everyone on the field trip brought their own lunch.

   B. I packed two sandwiches, some chips, and a granola bar.

11. ___ **A.** Speaking in a high voice, the dog became annoyed with its trainer.

   B. It tugged at its leash and tried to run away.

12. ___ **A.** There can be an understanding that's possible between teens and their parents.

   B. Parents must recall being young themselves.

13. ___ **A.** You have helped me in more ways than one; you're a real lifesaver.

   B. If you ever need help, please ask; I will try to help if I can.

14. ___ **A.** One of the boxed games is incomplete.

   B. One of its pieces are missing, so it can't be sold.

15. ___ **A.** I've worked for employers, and I've been self-employed.

   B. I like being self-employed because you can be your own boss.

PROOFREADING EXERCISE

Can you find and correct the sentence structure errors in the following essay?

Let's Get Technical

In my child development classes, I'm learning about ways to keep girls interested in technology. Studies shows that girls and boys begin their school years equally interested in technology. After elementary school is the time that computers are less of an interest for girls. Because boys keep up with computers and other technology throughout their educations more than girls, they get ahead in these fields. Experts have come up with some suggestions for teachers and parents of girls to help them.

Girls need opportunities to experiment with computers. Girls spend time on computers, but they usually just do their assignments then they log off. Since computer games and programs are often aimed at boys. Parents and teachers need to buy computer products that will challenge girls not only in literature and art, but also in math, science, and business is important.

Another suggestion is to put computers in places where girls can socialize. One reason many boys stay interested in technology is that it is something he can do on his own. Girls tend to be more interested in working with others and to share activities. When computer terminals are placed close to one another, girls work at them for much longer periods of time.

Finally, parents and teachers need to be aware that nothing beats positive role models. Teach them about successful women in the fields of business, scientific, and technology. And the earlier we start interesting girls in these fields, the better.

Source: "Let's Get Technical," *Technology & Learning,* Oct. 1998.

Punctuation and Capital Letters

Period, Question Mark, Exclamation Point, Semicolon, Colon, Dash

Every mark of punctuation should help the reader. Here are the rules for six marks of punctuation. The first three you have known for a long time and probably have no trouble with. The one about semicolons you learned when you studied independent clauses (p. 74). The ones about the colon and the dash may be less familiar.

Put a period (.) at the end of a sentence and after most abbreviations.

>   The students elected Ms. Daniels to represent the class.

>   Tues.   etc.   Jan.   Ph.D.   Ave.

Put a question mark (?) after a direct question but not after an indirect one.

>   Will the exam be an open-book or a closed-book test? (direct)

>   I wonder if the exam will be an open-book or a closed-book test. (indirect)

Put an exclamation point (!) after an expression that shows strong emotion. Use it sparingly.

>   I can't believe I did so well on my first exam!

Put a semicolon (;) between two independent clauses in a sentence *unless* they are joined by one of the connecting words *for, and, nor, but, or, yet, so.*

>   My mother co-signed for a loan; now I have my own car.

Some careers go in and out of fashion; however, people will always need doctors.

To be sure that you are using a semicolon correctly, see if a period and capital letter can be used in its place. If they can, you are putting the semicolon in the right spot.

My mother co-signed for a loan. Now I have my own car.

Some careers go in and out of fashion. However, people will always need doctors.

Put a colon (:) after a complete statement that introduces something: one item, a list, a direct question, or a quotation that follows.

The company announced its Employee-of-the-Month: Minh Tran. (The sentence before the colon introduces the name that follows.)

In London, we plan to visit the following famous sites: the Tower of London, Piccadilly Circus, and Madame Tussaud's Wax Museum. (Here *the following famous sites* ends a complete statement and introduces the list that follows, so a colon is used.)

In London, we plan to visit the Tower of London, Piccadilly Circus, and Madame Tussaud's Wax Museum. (Here *we plan to visit* does not end a complete statement, so no colon is used.)

All the kids in the class were wondering about the same thing: why is the sky blue? (Here *All the kids in the class were wondering about the same thing* is a complete statement that introduces a direct question, so a colon is used.)

All the kids in the class were wondering why the sky was blue. (Here *All the kids in the class were wondering* is not a complete statement, so a colon is not used.)

Thoreau had this to say about time: "Time is but the stream I go a-fishin in." (*Thoreau had this to say about time* is a complete statement. Therefore, a colon comes after it before adding the quotation.)

Thoreau said, "Time is but the stream I go a-fishin in."(*Thoreau said* is not a complete statement. Therefore, a colon does not come after it.)

Use a dash (—) to indicate an abrupt change of thought or to emphasize what follows. Use it sparingly.

I found out today — or was it yesterday? — that I have inherited a fortune.

We have exciting news for you — we're moving!

E X E R C I S E S

Add to these sentences the necessary punctuation (periods, question marks, exclamation points, semicolons, colons, and dashes). The commas used within the sentences are correct and do not need to be changed.

Exercise 1

1. My friend Adam and I were late for class yesterday it was a really important day

2. We had stayed up past midnight the night before perfecting our speech

3. The teacher had given us the best topic of all food irradiation

4. I wondered how the other students would react when they heard that they had been eating irradiated spices for years

5. Would they be alarmed or think it was cool

6. Adam and I had assembled several visual aids to accompany our speech a poster-sized chart of an irradiation facility, a photo of the glowing rods of radioactive material used to irradiate the food, and jars of both irradiated and nonirradiated spices

7. Adam thought that sterilizing food with radiation was a great idea

8. I had mixed feelings at least I think they were mixed about radiation used on food

9. By the time we arrived in class, another pair of students had started their speech

10. Now we have to wait until next week's class to give our speech this time we will not be late

Exercise 2

1. People have not stopped inventing mousetraps in fact, there are over 4000 different kinds

2. Some are simple however, some are complicated or weird

3. Nearly 50 new types of machines to kill mice are invented every year

4. The most enduring mousetrap was designed by John Mast it is the one most of us picture when we think of a mousetrap a piece of wood with a spring-loaded bar that snaps down on the mouse just as it takes the bait

5. John Mast created this version of the mousetrap in 1903 since then no other mousetrap has done a better job

6. There is a long list of technologies that have been used to trap mice electricity, sonar, lasers, super glues, etc

7. One mousetrap was built in the shape of a multi-level house with several stairways however, its elaborate design made it impractical and expensive

8. In 1878, one person invented a mousetrap for travellers it was a box that was supposed to hold men's removable collars and at night catch mice, but it was not a success

9. Who would want to put an article of clothing back into a box used to trap a mouse

10. Can you guess the name of the longest running play in Toronto it's *The Mousetrap*

Exercise 3

1. People in Australia are asking themselves a question why are some dolphins carrying big sponges around on their heads

2. First it was just one dolphin now several dolphins are doing it

3. Marine biologists all over the world are trying to understand this unusual sponge-carrying behaviour

4. They wonder about whether the sponges decrease the dolphins' ability to manoeuvre under water

5. If they do, then why would the dolphins sacrifice this ability

6. The dolphins might be using the sponges for a very important reason to help them find food

7. Some scientists think that the sponges may protect the dolphins' beaks in some way

8. The sponges might indicate position in the social order that's another explanation

9. Or the dolphins could be imitating each other a kind of dolphin "fad," in other words

10. Only one group of experts knows whether these sponges are hunting tools or just fashion statements that is the dolphins themselves

Source: Discover, Mar. 1998.

Exercise 4

1. Who would have thought that educators were a nomadic group

2. In 1899, Frontier College was founded by Alfred Fitzpatrick and a group of university students their aim was to make education available to the labourers in the work camps of Canada

3. Labourer-teachers were trained and sent to the camps where they worked alongside the labourers during the day then they taught reading and writing to them at night

4. Frontier College was also involved in encouraging Canadians to take up farming a woman by the name of Margaret Strang offered her tutorial and medical services for those who were interested at a model settlement at Edlund, Ontario

5. The Department of National Defence made an agreement with Frontier College, which placed labourer-teachers in Depression relief camps to provide recreation and tutoring

6. Some other projects that labourer-teachers were involved in were constructing the Alaska Highway, working in rail gangs after World War II, tutoring new Canadians, and working in long-term community development projects in northern settlements

7. In the mid-1970s, Frontier College enlarged its focus to include urban frontiers volunteers began working in prisons and with street youth, ex-offenders, and people with special needs

8. More than a decade ago, Frontier College began doing work with children, teens, and families, while at the same time developing the workplace literacy program, called Learning in the Workplace

9. The original idea to help out those isolated in work camps across Canada has changed a great deal since Frontier College's founding in 1899, but it continues to be an important aspect in today's education system

10. In 1999, Frontier College celebrated its centenary 100 Years of Teaching and Learning in Canada

Source: http://www.frontiercollege.ca

Exercise 5

1. Do you believe in ghosts

2. On Aug 14, 1999, the body of a young man was found on the Yukon and BC border by three teachers who went hunting for the day

3. The man he was named Kwaday Dan Sinchi by the Champagne and Aishihik First Nations was found on a northern BC glacier

4. Though the First Nations people in the area believed he was as old as 10 000 years, test results show the remains to be about 550 years old

5. Discovered along with the hunter were various artifacts a hat, a robe, made of animal skins, and spear tools

6. Radiocarbon dating was done on two samples the hat and the cloak The results are considered to be 95 percent accurate

7. The "ghost" is believed to be a hunter who is estimated to have lived between the years 1415 and 1445, about the time Henry V was king of England and the Black Plague ravaged Europe

8. This means the hunter died more than 300 years before the first known European contact on the northwest coast however, it is still not known if he is an ancestor of the Champagne and Aishihik First Nations

9. Scientists say that there are only two certainties the "ghost" is a young male, and he was on a trading route between the coast and the interior

10. The remains, which are now in the care of the Royal British Columbia Museum in Victoria BC, will be studied for further historic information

Source: "Do you believe in ghosts?" *The Toronto Star*, 29 Sept. 1999.

PROOFREADING EXERCISE

Can you find the six errors in this student paragraph?

In my design class, we are learning about the appeal of packages! Our instructor has asked us to think about the following question; do packages help sell products. During our last class meeting, we worked in groups to come up with examples of packages that have made us buy items in the past. The packages that my group thought of were: book jackets, album and CD covers, water bottles, and candy wrappers. By the end of the semester; each group will try to design a new successful package — based on what we've learned.

SENTENCE WRITING

Write ten sentences of your own that use periods, question marks, exclamation points, semicolons, colons, and dashes correctly. Imitate the examples used in the explanations if necessary. Write about an interesting assignment you have done for a class, or choose your own topic.

Comma Rules 1, 2, and 3

Commas and other pieces of punctuation guide the reader through sentence structures in the same way that signs guide drivers on the highway. Imagine what effects misplaced or incorrect road signs would have. Yet students often randomly place commas in their sentences. Try not to use a comma unless you know there is a need for it. Memorize this rhyme about comma use: *when in doubt, leave it out*.

Among all of the comma rules, six are most important. Learn these six rules, and your writing will be easier to read. You have already studied the first rule on page 75.

1. Put a comma before *for, and, nor, but, or, yet, so* (remember them as the *fanboys*) when they connect two independent clauses.

> The neighbours recently bought a minivan, and now they go everywhere together.

> We wrote our paragraphs in class today, but the teacher forgot to collect them.

> She was recently promoted, so she has moved to a better office.

If you use a comma alone between two independent clauses, the result is an error called a ***comma splice.***

> The ice cream looked delicious, it tasted good too. (comma splice)

> The ice cream looked delicious, and it tasted good too. (correct)

Before using a comma, be sure such words do connect two independent clauses. The following sentence is merely one independent clause with one subject and two verbs. Therefore, no comma should be used.

> The ice cream looked delicious and tasted good too.

2. Use a comma to separate three or more items in a series.

> Students in the literature class are reading short stories, poems, and plays.

> On Saturday I did my laundry, washed my car, and cleaned my room.

Occasionally, writers leave out the comma before the *and* connecting the last two items of a series, but it is more common to use it to separate all the items equally. Some words work together and don't need commas between them even though they do make up a kind of series.

> The team members wanted to wear their brand-new green uniforms.

> The bright white sunlight made the room glow.

To see whether a comma is needed between words in a series, ask yourself whether *and* could be used naturally between them. It would sound all right to say *short stories and poems and plays*; therefore, commas are used. But it would not sound right to say *brand and new and green uniforms* or *bright and white sunlight*; therefore, no commas are used.

If an address or date is used in a sentence, put a comma after every item, including the last.

> My father was born on August 19, 1941, in Saint John, New Brunswick, and grew up there.

> She lived in Vancouver, British Columbia, for two years.

When only the month and year are used in a date, no commas are needed.

> She graduated in May 1985 from McGill University.

3. Put a comma after an introductory expression (it may be a word, a phrase, or a dependent clause) or before a comment or question that is tacked on at the end.

> Finally, he was able to get through to his insurance company.

> During his last performance, the actor fell and broke his foot.

> Once I have finished my homework, I will call you.

> He said he needed to ruminate, whatever that means.

> The new chairs aren't very comfortable, are they?

E X E R C I S E S

Add commas to the following sentences according to the first three comma rules. Some sentences may not need any commas, and some may need more than one. Any other punctuation already in the sentences is correct. Check your answers after the first set.

Exercise 1

1. Whenever I ask my friend Nick a computer-related question I end up regretting it.

2. Once he gets started Nick is unable to stop talking about computers.

3. When I needed his help the last time my printer wasn't working.

4. Instead of just solving the problem Nick went on and on about print settings and font choices that I could be using.

5. When he gets like this his face lights up and I feel bad for not wanting to hear the latest news on software upgrades e-mail programs and hardware improvements.

6. I feel guilty but I know that I am the normal one.

7. I even pointed his problem out to him by asking, "You can't control yourself can you?"

8. He just grinned and kept trying to fix my printer.

9. Nick always solves my problem so I should be grateful.

10. When I ask for Nick's help in the future I plan to listen and try to learn something.

Exercise 2

1. Scientists have been studying the human face and they have been able to identify 5000 distinct facial expressions.

2. Researchers have identified and numbered every action of the human face.

3. Winking is action number 46 and we do it with the facial muscle that surrounds the eye.

4. People around the world make the same basic expressions when they are happy surprised sad disgusted afraid or angry.

5. These six categories of facial expressions are universally understood but different societies have different rules about showing their emotions.

6. The smile is one of the most powerful expressions for it changes the way we feel.

7. If we give someone a real smile showing genuine happiness then our brains react by producing a feeling of pleasure.

8. If we give more of a polite imitation smile then our brains show no change.

9. Even babies have been shown to smile one way for strangers and another way for their mothers.

10. A smile also wins the long-distance record for facial expressions for it can be seen from as far away as several hundred feet.

Source: Psychology Today, Oct. 1998.

Exercise 3

1. Edgar Allen Poe was born on January 19 1809 in Boston Massachusetts and he lived a life as full of suffering and sadness as any of the characters in his stories.

2. Nevertheless Poe became famous as an editor and as the author of short stories novels poems and critical essays.

3. Poe died under mysterious circumstances in October 1849 and was laid to rest in Westminster Burying Ground in Baltimore Maryland.

4. On the night of Poe's birth each year a person wearing a dark hat and light-coloured scarf visits Poe's grave.

5. The stranger approaches the author's stone monument lays down a small bunch of roses and toasts Poe's memory with a half-empty bottle of cognac.

6. These visitations began in 1949 and have been witnessed by many people.

7. Several years ago the stranger wrote a message that this ritual would be continued by others.

8. Since that time many people have taken the stranger's place at Westminster cemetery on Poe's birthday.

9. Jeff Jerome oversees the Poe House and Museum in Baltimore.

10. Jerome has faithfully followed the movements of these strangers at the grave site for more than twenty years so he knows that such stories are true.

Source: Biography Magazine, Oct. 1998.

Exercise 4

1. Long-playing vinyl records (LPs) have not been completely replaced by cassettes and compact discs.

2. Vinyl record albums may not be as easy to find as the other music formats but many people think that they still sound the best.

3. The vinyl format seems to capture the fullness of live music better than CDs or cassettes.

4. But there is no doubt that CDs are easier to package to handle and to maintain.

5. At the time CDs took over the music market vinyl records almost disappeared.

6. In the past few years musicians have begun releasing their work on CDs cassettes and LPs.

7. Nearly a quarter of the music currently being produced is available on vinyl records.

8. There are even new models of turntables but some are extremely expensive.

9. Most turntables are about the same price as a CD player but some can cost up to $40 000.

10. People can buy new LPs in music/video stores classic LPs in used-record stores and old LPs in thrift stores.

Source: Men's Fitness, Oct. 1998.

Exercise 5

1. Gold is amazing isn't it?

2. Unlike metals that change their appearance after contact with water oil and other substances gold maintains its shine and brilliant colour under almost any circumstances.

3. When a miner named James Marshall found gold in the dark soil of California in 1848 the gold rush began.

4. Though few people are aware of it the first gold in Canada was found in small deposits in central Nova Scotia and the Eastern Townships of Quebec.

5. Harry Oakes developed the deepest gold mine in North America at Kirkland Lake Ontario.

6. Beginning with the Fraser River Gold Rush in 1858 a series of gold discoveries in British Columbia transformed the colony's history.

7. During the famous Klondike Gold Rush the huge influx of people searching for gold prompted the Canadian government to establish the Yukon Territory in 1898.

8. Canada was the world's third largest gold producer but remained far behind South Africa and Russia.

9. Some people have become rich directly because of gold and some have become rich indirectly because of gold.

10. For example if it had not been for the gold rush Levi Strauss would not have had any customers and the world would not have blue jeans.

Sources: 1) *Smithsonian*, July 1998.
2) *The Canadian Encyclopedia* (Edmonton: Hurtig, 1985).

PROOFREADING EXERCISE

Apply the first three comma rules to the following paragraph:

When you belong to a large family holidays are a mixed blessing. They are certainly times to see one another but how do you choose where to go and whom to see? For example I have sets of relatives living in four different areas and they all want to get together for the holidays. If I accept one group's invitation I disappoint the others. If I turn them all down and stay home with my immediate family I make them all mad. I guess I will just have to invite the whole clan to spend the holidays at my house won't I?

SENTENCE WRITING

Combine the following sets of sentences in different ways using all of the first three comma rules. You may need to reorder the details and change the phrasing. Compare your answers with those at the back of the book.

I like to swim.

I have never taken lessons.

The alarm rings.

I get up and get ready for school.

He is currently an elementary schoolteacher.

He was a math tutor in college.

He worked as a ski instructor.

Tricia and James are equal partners in their business.

Both of them are practical.

They are both organized.

Both of them graduated from university.

Comma Rules 4, 5, and 6

The next three comma rules all involve using a pair of commas to enclose information that is not needed in a sentence — information that could be taken out of the sentence without affecting its meaning. Two commas are used — one before and one after — to signal unnecessary words, phrases, and clauses.

4. Put commas around the name of a person spoken to.

> Did you know, Danielle, that you left your backpack at the library?

> We regret to inform you, Mr. Chen, that your policy has been cancelled.

5. Put commas around expressions that interrupt the flow of the sentence (such as *however, moreover, therefore, of course, by the way, on the other hand, I believe, I think*).

> I know, of course, that I have missed the deadline.

> They will try, however, to use the rest of their time wisely.

> Today's exam, I think, is only a practice test.

Read the preceding sentences aloud, and you'll hear how those expressions interrupt the flow of the sentence. But sometimes such expressions flow smoothly into the sentence and don't need commas around them.

> Of course he checked to see if their plane had been delayed.

> We therefore decided to stay out of it.

> I think you made the right decision.

Remember that when one of the previous words like *however* joins two independent clauses, that word needs a semicolon before it. It may also have a comma after it, especially if there seems to be a pause between the word and the rest of the sentence. (See p. 74.)

> The bus was late; *however,* we still made it to the museum before it closed.

> I am improving my study habits; *furthermore,* I am getting better grades.

> She was interested in journalism; *therefore,* she took a job at a local newspaper.

> I spent hours studying for the test; *finally,* I felt prepared.

Thus words like *however* or *therefore* may be used in three ways:

1. as an interrupter (commas around it)

2. as a word that flows into the sentence (no commas needed)

3. as a connecting word between two independent clauses (semicolon before and often a comma after)

6. Put commas around additional information that is not needed in a sentence.

Such information may be interesting, but the subject and main idea of the sentence would be clear without it. In the following sentence

Maxine Taylor, who organized the fundraiser, will introduce the candidates.

the clause *who organized the fundraiser* is not needed in the sentence. Without it, we still know exactly who the sentence is about and what she is going to do: Maxine Taylor will introduce the candidates. Therefore, the additional information is set off from the rest of the sentence by commas to show that it could be left out. But in the following sentence

The woman who organized the fundraiser will introduce the candidates.

The clause *who organized the fundraiser* is needed in the sentence. Without it, the sentence would read: The woman will introduce the candidates. We would have no idea which woman. The clause *who organized the fundraiser* couldn't be left out because it tells us which woman. Therefore, commas are not used around it. In this sentence

Hamlet, Shakespeare's famous play, has been made into a movie many times.

the additional information *Shakespeare's famous play* could be left out, and we would still know the main meaning of the sentence: *Hamlet* has been made into a movie many times. Therefore, the commas surround the added material to show that it could be omitted. But in this sentence

Shakespeare's famous play *Hamlet* has been made into a movie many times.

the title of the play is necessary. Without it, the sentence would read: Shakespeare's famous play has been made into a movie many times. We would have no idea which of Shakespeare's famous plays was being discussed. Therefore, the title couldn't be left out, and commas are not used around it.

The trick in deciding whether additional information is necessary is to say, "If I don't need it, I'll put commas around it."

E X E R C I S E S

Add any necessary commas to these sentences according to Comma Rules 4, 5, and 6. Any commas already in the sentences follow Comma Rules 1, 2, and 3. Some sentences may be correct.

Exercise 1

1. This year's class pictures I believe turned out better than last year's.

2. I believe this year's class pictures turned out better than last year's.

3. There were however a few problems.

4. However there were a few problems.

5. The boy who is wearing a red sweater is my little brother, but it's hard to see him.

6. My little brother who is wearing a red sweater is sitting on the left, but it's hard to see him.

7. Ms. Patel the teacher who took the picture needed to stand a little closer to the group.

8. The teacher who took the picture needed to stand a little closer to the group.

9. And no one it seems had time to comb the children's hair.

10. And it seems that no one had time to comb the children's hair.

Exercise 2

1. We hope of course that people will remember to vote on Tuesday.

2. Of course we hope that people will remember to vote on Tuesday.

3. The organizations that volunteer their buildings as polling stations make elections more convenient for voters in their neighbourhood.

4. The elementary school which volunteers its gym as a polling station makes elections more convenient for voters in the neighbourhood.

5. We may therefore run into people that we know at the polling station.

6. Therefore we may run into people that we know at the polling station.

7. The voting booth a small cubicle where each person casts a vote is meant to be a private place.

8. The small cubicle where each person casts a vote is meant to be a private place.

9. We trust that no one will influence our thoughts there.

10. No one we trust will influence our thoughts there.

Exercise 3

1. The geology teacher Ms. Sousa looks like the chemistry teacher Ms. Riel.

2. Ms. Sousa the geology teacher looks like Ms. Riel the chemistry teacher.

3. My clothes iron which has an automatic shut-off switch is safer to use than yours which doesn't.

4. An appliance that has an automatic shut-off switch is safer to use than one that doesn't.

5. Students who ask a lot of questions usually do well on their assignments.

6. Claire and André who ask a lot of questions usually do well on their assignments.

7. The Ahmeds who left before the concert was over missed the grand finale.

8. The people who left before the concert was over missed the grand finale.

9. The teacher posted the results of the test that we took last week.

10. The teacher posted the results of the exam which we took last week.

Exercise 4

1. England's Prince Charles has two sons William and Harry.

2. William is the son who will someday inherit the throne.

3. William whose full name is His Royal Highness Prince William Arthur Philip Louis of Wales was named after William the Conqueror.

4. The princes' grandmother Queen Elizabeth II will pass the crown to her son Charles who will then pass it on to William.

5. William who was born in 1982 stands over six feet tall and has become as popular as a movie star.

6. He appears overwhelmed by the attention of girls who throw him bouquets decorated with their phone numbers.

7. Charles and Harry have met the Spice Girls who posed for pictures with them.

8. William is well read and intelligent; however he is also athletic and fun-loving.

9. Polls from the mid-1990s showed that the majority of British citizens favoured William as the next king instead of his father.

10. However, it will probably be many years before William takes on his future title which will be King William V.

Source: Biography Magazine, Oct. 1998.

Exercise 5

1. Jim Henson who created the Muppets began his television career in the mid-1950s.

2. He was it seems eager to be on TV, and there was an opening for someone who worked with puppets.

3. Henson and a buddy of his quickly fabricated a few puppets including one called Pierre the French Rat and they got the job.

4. Henson's next project *Sam and Friends* also starred puppets.

5. *Sam and Friends* was a live broadcast lasting only five minutes; however it was on twice a day and ran for six years.

6. Kermit the Frog a character that we now associate with *Sesame Street* and *The Muppet Show* was part of the cast of *Sam and Friends*.

7. Henson provided the voice and animated the movements of Kermit and a few others from the beginning, and he worked with Frank Oz who helped round out the cast of Muppet characters.

8. In 1969, the Muppets moved to *Sesame Street*; however they graduated to their own prime-time program *The Muppet Show* in the late 1970s.

9. At the high point of its popularity worldwide, more than 200 million people adults and children tuned in to a single broadcast of *The Muppet Show*.

10. Jim Henson continued as a highly creative force in television until his death from a sudden and severe case of pneumonia in 1990.

Source: Time, June 8, 1998.

PROOFREADING EXERCISE

Insert the necessary commas into this paragraph according to Comma Rules 4, 5, and 6.

Unlike my mom and my sister who generally don't like dealing with food I love to cook. I think I inherited this passion for cooking from my dad who is always interested in trying out new recipes. He has a whole bookshelf full of cookbooks; what's more he likes to read them from cover to cover in his spare time. Most of the meals we eat are of course prepared by him. But sometimes when I have enough time and energy I cook a special meal. My sister and her husband Ted have recently asked me to cook brunch for them and eight of their friends on New Year's Eve. Believe it or not I can't wait!

SENTENCE WRITING

Combine the following sets of sentences in different ways using Comma Rules 4, 5, and 6. Try to combine each set in a way that needs commas and in a way that doesn't need commas. You may reorder the details and change the phrasing. Compare your answers with those at the back of the book.

Titanic is a famous movie.

I have seen it several times.

I believe.

I could learn a few more study skills.

My friend has curly hair.

He sits in the back of the class.

He wrote a good paper.

REVIEW OF THE COMMA

SIX COMMA RULES

1. Put a comma before *for, and, nor, but, or, yet, so* when they connect two independent clauses.

2. Put a comma between three or more items in a series.

3. Put a comma after an introductory expression or before an after-thought.

4. Put commas around the name of a person spoken to.

5. Put commas around an interrupter, like *however* or *therefore*.

6. Put commas around unnecessary additional information.

PROOFREADING EXERCISE

Add the missing commas, and identify which one of the six comma rules applies in the brackets at the *end* of each sentence. Each of the six sentences illustrates a different rule.

I am writing you this note Helen to ask you to do me a favour. [   ] When you get home from work tonight would you take the turkey out of the freezer? [   ] I plan to get started on the pies the rolls and the sweet potatoes as soon as I walk in the door after work. [   ] I will be so busy however that I might forget to thaw out the turkey. [   ] It's the first time I've made the holiday meal by myself and I want everything to be perfect. [   ] My big enamel roasting pan which is in the back of the cupboard under the counter will be the best place to keep the turkey as it thaws. [   ] Thanks for your help.

SENTENCE WRITING

Write at least one sentence of your own to demonstrate each of the six comma rules.

Quotation Marks and Underlining / Italics

Put quotation marks around a direct quotation (the exact words of a speaker) but not around an indirect quotation.

The officer said, "Please show me your driver's licence." (a direct quotation)

The officer asked to see my driver's licence. (an indirect quotation)

John Keats said that "Heard melodies are sweet, but those unheard are sweeter."

John Keats said that the melodies that can be heard are sweet, but those that cannot be heard are even sweeter.

If the speaker says more than one sentence, quotation marks are used before and after the entire speech.

She said, "One of your brake lights is out. You need to take care of the problem right away."

If the quotation begins the sentence, the words telling who is speaking are set off with a comma unless, of course, a question mark or an exclamation point is needed.

"I didn't even know it was broken," I said.

"Do you have any questions?" she asked.

"You mean I can go!" I yelled.

"Yes, consider this just a warning," she said.

Each of the preceding quotations begins with a capital letter. But when a quotation is broken, the second part doesn't begin with a capital letter unless it's a new sentence.

"If you knew how much time I spent on the essay," the student said, "you would give me an A."

"A chef might work on a meal for days," the teacher replied. "That doesn't mean the results will taste good."

Put quotation marks around the titles of short stories, poems, songs, essays, TV program episodes, or other short works.

I couldn't sleep after I read "Friend of My Youth," a short story by Alice Munro.

My favourite Gordon Lightfoot song is "Early Morning Rain."

We had to read George Orwell's essay "A Hanging" for my English class.

Jerry Seinfeld's troubles in "The Puffy Shirt" episode are some of the funniest moments in TV history.

***Italicize* titles of longer works such as books, newspapers, magazines, plays, record albums or CDs, movies, or TV or radio series.**

The Handmaid's Tale is a novel by Margaret Atwood.

I read about the latest discovery of dinosaur footprints in *Maclean's*.

Gone with the Wind was re-released in movie theatres in 1998.

My mother watches *Canada AM* on TV every morning.

You may need to underline instead of italicizing if you are working on a typewriter. Just be consistent throughout any paper in which you use underlining or italics.

The Handmaid's Tale is a novel by Margaret Atwood.

I read about the latest discovery of dinosaur footprints in Maclean's.

Gone with the Wind was re-released in movie theaters in 1998.

My mother watches Canada AM on TV every morning.

E X E R C I S E S

Punctuate the quotations, and italicize or put quotation marks around each title.

Exercise 1

1. The fifth estate is still a popular television series.

2. I don't explain said Marshall McLuhan I explore.

3. Do I have to do all of the dishes by myself my roommate asked.

4. Last night we watched the movie Wag the Dog on video.

5. Oscar Wilde wrote the play The Importance of Being Earnest, the novel The Picture of Dorian Gray, the poem The Ballad of Reading Gaol, and the children's story The Selfish Giant.

6. Never use a big word if a little one will do Emily Carr once said

7. The class period can't be over said the student I haven't even started my concluding paragraph yet.

8. I found my friend in the library reading the latest issue of Flare magazine.

9. We were asked to read the essay Thinking as a Hobby for Wednesday's class.

10. The movie version of The English Patient was just as poetic as the book.

Exercise 2

1. The Precambrian Shield is a poem by E.J. Pratt.

2. Once you fill in all the answers the teacher said turn your quiz papers over on your desks.

3. I have a subscription to several magazines, including Canadian Living.

4. Everything exists in limited quantities Pablo Picasso perceived even happiness.

5. How many times she asked are you going to mention the price we paid for dinner.

6. After Babe Ruth's death, his wife remarked I don't even have an autographed ball. You don't ask your husband for an autographed ball. He'd probably think you were nuts.

7. Sophocles, the Greek playwright, wrote the tragedy Oedipus Rex in the fifth century BC.

8. When you go by on a train, everything looks beautiful. But if you stop Edward Hopper explained it becomes drab.

9. There is a Mexican proverb that says Whoever sells land sells his mother.

10. When Allan Lamport, who was mayor of the city, was asked about Toronto, he answered Nobody should visit Toronto for the first time.

Exercise 3

1. In her book Orlando, Virginia Woolf has this to say about art Green in nature is one thing, green in literature another.

2. Phil Hartman was the voice of Troy McClure on the animated TV series The Simpsons.

3. Hold fast to your dreams wrote Langston Hughes for if dreams die, then life is like a broken-winged bird that cannot fly.

4. David Suzuki wrote of his childhood in a chapter entitled A New Generation; it is part of his larger autobiography Metamorphosis: Stages in a Life.

5. Joan Didion describes her relationship with migraine headaches in her essay In Bed.

6. Where can I buy some poster board he asked.

7. There is a school-supply store around the corner his friend replied but I don't think that it's open this late.

8. Sylvia asked the other students if they had seen the Alfred Hitchcock movie called The Birds.

9. I don't remember James answered.

10. It's not something you could ever forget she yelled.

Exercise 4

1. Kurt Vonnegut, in his novel Slapstick, describes New York City as Skyscraper National Park.

2. The past is still, for us, a place that is not safely settled wrote Michael Ondaatje.

3. In her book The Mysterious Affair at Styles, Agatha Christie wrote that Every murderer is probably somebody's old friend.

4. Swear not by the moon says Juliet to Romeo.

5. Pierre Trudeau told a U.S. audience Living next to you is like sleeping next to an elephant.

6. Norman Bethune stated that The function of the artist is to disturb.

7. Writers are always selling somebody out Joan Didion observed.

8. The expression All animals are equal, but some animals are more equal than others can be found in George Orwell's novel Animal Farm.

9. A Swahili proverb warns, To the person who seizes two things, one always slips from his grasp!

10. Groucho Marx once remarked I wouldn't want to belong to any club that would accept me as a member.

Exercise 5

1. Ovid reminded us that we can learn from our enemies.

2. We know what a person thinks not when he tells us what he thinks said Isaac Bashevis Singer but by his actions.

3. The Spanish proverb El pez muere por la boca translated means The fish dies because it opens its mouth.

4. Ask yourself whether you are happy, and you cease to be so John Stuart Mill wrote.

5. A Russian proverb states Without a shepherd, sheep are not a flock.

6. Stephen Leacock felt that The essence of humour is human kindliness.

7. St. Jerome had the following insight The friendship that can cease has never been real.

8. Oscar Wilde found that In this world there are only two tragedies. One is not getting what one wants, and the other is getting it.

9. Self-respect observed Joe Clark permeates every aspect of your life.

10. Choose a job you love Confucius suggested and you will never have to work a day in your life.

PROOFREADING EXERCISE

Punctuate quotations, and underline or put quotation marks around titles used in the following paragraph.

It may be decided, sometime off in the future, that the sum of Douglas Coupland's literary contribution equals the two words he used for the title of his 1991 debut as a novelist. In Generation X, Coupland pointed and clicked onto the generation born in the late 1950s and the 1960s as it stared into the future and tried to figure out what was going to fulfill it there. If the book didn't attract universally favourable reviews, it was a resounding commercial success and made Coupland an instant spokesman for his generation. It didn't matter so much that he didn't want the job — I speak for myself, he's said, repeatedly, not for a generation. No, he'd been deemed a sociological seer and, like it or not, each of his subsequent novels — books like Microserfs (1995) and Girlfriend in a Coma (1998) — would find itself judged less as fiction than as the words of an oracle between hard covers.

Source: Quill and Quire: Canada's Magazine of Books and News, January 2000, Vol. 66, No. 1: 20.

SENTENCE WRITING

Write ten sentences that list and discuss your favourite songs, TV shows, characters' expressions, movies, books, and so on. Be sure to punctuate titles and quotations correctly. Refer to the rules at the beginning of this section if necessary.

Capital Letters

1. Capitalize the first word of every sentence.

Peaches taste best when they are cold.

2. Capitalize the first word of a direct quotation.

She said, "I've never worked so hard before."

"I have finished most of my homework," she said, "but I still have a lot to do." (The *but* is not capitalized because it continues the same quotation and does not begin a new sentence.)

"I love my English class," she said. "Maybe I'll change my program." (*Maybe* is capitalized because it begins a new sentence.)

3. Capitalize the first, last, and every important word in a title. Don't capitalize prepositions (such as *in, of, at, with*), short connecting words, the *to* in front of a verb, or *a, an,* or *the.*

I saw a copy of Darwin's *The Origin of Species* at a yard sale.

The class enjoyed the essay "How to Write a Rotten Poem with Almost No Effort."

Shakespeare in Love is a comedy based on Shakespeare's writing of the play *Romeo and Juliet.*

4. Capitalize specific names of people, places, languages, races, and nationalities.

Dr. Norman Bethune	China	Leonard Cohen
Ireland	Spanish	Japanese
Ujjal Dosanjh	Saskatoon	Dundas Street

5. Capitalize the names of months, days of the week, and special days, but not the seasons.

March	Victoria Day	spring
Tuesday	Easter	winter
Valentine's Day	Labour Day	fall

6. Capitalize a title of relationship if it takes the place of the person's name. If *my* **(or** *your, her, his, our, their***) is in front of the word, a capital is not used.**

I think Dad wrote to her.	*but*	I think my dad wrote to her.
She visited Aunt Sophia.	*but*	She visited her aunt.
We spoke with Grandpa.	*but*	We spoke with our grandpa.

7. Capitalize names of particular people or things, but not general terms.

I admire Professor Schwartz.	*but*	I admire my professor.
We saw the famous St. Lawrence River.	*but*	We saw the famous river.
Are you from the West?	*but*	Is your house west of the mountains?
I will take Philosophy 120 and English 100.	*but*	I will take philosophy and English.
She graduated from Sutter High School.	*but*	She graduated from high school.
They live at 119 Forest St.	*but*	They live on a beautiful street.
We enjoyed the Royal Ontario Museum.	*but*	We enjoyed the museum.

E X E R C I S E S

Add all of the necessary capital letters to the sentences that follow.

Exercise 1

1. mom and i have both decided to take classes next fall.

2. fortunately, in toronto we live near several colleges and universities.

3. classes at the community colleges usually begin in late august or early september.

4. we could easily drive to the university of toronto, ryerson polytechnic university, humber college, george brown college, or sheridan college.

5. i want to take credit classes, and my mom wants to sign up for community education classes.

6. for instance, i will enroll in the academic courses necessary to transfer to a university.

7. these include english, math, science, and history classes.

8. my mother, on the other hand, wants to take noncredit classes with titles like "learn to play keyboards," "web pages made easy," and "be your own real estate agent."

9. mom already has a great job, so she can take classes just for fun.

10. i know that if i want to go to one of the colleges at the university of toronto, i will have to be serious from the start.

Exercise 2

1. born alice laidlaw in wingham, ontario, short story writer alice munro began to write fiction in her early teens.

2. after studying english for two years at the university of western ontario, she moved to british columbia, where her husband established a bookstore.

3. her early short stories were published in national magazines and broadcast on the cbc.

4. after the breakup of her marriage in 1976, she returned to southwestern ontario.

5. munro published her first book of short stories, *dance of the happy shades,* for which she won her first governor general's award.

6. *lives of girls and women,* one of munro's most famous works, received the canadian booksellers award.

7. when the cbc filmed a dramatization of this work, munro's daughter jenny was cast in the main role.

8. some of the stories in *the moons of jupiter* previously appeared in *the new yorker,* where munro has continued to publish her work.

9. munro sets some of her stories in british columbia, in toronto, and even in albania, but her stories are mostly based in southwestern Ontario.

10. students in literature classes study many of munro's stories, including "friend of my youth" and "lives of girls and women."

Source: Eugene Benson & William Toye, eds., *The Oxford Companion to Canadian Literature,* 2nd. ed. (Toronto: Oxford, 1997). Copyright © Oxford University Press Canada 1997.

Exercise 3

1. tom cruise's family lived in syracuse, new york, when he was born in 1962.

2. his original name was thomas cruise mapother iv [the fourth].

3. before he became a famous actor, tom cruise didn't do as well in school as he wanted to because he had dyslexia, which causes reading problems.

4. tom discovered acting when he was still a high school student in new jersey.

5. he played the part of nathan detroit in glen ridge high school's production of the musical *guys and dolls*.

6. tom cruise then moved to new york city to find other jobs as an actor.

7. he was in a movie called *endless love* with brooke shields, but it was not successful.

8. the film that made tom cruise a star was *risky business*, in which he sang along to the bob seeger song "old time rock & roll."

9. *people* magazine has put tom cruise on its list of "most beautiful people" many times.

10. cruise married another famous actor, nicole kidman, in december 1990, and they have adopted two children, isabella and connor.

Source: Biography Magazine, Oct. 1998.

Exercise 4

1. i grew up watching *the wizard of oz* once a year on tv before video stores like blockbuster even rented movies to watch at home.

2. i especially remember enjoying it with my brother and sisters when we lived on maple drive.

3. mom would remind us early in the day to get all of our homework done.

4. "if your homework isn't finished," she'd say, "you can't see the munchkins!"

5. my favourite part has always been when dorothy's house drops on one of the wicked witches and her feet shrivel up under the house.

6. the wicked witch of the west wants revenge after that, but dorothy and toto get help from glinda, the good witch of the north.

7. glinda tells dorothy about the emerald city and the wizard of oz.

8. on their way, toto and dorothy meet the scarecrow, the tin man, and the cowardly lion.

9. together they conquer the witch and meet professor marvel, the real man who has been pretending to be a wizard.

10. The ruby slippers give dorothy the power to get back to kansas and to her aunt em and uncle henry.

Exercise 5

1. oscar wilde was an irish-born writer who lived and wrote in england for much of his life during the late 1800s.

2. he was famous for his refined ideas about art and literature.

3. while still a young man, wilde travelled to america.

4. contrary to what many people expected, he was well received in rough mining towns such as leadville, colorado.

5. he gave one particularly long speech to the miners who lived in leadville.

6. wilde spoke on the following topic: "the practical application of the aesthetic theory to exterior and interior house decoration, with observations on dress and personal ornament."

7. during his stay in leadville, wilde had gained the miners' respect by visiting them down in the mines and by proving that he could drink as much whiskey as they could without getting drunk.

8. wilde wrote about one incident that took place in leadville.

9. before giving a lecture he called "the ethics of art," wilde was told that two criminals accused of murder had been found in town.

10. earlier that evening, on the same stage where wilde was about to give his speech, the two men were convicted of the crime and were then executed by leadville officials.

Source: Saloons of the Old West (Toronto: Knopf, 1979).

REVIEW OF PUNCTUATION AND CAPITAL LETTERS

Punctuate these sentences. They include all the rules for punctuation and capitalization you have learned. Compare your answers carefully with those at the back of the book. Sentences may require several pieces of punctuation or capital letters.

1. The height of the cn tower, located in toronto, is 553 m.

2. Have you ever read helen weinzweigs short story a view from the roof

3. We drove around the country all summer now were ready to stay right here

4. How much does a one-way ticket to paris cost she asked

5. We received your application ms kovac and will contact you soon with our response

6. The dog that receives the highest number of points wins the blue ribbon

7. Mr michaels teaches music 201 which is the intermediate voice class

8. Whenever we eat there we leave something behind at our table then we have to drive back and get it

9. We brought the plates forks cups and napkins but we forgot the bag with the food

10. Hamlet doesnt *give* the famous advice to thine own self be true but he *follows* it

11. I love to read the cartoons in the calgary sun its my favourite newspaper

12. Packing for a long trip requires patience planning and previous experience

13. Our french instructor told us the following think french when you speak french

14. I wonder if we need to bring our english books to class today

15. I think it was john lennon who said life is what happens when youre busy making other plans

Comprehensive Test

In these sentences you'll find all the errors that have been discussed in the entire text. Try to name the error in the blank before each sentence, and then correct the error if you can. You may find any of these errors:

awk	awkward phrasing
apos	apostrophe
c	comma needed
cap	capitalization
cliché	overused expression
cs	comma splice
dm	dangling modifier
frag	fragment
mm	misplaced modifier
p	punctuation
pro	incorrect pronoun
pro agr	pronoun agreement
pro ref	pronoun reference
ro	run-on sentence
shift	shift in time or person
sp	misspelled word
s/v agr	subject/verb agreement
wordy	wordiness
ww	wrong word
//	not parallel

A perfect — or almost perfect — score will mean you've mastered the first part of the text.

1. _____ I am delighted to except an invitation to your wedding.

2. _____ Our company is commited to excellence.

3. _____ There is a need to give the students better food choices on campus.

4. _____ The art class took a trip to the museum of civilization.

5. _____ Our neighbour paid my brother and I to paint her fence.

6. _____ I knew that I had not studied for the test, that I missed several easy questions, and definitely wasn't going to pass it.

7. _____ The grass needs to be mowed and the gutters need to be cleared before it rains.

8. _____ Sitting at the bus stop, a car swerved and ended up facing the wrong direction.

9. _____ He told Mr. Keely that he lost his notebook.

10. _____ I eat pizza because it always tasted so good.

11. _____ I didn't know that you played the violin?

12. _____ The childrens' toys were scattered around the room.

13. _____ At the age of 18, my parents bought me a car.

14. _____ They didn't know what time it was neither of them wore a watch that day.

15. _____ Last but not least, nicotine patches help smokers kick the habit.

16. _____ With a little advance planning, it is easy to throw a very unique party.

17. _____ Everyone in the class forgot to bring their book.

18. _____ Because the gate was open and music was playing in the back-yard.

19. _____ I enjoy buying birthday presents, they bring a special kind of joy.

20. _____ Each of the cookies were burned on the bottom.

PART 4

Writing

Aside from the basics of spelling, sentence structure, and punctuation, what else do you need to understand to write better? Just as sentences are built according to accepted patterns, so are other structures of English — paragraphs and essays, for example.

Think of writing as including levels of structure, beginning small with words connecting to form phrases, clauses, and sentences — and then sentences connecting to form paragraphs and essays. Each level has its own set of "blueprints." To communicate clearly in writing, words must be spelled correctly; a sentence needs a subject, a verb, and a complete thought; paragraphs are indented and contain a main idea and support; and essays explore a topic in several paragraphs, usually including an introduction, body, and conclusion. These consistent structures comfort beginning writers as patterns that they can learn to use themselves.

Not everyone approaches writing as structure, however. One can write better without thinking about structure at all. A good place to start might be to write what you care about and care about what you write. You can make an amazing amount of progress by simply being genuine, being who you are naturally. No one has to tell you to be yourself when you speak, but beginning writers often need encouragement to be themselves in their writing.

Writing is almost never done without a reason. The reason may come from an experience, such as fighting an unfair parking ticket, or from a requirement in a class. And when you are asked to write, you often receive guidance in the form of an assignment: tell a story to prove a point, paint a picture with your words, summarize an article, compare two subjects, share what you know about something, explain why you agree with or disagree with an idea.

Learning to write well is important, one of the most important things you will do in your education. Confidence is the key. The Writing sections will help you build confidence, whether you are expressing your own ideas or summarizing and responding to the ideas of others. Like the Sentence Structure sections, the Writing sections are best taken in order. However, each one discusses an aspect of writing that can be reviewed on its own at any time.

What Is the Least You Should Know About Writing?

"Unlike medicine or the other sciences," William Zinsser points out, "writing has no new discoveries to spring on us. We're in no danger of reading in our morning newspaper that a breakthrough has been made in how to write [clearly]. ... We may be given new technologies like the word processor to ease the burdens of composition, but on the whole we know what we need to know."

One thing we know is that we learn to write by *writing* — not by reading long discussions about writing. Therefore the explanations and instructions in this section are as brief as they can be, followed by samples from student and professional writers.

Understanding the basic structures and learning the essential skills covered in this section will help you become a better writer.

BASIC STRUCTURES	WRITING SKILLS
I. The Paragraph	**III.** Writing in Your Own Voice
II. The Essay	**IV.** Finding a Topic
	V. Organizing Ideas
	VI. Supporting with Details
	VII. Revising Your Papers
	VIII. Presenting Your Work
	IX. Writing about What You Read

Basic Structures

I. THE PARAGRAPH

A paragraph is unlike any other structure in English. Visually, it has its own profile: the first line is usually indented about five spaces, and sentences continue to fill the space between both margins until the paragraph ends (which may be in the middle of the line).

_____

_____

_____

_____

_____

_____ .

Beginning writers often forget to indent their paragraphs, or they break off in the middle of a line within a paragraph, especially when writing in class. You must remember to indent whenever you begin a new paragraph and fill the space between the margins until it ends. (Note: In business writing, paragraphs are not indented but double-spaced in-between.)

Defining a Paragraph

A typical paragraph centres on one idea, usually phrased in a topic sentence from which all the other sentences in the paragraph radiate. The topic sentence does not need to begin the paragraph, but it most often does, and the other sentences support it with specific details. (For more on topic sentences and organizing paragraphs, see p. 209.) Paragraphs usually contain several sentences, though no set number is required. A paragraph can stand alone, but more commonly paragraphs are part of a larger composition, such as an essay. There are different kinds of paragraphs, based on the jobs they are supposed to do.

Types of Paragraphs

Introductory paragraphs begin essays. They provide background information about the essay's topic and usually include the thesis statement or main idea of the essay. (See p. 207 for information on how to write a thesis statement.) Here is the introductory paragraph of a student essay entitled "A Cure for My Premature Old Age":

> Most people would love to live in a quiet neighbourhood. I have heard that some people even camp out in front of a house they are planning to buy just to see if the block is as quiet as they have been told. Maybe I am unusual, but not long ago I felt that my community was too quiet. It was a problem for me, but I didn't get much sympathy when I told people about it. I learned that, from the problems in our lives, we become who we are.

In this opening paragraph, the student leads up to the main idea that "we become who we are" as a result of the challenges in our lives with background information about the "problem" of living in a quiet neighbourhood.

Body paragraphs are those in the middle of essays. Each body paragraph contains a topic sentence and presents detailed information about one subtopic or idea that relates directly to the essay's thesis. (See p. 209 for more information on organizing body paragraphs.) Here are the body paragraphs of the same essay:

> The silence of my neighbourhood affected me. Everyday I woke up to an alarm clock of quiet. There were no birds chirping, no cars passing by,

nothing noisy around to comfort me. I lived then (and still do) in a cul-de-sac next to a home for senior citizens. Even the ambulances that came to transport the old folks never used their sirens. I often felt lonely and spent time looking out the window at the bushes and the badly painted fence. I too was becoming old, but I was only 19. I found myself actually whispering at times.

There was no easy solution to my problem. My grandmother hated loud sounds, and she would never consider moving. We didn't even watch television because the blaring commercials upset her. I wanted to get out of the house with friends and visit noisy places, but my grandmother needed me to help her while my parents were at work. I didn't mind spending time with her, and she did teach me to make an incredible spaghetti sauce.

One day, I finally discovered a remedy for my problem. I took my grandmother to visit her friend Irene at the nursing home next door, and — no, I didn't leave her there. I started reading out loud to both of them. At first I read from the newspaper, but then someone suggested that I read a short story instead. As I read them the story, I realized that I had been silent for so long that I loved to hear my own voice, to act out the characters' personalities, and to live through the actions of the characters. Grandma and Irene loved it, too.

Notice that each of the three body paragraphs discusses a single aspect of the student's response to the problem — the ways it affected him, the lack of a simple solution, and finally the "cure."

Concluding paragraphs are the final paragraphs in essays. They bring the discussion to a close and share the writer's final thoughts on the subject. (See p. 221 for more about concluding paragraphs.) Here is the conclusion of the sample essay:

Now I am in my first year of university, and I've chosen English as a major. My grandmother spends three days a week visiting Irene next door. After school, I read them the essays I write for my classes, and they give me advice on how to make them better. I also work on campus, making recordings of books for visually impaired students. And I will be playing the part of Mercutio in our theatre department's production of *Romeo and Juliet*. I never imagined that the solution to my problem would turn out to be the beginning of my adult life.

In this concluding paragraph, the student describes his transformation from depressed "aging" teen to promising student and aspiring actor — all as a result of living in a quiet cul-de-sac and caring for his grandmother.

SAMPLE OF A PARAGRAPH ALONE

Single-paragraph writing assignments may be given in class or as homework. They test the beginning writer's understanding of the unique structure of a paragraph. They may ask the writer to answer a single question, perhaps following a reading, or to provide details about a limited topic. Look at this student paragraph, the result of a homework assignment asking students to report on a technological development in the news:

> I learned on the evening news last night that in the future we will still be reading books, magazines, and newspapers made of paper, but the words and pictures will be printed with electronic ink. This special ink will turn a piece of paper into something like a computer screen. So the information on the page will change completely when new data is sent to it through a kind of pager device. The same sheets of electronic paper that had yesterday's news printed on them will be able to be cleared so that today's news is printed on them. The ink will work like the cards that crowds of people in sports stadiums hold and turn over in patterns to display a message or a picture. Each tiny bit of the ink will have a white and a black side that flips one way or the other, forming letters and pictures on the page. Paper and books using electronic ink will be here in a few years, and I can't wait.

Source: ABC News, 16 July 1998.

These shorter writing assignments help students practise presenting information within the limited structure of a paragraph.

The assignments in the upcoming Writing Skills section will sometimes ask you to write paragraphs. Remember that you may review the previous pages as often as you wish until you understand the unique structure of the paragraph.

II. The Essay

Like the paragraph, an essay has its own profile, usually including a title and several paragraphs.

Title

_____

_____
_____
_____
_____
_____ .

_____
_____
_____
_____
_____
_____ .

_____

_____

_____

_____

_____

_____ .

_____

_____

_____

_____

_____

_____

_____ .

_____

_____

_____

_____ .

While the paragraph is the single building block of text used in almost all forms of writing (letters, novels, newspaper stories, and so on), an essay is a more complex structure.

The Five-Paragraph Essay and Beyond

On pp. 194–95, you read a five-paragraph student essay illustrating the different kinds of paragraphs within essays. Many people like to include five paragraphs in an essay: an introductory paragraph, three body paragraphs, and a concluding paragraph. Three is a comfortable number of body paragraphs — it is not two, which makes an essay seem like a comparison even when it isn't; and it is not four, which may be too many subtopics for the beginning writer to organize clearly.

However, as writers become more comfortable with the flow of their ideas and gain confidence in their ability to express themselves, they are free to create essays of many different shapes and sizes. As in all things, learning about writing begins with structure and then expands to include all possibilities.

Defining an Essay

There is no such thing as a typical essay. Essays may be serious or humorous, but the best of them are thought-provoking and — of course — informative. Try looking up the word _essay_ in a dictionary right now. Some words used to define what an essay is might need to be explained themselves:

An essay is _prose_ (meaning it is written in the ordinary language of sentences and paragraphs).

An essay is *nonfiction* (meaning it deals with real people, factual information, and actual opinions and events).

An essay is a *composition* (meaning it is created in parts that make up the whole, several paragraphs that explore a single topic).

An essay is *personal* (meaning it shares the writer's unique perspective, even if only in the choice of topic, method of analysis, and details).

An essay is *analytical* and *instructive* (meaning it examines the workings of a subject and shares the results with the reader).

A SAMPLE ESSAY

For an example of a piece of writing that fits the above definition, read the following biographical essay about the woman responsible for inventing the Melitta coffeemaker (from the book *Mothers of Invention*, by Ethlie Ann Vare and Greg Ptacek).

Drip Coffee

In 1908 a housewife in Dresden, Germany, became annoyed with the time-consuming method of brewing coffee by wrapping the loose grounds in a cloth bag and boiling water around it. Worse, coffee made that way (or by the shortcut of boiling coffee grounds right in the water) was bitter-tasting and grainy.

So Melitta Bentz ripped a sheet of blotting paper from her son's schoolbook, cut a circle of the porous paper, and stuck it in the bottom of a brass pot that she had poked full of holes. She reasoned that if she put the coffee grounds on top of this filter and poured the boiling water over it, she could get the taste of the coffee without the bad side effects.

Melitta Bentz was right about the coffee filtration system — so right, in fact, that she and her husband, Hugo, hired a tinsmith to produce the new-fangled coffeepots for sale. In 1909 they brought their drip system to the Leipzig trade fair and sold more than 1200 "coffeemakers," as they called them. The Melitta company was born.

By 1912 Melitta was manufacturing its own line of coffee filters. Frau Bentz's company continued to grow, owned and operated by her children and her children's children. Her original disk-shaped filter was replaced by the familiar cone shape of today, and early metal pots were replaced by porcelain and plastic models. The Melitta coffeemaker is used today in 150 countries worldwide; a majority of coffee drinkers use the drip preparation method.

From a cottage in Dresden and a hausfrau with a taste for good coffee grew an international concern and a woman's first name that will forever remain synonymous with this omnipresent appliance.

Now that you have learned more about the basic structures of the paragraph and the essay, you are ready to practise the skills necessary to write them.

Writing Skills

III. WRITING IN YOUR OWN VOICE

All writing "speaks" on paper. And the person "listening" is the reader. Some beginning writers forget that writing and reading are two-way methods of communication, just like spoken conversations between two people. When you write, your reader listens; when you read, you also listen.

When speaking, you express a personality in your choice of phrases, your movements, your tone of voice. Family and friends probably recognize your voice messages on their answering machines without your having to identify yourself. Would they also be able to recognize your writing? They would if you extended your "voice" into your writing.

Writing should not sound like talking, necessarily, but it should have a "personality" that comes from the way you decide to approach a topic, to develop it with details, to say it your way.

The beginning of this book discusses the difference between spoken English (following looser patterns of speaking) and Standard Written English (following accepted patterns of writing). Don't think that the only way to add "voice" to your writing is to use the patterns of spoken English. Remember that Standard Written English does not have to be dull or sound "academic." Look at this example of Standard Written English that has a distinct voice, part of the preface to John A. Murray's book *Grizzly Bears: An Illustrated Field Guide*:

Whatever I know of grizzlies has been learned primarily ... by watching bears in the field. ... I have sat on the cold spring ground and photographed a sow grizzly as she nibbled horsetail sprouts from earth that ten days earlier had snow on it. ... I have watched in amazement as a boar grizzly dragged the remains of a spike bull across a meadow and into a forest. The only hold it had on the carcass was a bit of neck muscle in the teeth. I have videotaped a young female grizzly as she successfully battled a subarctic wolf for possession of a caribou carcass. I have watched grizzlies play, fight, eat, sleep, nurse cubs, explore, make love and go about their daily affairs in the wild, and I am deeply appreciative. Each sighting has been a gift, every moment a privilege. I never tire of watching grizzlies, or of sharing them with my guests. ...

Murray's preface illustrates Standard Written English at its best — from its solid sentence structures to its precise use of words. But more importantly, Murray's clear voice speaks to us and involves us in his world, in his appreciation of grizzly bears. Students can involve us in their writing, too, when they let their own voices through. Writing does not need to be about something personal to have a voice. Here is an example of a student writing about computer hackers:

> Some mischievous hackers are only out to play a joke. One of the first examples was a group who created the famous "Cookie Monster" program at Massachusetts Institute of Technology. Several hackers programmed MIT's computer to display the word "cookie" all over the screens of its users. In order for users to clear this problem, they had to "feed" the Cookie Monster by entering the word "cookie" or lose all the data on their screens.

Notice that both the professional and the student writer tell stories (narration) and paint pictures (description) in the sample paragraphs. Narration and description require practice, but once you master them, you will gain a stronger voice and will be able to add interest and clarity to even the most challenging academic writing assignments.

Narration

Narrative writing tells the reader a story, and since most of us like to tell stories, it is a good place to begin writing in your own voice. An effective narration allows readers to experience an event with the writer. Since we all see the world differently and feel unique emotions, the purpose of narration is to take readers with us through an experience. As a result, the writer gains a better understanding of what happened, and readers get to live other lives momentarily. Listen to the "voice" of this student writer telling the story of a difficult lesson she learned in her childhood:

```
                    Bedtime Is a Good Thing


    There I was, a rebellious 7-year-old, telling, begging
my father to let me stay up past my bedtime. It was Sat-
urday night, and the big "Movie of the Week" was on.
After I jumped up and down for about 30 minutes, my
father bellowed at me, "Fine! But you have to watch
```

what we're going to watch." "We" stood for my father, my stepmother, and my two *older* brothers. In the excitement of being allowed to stay up, I didn't care what we were going to watch. I soon found out that I should have cared.

The theme music gradually became louder and louder. It was just music, no words. "Duh nuh" ... "Duh nuh" ... "Duh nuh, duh nuh, duh nuh!" All of a sudden the word *JAWS* flashed on the screen. I didn't say anything. If I had, I would have been sent straight to bed. After the accomplishment I had just achieved, I was not about to surrender. The room was dim, like a movie theatre, and a 7-year-old *little* girl sat there secretly terrified. The movie ended, and by that time I was so tired I went to bed and fell asleep instantly.

But the next three nights in a row, just as I closed my eyes, flashes of a huge shark biting my leg came into my mind and would not stop. The first night I cried out for my dad. He came running in and listened to my story. He started to laugh, saying, "I told you so." He hugged me and stayed until I fell asleep. But this went on until finally my dad allowed our big dog to come in the house and sleep with me. I was getting better with my "protector" next to me. Every time I imagined the shark's jaws coming at me, I opened my eyes and saw the big floppy face of our old dog looking back with sleepy eyes. It took the rest of the week for the shark to leave.

The following weekend I did not beg my father to let me stay up. I simply gave him a kiss goodnight and marched happily back to my room. I had learned that there were reasons for my dad's rules. They were there to protect me. I was too young to see that movie, and that's why it was on after my bedtime. I wouldn't have believed my dad if he had just told me. I had to find out the hard way.

Description

Descriptive writing paints word pictures with details that appeal to the reader's five senses — sight, sound, touch, taste, and smell. The writer of description often uses comparisons to help readers picture one thing by imagining something else, just as the writer of "Bedtime Is a Good Thing" compared her dim living room to a movie theatre. In the short paragraph below, a student uses several comparisons to help describe a problem in her neighbourhood that she would like to have solved:

> A complaint I have about my community has to do with young children playing in the street. These are small, troll-like children between 6 and 10 years old, scattered like a broken jar of jellybeans along the street. They chase each other carelessly through car gaps and vanish instantly like puffs of smoke.

Here is another example, from writer Michael Ondaatje's short story "The Bridge." As we read his description, we feel as though we are there with the men on the flatbed of the truck, travelling through the streets of Toronto at dawn.

> A truck carries fire at five A.M. through central Toronto, along Dundas Street and up Parliament Street, moving north. Aboard the flatbed, three men stare into passing darkness — their muscles relaxed in this last half-hour before work — as if they don't own the legs or the arms jostling against their bodies and the backboard of the Ford.
>
> Written in yellow over the green door is DOMINION BRIDGE COMPANY. But for now all that is visible is the fire on the flatbed burning over the three-foot by three-foot metal dish, cooking the tar in a cauldron, leaving this odour on the streets for anyone who would step out into the early morning and swallow the air.
>
> The truck rolls burly under the arching trees, pauses at certain intersections where more workers jump onto the flatbed, and soon there are eight men, the fire crackling, hot tar now and then spitting onto the back of a neck or an ear. Soon there are twenty, crowded and silent.
>
> The light begins to come out of the earth. They see their hands, the textures on a coat, the trees they had known were there. At the top of Parliament Street the truck turns east, passes the Rosedale fill, and moves towards the half-built viaduct.
>
> The men jump off. The unfinished road is full of ruts and the fire and the lights of the truck bounce, the suspension wheezing. The truck travels so slowly the men are walking faster, in the cold dawn air, even though it is summer.

Source: Michael Ondaatje "The Bridge," *In the Skin of the Lion.* Toronto: McClelland & Stewart, 1987.

You may have noticed that all of the examples in this section use both narration and description. In fact, most effective writing — even a good résumé or biology lab report — calls for clear storytelling and the creation of vivid word pictures for the reader.

Writing Assignments

The following two assignments will help you develop your voice as a writer. For now, don't worry about topic sentences or thesis statements or any of the things we'll consider later. Narration and description have their own logical structures. A story has a beginning, a middle, and an end. And we describe things from top to bottom, side to side, and so on.

Assignment 1

NARRATION: FAMOUS SAYINGS

The following is a list of well-known expressions. No doubt you have had an experience that proves at least one of these to be true. Write a short essay that tells a story from your own life that relates to one of these sayings. (See if you can tell which of the sayings fits the experience narrated in the student essay "Bedtime Is a Good Thing" on p. 200.) You might want to identify the expression you have chosen in your introductory paragraph. Then tell the beginning, middle, and end of the story. Be sure to use vivid details to bring the story to life. Finish with a brief concluding paragraph in which you share your final thoughts on the experience.

> Fools and their money are soon parted.
>
> No good deed goes unpunished.
>
> If at first you don't succeed ... try, try again.
>
> Money can't buy happiness.
>
> We learn best from our mistakes.
>
> You can't judge a book by its cover.

Assignment 2

DESCRIPTION: A PICTURE WORTH 250 WORDS?

Describe a picture that means a lot to you. It could be a favourite family photo, a well-known news image, a famous drawing or painting, or a moment from a popular movie or TV commercial. Your goal is to make the reader *visualize* the picture. Try to use details and comparisons that appeal to the reader's senses in some way. Look back at the examples for inspiration. Be sure the reader knows — from your choice of details — what the picture means to you.

IV. FINDING A TOPIC

You will most often be given a topic to write about, perhaps based on a reading assignment. However, when the assignment of a paper calls for you to choose your own topic without any further assistance, try to go immediately to your interests.

Look to Your Interests

If the topic of your paper is something you know about and — more important — something you *care* about, then the whole process of writing will be smoother and more enjoyable for you. If you ski, if you are a musician, or even if you just enjoy watching a lot of television, bring that knowledge and enthusiasm into your papers.

Take a moment to think about and jot down a few of your interests now (no matter how unrelated to school they may seem), and then save the list for use later when deciding what to write about. One student's list of interests might look like this:

surfing the Internet

playing video games with friends

skateboarding in summer

collecting hockey cards

Another student's list might be very different:

playing the violin

going to concerts

watching old musicals on video

drawing caricatures of my friends

While still another student might list the following interests:

going to the horse races

reading for my book club

travelling in the summer

buying lottery tickets

These students have listed several worthy topics for papers. And because they are personal interests, the students have the details needed to support them.

Starting with a general topic, you can use several ways to gather the details needed to support it in a paragraph or an essay.

Focussed Free Writing (or Brainstorming)

Free writing is a good way to begin. When you are assigned a paper, try writing for ten minutes, putting down all your thoughts on one subject — watching old movies on video, for example. Don't stop to think about organization, sentence structures, capitalization, or spelling — just let details flow onto the page. Free writing will help you see what material you have and will help you figure out what aspects of the subject to write about.

Here is an example:

When I watch old movie musicals, I want to live back then. All the clothes were so fancy and it looks like people cared about each other more than they do now. I was watching a movie called guys and dolls the other night, and it was all about a bunch of gamblers in NYC who knew each other and one of them fell in love with a girl who worked for the salvation army. She hated gambling, and he hated her snooty attitude. But they fell in love anyway I guess opposites do attract after all. It had M. Brando, Frank Sinatra, and Jean somebody in it. I also saw the music man which was kind of similar. It was also about a criminal a con-man but in this one he was in a town full of backwards people and he fell for a woman a librarian so I guess she had a more open mind.

Now the result of this free writing session is certainly not ready to be typed and turned in as a paragraph. But what did become clear in it was that the student could probably compare the two musicals to show how they told the same story — that opposites attract — in two different ways.

Clustering

Clustering is another way of thinking a topic through on paper before you begin to write. A cluster is more visual than free writing. You could cluster the topic of "going to the horse races," for instance, by putting it in a circle in the centre of a piece of paper and then drawing lines to new circles as ideas or details occur to you. The idea is to free your mind from the limits of sentences and paragraphs to generate pure details and ideas. When you are finished clustering, you can see where you want to go with a topic.

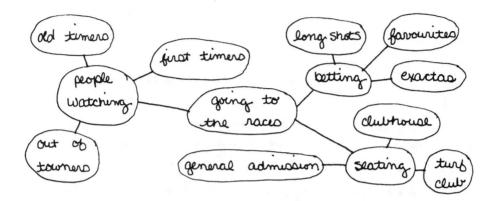

This cluster shows that the student has found three general aspects of attending the horse races: the variety of seating, types of bets, and groups of people to watch. This cluster might lead to another where the student chooses one aspect — groups of people to watch, for instance — and thinks of more details about it.

Talking with Other Students

It may help to talk to others when deciding on a topic. Many teachers break their classes up into groups at the beginning of an assignment. Talking with other students helps you realize that you see things just a little differently. Value the difference — it will help your written voice that we discussed earlier emerge.

Assignment 3
LIST YOUR INTERESTS

Make a list of four or five of your own interests. Be sure that they are as specific as the examples listed on p. 204. Keep the list for later assignments.

Assignment 4
DO SOME FREE WRITING

Choose one of your interests, and do some focussed free writing about it. Write for ten minutes with that topic in mind but without stopping. Don't worry about anything such as spelling or sentence structures while you are free writing. The results are meant to help you find out what you have to say about the topic *before* you start to write a paper about it. Save the results for a later assignment.

Assignment 5
TRY CLUSTERING IDEAS

Choose another of your interests. Put it in the centre of a piece of paper, and draw a cluster of details and ideas relating to it, following the sample on page 206. Take the cluster as far as it will go. Then choose one aspect to cluster again on its own. This way you will arrive at specific, interesting details and ideas — not just the first ones that come to mind. Save the results of all your efforts.

V. Organizing Ideas

The most important thing to keep in mind, no matter what you are writing, is the idea you want to get across to your reader. Whether you are writing a paragraph or an essay, you must have in mind a single idea that you want to express. In a paragraph, such an idea is called a topic sentence; in an essay, it's called a thesis statement, but they mean the same thing — an idea you want to get across. We will begin with a discussion of thesis statements.

Thesis Statements

Let's choose one of the students' interests listed on page 204 as a general topic. "Surfing the Internet" by itself doesn't make any point. What about it? What does it do for you? What point about surfing the Internet would you like to present to your reader? You might write

Surfing the Internet is a good way to discover new things.

But this is a vague statement, not worth developing. You might move into more specific territory and write

I have improved my reading and writing skills by surfing the Internet.

Now you have said something specific. *When you write in one sentence the point you want to present to your reader, you have written a thesis statement.*

All good writers either have a thesis in mind when they begin to write or develop the thesis as they write. Whether they are writing essays, novels, poems, or plays, they eventually have in mind an idea they want to present to the reader. They may develop it in various ways, but behind whatever they write is their ruling thought, their reason for writing, their thesis.

For any writing assignment, after you have done some free writing or clustering to explore your topic, the next step is to write a thesis statement. As you write your thesis statement, keep two things in mind:

1. A thesis statement must be a sentence *with a subject and a verb* (not merely a topic).

2. A thesis statement must be *an idea that you can explain or defend* (not simply a statement of fact).

Exercise 1
THESIS OR FACT?

Which of the following are merely topics or facts, and which are thesis statements that you could explain or defend? In front of each one that could be a thesis statement, write THESIS. In front of each one that is a fact, write FACT. Check your answers with those at the back of the book.

1. _____ We travelled to London last spring.

2. _____ Getting my first car took away my freedom.

3. _____ A computer could easily do my job.

4. _____ College bookstores could serve students better than they do now.

5. _____ Ice was recently found on the moon.

6. _____ As predicted, killer bees have made their way to North America.

7. _____ I have finally learned how to successfully apply for a scholarship.

8. _____ Some people can only tell the time using digital clocks and watches.

9. _____ People using e-mail have invented new uses for punctuation marks, called "emoticons."

10. _____ Sharks have no bones in their bodies.

Assignment 6
WRITE A THESIS STATEMENT

Use your free writing or clustering results from Assignments 4 and 5 (pp. 206–7) and write at least one thesis statement based on one of your interests. Be sure that the thesis you write is phrased as a complete thought that can be defended or explained in an essay.

Organizing an Essay

Once you have written a good thesis and explored your topic through discussion with others or by free writing and clustering, you are ready to organize your essay.

First you need an introductory paragraph. It should catch your reader's interest, provide necessary background information, and either include or suggest your thesis statement. (See p. 194 and p. 200 for two examples of student writers' introductory paragraphs.) In your introductory paragraph, you may also list supporting points, but a more effective way is to let them unfold paragraph by paragraph rather than to give them all away in the beginning of the essay. Even if your supporting points don't appear in your introduction, your reader will easily spot them later if your paper is clearly organized.

Your second paragraph will present your first supporting point — everything about it and nothing more.

Your next paragraph will be about your second supporting point — all about it and nothing more.

Each additional paragraph will develop another supporting point.

Finally, you'll need a concluding paragraph. In a short paper, it isn't necessary to restate all your points. Your conclusion may be brief; even a single sentence to round out the paper may do the job. Remember that the main purpose of a concluding paragraph is to bring the paper to a close by sharing your final thoughts on the subject. (See p. 195 and p. 201 for two examples of concluding paragraphs.)

Learning to write this kind of paper will teach you to distinguish between the parts of an essay. Then when you're ready to write a longer paper, you'll be able to organize it clearly and elaborate on its design and content.

Topic Sentences

A topic sentence does for a paragraph what a thesis statement does for an essay — it states the main idea. Like thesis statements, topic sentences must be phrased as complete thoughts to be proven or developed through the presentation of details. But the topic sentence introduces an idea or subtopic that is the right size to cover in a paragraph. The topic sentence doesn't have to be the first sentence in a paragraph. It may come at the end or even in the middle, but putting it first is most common.

Each body paragraph should contain only one main idea, and no detail or example should be allowed to creep into the paragraph if it doesn't support the topic sentence. (See pp. 194–95 and pp. 199–202 for more examples of body paragraphs within essays and of paragraphs alone.)

Organizing Body Paragraphs (or Single Paragraphs)

A single paragraph or a body paragraph within an essay is organized in the same way as an entire essay but on a smaller scale. Here's the way you learned to organize an essay:

Thesis: stated or suggested in introductory paragraph

First supporting paragraph

Second supporting paragraph

Additional supporting paragraphs

Concluding paragraph

And here's the way to organize a paragraph:

> Topic sentence
>
> First supporting detail or example
>
> Second supporting detail or example
>
> Additional supporting details or examples
>
> Concluding or transitional sentence

You should have several details to support each topic sentence. If you find that you have little to say after writing the topic sentence, ask yourself what details or examples will make your reader believe that the topic sentence is true for you.

Transitional Expressions

Transitional expressions within a paragraph and between paragraphs in an essay help the reader move from one detail or example to the next and from one supporting point to the next. When first learning to organize an essay, you might start each supporting paragraph in a paper with a transitional expression.

There are transitions to show addition:

> Also
>
> Furthermore
>
> Another (example, point, step, etc. ...)
>
> In addition

There are transitions to show sequence:

First	One reason	One example
Second	Another reason	Another example
Finally	Most important	In conclusion

There are transitions to show contrast:

However	On the other hand	In contrast

Exercise 2

ADDING TRANSITIONAL EXPRESSIONS

Place the transitional expressions from the following list into the blanks in the following paragraph to make it read smoothly. Check your answers with those in the back of the book.

Therefore	Finally	Next	First of all

When I moved into my own apartment for the first time last month, I discovered the many hidden expenses of entering "the real world." _____ , I had no idea that utility companies needed a security deposit from anyone who hasn't rented before. Each utility required a $30 to $50 deposit. _____ , my start-up costs just for gas, electricity, and phone used up all the money I had saved for furnishings. _____ , I found out how expensive it was to supply a kitchen with the basic staples of food and cleaning supplies. My initial trip to the grocery store cost $125, and I hadn't even bought my curtains at that point. _____ , I was able to budget my money and keep a little aside for any other unexpected expenses of living on my own.

Assignment 7
SHOULD THERE BE AGE LIMITS FOR PARENTS?

New methods of fertilization have made it possible for at least one woman in her 60s to give birth to her first child, and men 70 and older have naturally fathered children. Write a long paragraph or a short essay in which you briefly answer the question "Do you believe there should be age limits for parents?" Your answer to the question will be your main idea, and the reasons and details that support it should be your own opinions. Try free writing, clustering, or discussing the subject with others to find out how you feel and what you think about the topic before you begin to write.

VI. SUPPORTING WITH DETAILS

Now you're ready to support your main ideas with subtopics and specific details. That is, you'll think of ways to convince your reader that what you say in your thesis is true. How could you convince your reader that surfing the Internet has improved your reading and writing skills? You might write

> My reading and writing skills have improved since I began surfing the Internet. (because)

1. The computer won't respond to sloppy spelling and punctuation.

2. I read much more on screen than I ever did on paper, and much faster.

3. I write e-mail to friends and family, but I never wrote real letters to them before.

> **NOTE:** Sometimes if you imagine a *because* at the end of your thesis statement, it will help you write your reasons or subtopics clearly and in parallel form.

Types of Support

The subtopics developing a thesis and the details presented in a paragraph are not always reasons. Supporting points may take many forms based on the purpose of the essay or paragraph. They may be

examples (in an illustration)

steps (in a how-to or process paper)

types or kinds (in a classification)

meanings (in a definition)

similarities and/or differences (in a comparison/contrast)

effects (in a cause-and-effect analysis)

Whatever they are, supporting points should develop the main idea expressed in the thesis or topic sentence and prove it to be true.

Here is the final draft of a student essay on the problem of not being able to trust instincts. Notice how the body paragraphs present examples of the student's indecision. And all of the details within the body paragraphs support her topic sentences.

Indecision

As far back as I can remember, I've always been fickle-minded. At first, my mind would settle on one decision. Then suddenly, in a snap, I would change it. I have trouble with everything from choosing birthday presents for my friends to deciding what to eat for dinner every night. My problem of indecision is worst at school, where I have never trusted my instincts.

For instance, whenever I take multiple-choice tests, I get two points lower than an *A* because of last-minute changes. I get the right answer first, yet I frequently hear this inner voice tell me to change it when I review my answers. It feels as though I'm being torn between my left hand urging me to erase my first answer and my right hand trying to stop the other one from doing it. Then this weird voice orders me to change the answer anyway.

The sad part comes after the test. I open my notes and scan for the right answer. Then I realize that once again I have wasted my energy, my eraser, and most of all the point or points on the test. Next is the indescribable feeling of a "lump" in my throat and pressure on my chest when the tests are given back. I usually get *B*'s just because of erasures. This has happened in my anatomy, history, and psychology classes. I guess something in me is afraid of getting *A*'s.

The same problem of indecision occurred last week outside of school. We were assigned to purchase a basal thermometer for an experiment in my anatomy class. So I went to the pharmacy near my house, and I found two — one just like the sample the teacher showed us in class and another brand with the same information on the label. Once more my hands fought with my brain. Incredibly, I chose the off brand. I came home and tried it. The mercury read my temperature, but the silver line didn't go down when I shook the thermometer afterward. Once again I should have trusted my instincts and bought the one the teacher showed us. The following day, I had to take an extra trip on the bus just to exchange it.

After this incident, I have resolved to value my first judgements. I know that if I trust my initial decisions, I will be trusting myself. I will still go through my test papers a second time, but I won't change a thing unless I know an answer is 100 percent wrong. With this plan, I may become an *A* student yet.

(Note: See pp. 215–16 for a rough draft of the above essay, before its final revisions.)

Learning to support your main ideas with vivid details is perhaps the most important thing you can accomplish in this course. Many writing problems are not really *writing* problems but *thinking* problems. Whether you're writing a term paper or merely an answer to a test question, if you take enough time to think, you'll be able to write a clear thesis statement and support it with paragraphs loaded with meaningful details.

Assignment 8

WRITE AN ESSAY ON ONE OF YOUR INTERESTS

Return to the thesis statement you wrote about one of your interests for Assignment 6 on page 208. Now write a short essay to support it. You can explain the allure of your interest, its drawbacks, or its benefits (such as the one about the Internet improving the student's reading and writing skills). Don't forget to use any free writing or clustering you may have done on the topic beforehand.

Assignment 9

A WEAKNESS

Like the student writer of "Indecision," we all have minor personality weaknesses. We may procrastinate (put things off until the last minute), hide our true feelings, or gossip about people we know. These weaknesses affect our lives, yet we are usually aware of them. Write an essay about one of your minor personality weaknesses, and give examples of the effects it has had on your life. You may want to include how you might solve the problem.

VII. REVISING YOUR PAPERS

Great writers don't just sit down and write a final draft. They write and revise. You may have heard the expression, "Easy writing makes hard reading." True, it is *easier* to turn in a piece of writing the first time it lands on paper. But you and your reader will be disappointed by the results. Try to think of revision as an opportunity instead of a chore, as a necessity instead of a choice.

Whenever possible, write the paper several days before the first draft is due. Let it sit for a while. When you reread it, you'll see ways to improve the organization or to add more details to a weak paragraph. After revising the paper, put it away for another day, and try again to improve it. Save all of your drafts along the way to see the progress that you've made or possibly to return to an area left out in later drafts but which fits in again after revision.

Don't call any paper finished until you have worked it through several times. Revising is one of the best ways to improve your writing.

Take a look at an early draft of the student essay you read on page 212 on the problem of indecision. Notice that the student has revised her rough draft by crossing out some parts, correcting word forms, and adding new phrasing or reminders for later improvement.

Indecision

give more background

As far back as I can remember, I've always been fickle-minded. At first, my mind would settle on one decision. Then suddenly, in a snap, I would change it.* I have never trusted my instincts.

For instance, whenever I ~~have~~ take tests ~~like scantrons or~~ multiple-choice, I get two points lower than ~~the grade I want~~ an "A" because of last-minute changes. I ~~always~~ get the right answer ~~on my~~ first ~~choice~~, yet I frequently hear this inner voice say to change it when I ~~go back and~~ review my answers. It ~~always~~ feels ~~like~~ as though I'm being torn between by left hand's urge to erase my first answer and my right hand trying to keep ~~holding~~ my left hand ~~to keep~~ from doing it. Then comes the ~~wierd~~ weird voice that orders me to ~~do erase it~~ change the answer anyway.

The sad part comes after the test. I open my notes ~~and scan for the the question and~~ once again the right answer. Then I realize that ~~I went through all that trouble only to find out~~ I wasted my energy, eraser, ~~temptation,~~ and most of all the point or points on the test.

~~same paragraph~~ Next ~~comes~~ is the indescribable feeling of a "lump" ~~sensation~~ pressure on my throat and chest when the ~~papers~~ tests are given back. I usually get B's just because of erasures. This has happened in ~~a lot of my subjects, like~~ my classes, Anatomy, History, and Psychology, ~~and a lot more.~~ I guess something in me is afraid of getting A's.

The same problem of indecision occurred last week. We were assigned outside of school to purchase a basal thermometer for an experiment in my anatomy class. So I went to the pharmacy near my house, and I found two—one just like the ~~one~~ sample the teacher showed

201

us in class and another ~~one a little different but~~ _brand_ with
the same information on the label. Once more my hands
fought with my brain. _Incredibly_ I chose the ~~new one~~ _off brand_. I came home
and tried it. The mercury read my temperature, but ~~it~~ _the silver line_ _the thermometer afterwards_
didn't go down when I shook ~~it~~. Again_,_ I should have
trusted my instincts and ~~got~~ _bought_ the one the teacher showed
us. The following day, I had to take an extra trip on the
bus just to exchange it.

  After this incident, I _have_ resolve_d_ to ~~trust~~ _value_ my first
judgements. I know that if I trust my initial decisions, I
will be trusting myself. I will still go through my test
papers a second time, but I won't change a thing unless I
know an answer is one hundre_d_ percent wrong. With this
plan, I ~~hope things will turn out better.~~ _may become an A student yet._

Can you see why each change was made? Analyzing the reasons for the changes will help you improve your own revision skills.

Assignment 10

AN INVENTION

You've read a lot about famous inventions in this text. If you could invent something that would make some aspect of our lives easier, more fun, or more productive, what would it be? You might choose to write about why you believe your invention is necessary, who would benefit from your invention, or what kind of help you would need to produce it.

  Write a rough draft of the paper and then set it aside. When you finish writing about your invention (Assignment 10), reread your paper to see what improvements you can make to your rough draft. Use the following checklist to help guide you through this or any other revision.

REVISION CHECKLIST

Here's a checklist of revision questions. If the answer to any of these questions is no, revise that part of your paper until you're satisfied that the answer is yes.

continued

1. Does the introductory paragraph introduce the topic clearly and suggest or include a thesis statement that the paper will explain or defend?

2. Does each of the other paragraphs support the thesis statement?

3. Does each body paragraph contain a clear topic sentence and focus on only one supporting point?

4. Do the body paragraphs contain enough details, and are transitional expressions well used?

5. Do the final thoughts expressed in the concluding paragraph bring the paper to a smooth close?

6. Does your (the writer's) voice come through?

7. Do the sentences read smoothly and appear to be correct?

8. Are the spelling and punctuation consistent and correct?

Exchanging Papers

This checklist could also be used when you exchange papers with another student in your class. Since you both have written a response to the same assignment, you will understand what the other writer went through and learn from the differences between the two papers.

Proofreading Aloud

Finally, read your finished paper *aloud*. If you read it silently, you will see what you *think* is there, but you are sure to miss some errors. Read your paper aloud slowly, pointing to each word as you read it to catch omissions and errors in spelling and punctuation. Reading a paper to yourself this way may take fifteen minutes to half an hour, but it will be time well spent. There are even word processing programs that will "speak" your text in a computer's voice. Using your computer to read your paper to you can be fun as well as helpful. If you don't like the way something sounds, don't be afraid to change it! Make it a rule to read each of your papers *aloud* before handing it in.

Here are four additional writing assignments to help you practise the skills of writing and revising.

Assignment 11

WHAT'S IN A NAME?

Write about your name — any part or all of it. Are there any special stories behind your name? Do you know its meaning, if any? Are you named after anyone special?

How do you feel about your name — would you ever consider changing it? Organize your responses to these questions into the structure of a brief essay.

Assignment 12
PICK A NUMBER, ANY NUMBER

We are all identified at times by numbers — birthdates, social insurance numbers, phone numbers, PIN numbers, credit card numbers, just to name a few. What do you think about all of the numbers in your life? Which ones are most important to you, and which would you gladly get rid of, if any? Write a thesis statement that you then support with detailed body paragraphs.

Assignment 13
A BOOK OR MOVIE THAT MADE AN IMPRESSION

Choose a book you have read or a movie or TV show you have seen that made a strong impression on you. Write a brief overview of the book or movie, and then describe your reactions to it. Think back over all the stages of your life to find one that really made an impact. Be sure to explain why it affected you.

Assignment 14
A QUOTATION

Look through the quotations in Exercise 5 on page 182. Does one of them apply to you? Could you profit from following one of them? Write a short paper in which you react to or offer an explanation of one of the quotations and then support your reaction or explanation with examples from your own experiences.

VIII. PRESENTING YOUR WORK

Part of the success of a paper could depend on how it looks. The same paper written sloppily or typed neatly might even receive different grades. It is human nature to respond positively when a paper has been presented with care. Here are some general guidelines to follow.

Paper Formats

Your paper should be written on a computer or typed, double-spaced, or copied neatly in ink on 8 ½-by-11 paper on one side only. A one-inch margin should be left around the text on all sides for your instructor's comments. The beginning of each paragraph should be indented five spaces.

Most instructors have a particular format for presenting your name and the course material on your papers. Always follow such instructions carefully.

Titles

Finally, spend some time thinking of a good title. Just as you're more likely to read a magazine article with an interesting title, so your readers will be more eager to read your paper if you give it a good title. Which of these titles from student papers would make you want to read further?

An Embarrassing Experience	Super Salad?
Falling into The Gap	Buying Clothes Can Be Depressing
Hunting: The Best Sport of All?	Got Elk?

Remember these three things about titles:

1. Only the first letter of the important words in a title should be capitalized.

   A Night at the Races

2. Don't put quotation marks around your own titles unless they include a quotation or title of an article, short story, or poem within them.

   "To Be or Not to Be" Is Not for Me

3. Don't *italicize* or underline your own titles unless they include the title of a book, play, movie, or magazine within them.

   Still Stuck on *Titanic*

A wise person once said, "Haste is the assassin of elegance." Instead of rushing to finish a paper and turn it in, take the time to give your writing the polish it deserves.

IX. WRITING ABOUT WHAT YOU READ

Reading and writing are related skills. The more you read, the better you will write. When you are asked to prepare for a writing assignment by reading a newspaper story, a magazine article, a professional essay, or part of a book, there are many ways to respond in writing. Among them, you may be asked to write your reaction to a reading assignment or a summary of a reading assignment.

Writing a Reaction

Reading assignments become writing assignments when your teacher asks you to share your opinion about the subject matter or to relate the topic to your own experiences. In a paragraph, you would have enough space to offer only the most immediate impressions about the topic. However, in an essay you could share your personal reactions, as well as your opinions on the value of the writer's ideas and support. Of course, the first step is always to read the selection carefully, looking up unfamiliar words in a dictionary.

SAMPLE REACTION PARAGRAPH

Here is a sample paragraph-length response following several readings about controversial court cases in history to the question "Choose any one of the cases we have read about and explain your reaction to it." This student chose the case of Sue Rodriguez, a victim of ALS (more commonly known as Lou Gehrig's disease). ALS causes the slow deterioration of the nervous system while leaving the mind intact. It is a painful condition and has no cure. Rodriguez challenged the Canadian courts on the right-to-choose-to-die issue. Her case led to a close examination of the Criminal Code and the Charter of Rights concerning suicide.

> When I read Sue Rodriguez's case, I was moved, saddened, confused, and sometimes angry. She was a 41-year-old woman, with a teenage son, who loved life and was very physically active prior to the onset of the disease in 1992. She wanted, however, to end her life prematurely so that her son would not have to witness her slow deterioration. Rodriguez chose what she thought was best for her son and ultimately for herself — assisted suicide. The current Criminal Code states that anyone who counsels or assists in suicide faces a fourteen-year prison term. Section 7 of the Charter of Rights gives Canadians the right to life, liberty, and the security of person. Rodriguez argued that the right to life also included the right to a dignified death, and she wanted to achieve this with the help of her physician. In the end, the Supreme Court of Canada maintained that Sue Rodriguez did not have the right to end her own life, so she had to act in secret with the help of friends to achieve her wish. It's strange. I always thought the government created legislation that was supposed to be in the best interest of all Canadians. I guess I was wrong.

> *Sources:* 1) http://www.newsworld.cbc.ca/flashback/1993/sue1.html
> 2) http://www.newsworld.cbc.ca/flashback/1993/sue2.html
> 3) http://www.newsworld.cbc.ca/flashback/1993/sue3.html
> 4) http://www.web.apc.org/dwd/canlaw/html/#SEC1F

If this had been an essay-length assignment, the student would have included more details about the case. Perhaps he would have compared it with another case to broaden the discussion, or he would have explored at depth the reasons why he believed the laws governing assisted suicide are wrong.

Assignment 15

WRITE A REACTION PARAGRAPH

The following are the first two paragraphs of a book entitled *Achieving Gender Equity: Strategies for the Classroom,* by Dianne D. Horgan of the University of

Memphis. Write a paragraph in which you respond thoughtfully to Horgan's topic and to the details she uses to support it.

Typically, girls earn better grades than boys and present far fewer disciplinary problems. Yet they are more likely to suffer from low self-esteem and low self-confidence. They are less likely to select challenging courses, particularly in math and science. When faced with a difficult problem, girls are less likely than boys to persist. Girls are more likely to avoid tasks in which there is a likelihood of failure. When they are adults, young women then enter the workplace with serious internal barriers to success. They don't believe in themselves, and they haven't subjected themselves to the most challenging learning situations.

Many boys, especially minority boys and boys of lower socio-economic status, are also at risk. Teachers often assume that boys will misbehave and dislike school. Often, they are treated more harshly than girls. Boys are more likely to fail, drop out, misbehave, and exhibit poor motivation. Minority boys may feel serious peer pressure to resist Anglo-[society's], middle class school values. The situation for minority boys and for all girls is similar in that — with all good intentions — teachers expect less from them, interact less with them, and send them "low-ability" messages.

Before starting your paragraph, *read the selection again carefully*. Be sure to use a dictionary to look up any words you don't know. You can also use the free writing and clustering techniques explained on pages 204–6. Or your instructor may want you to discuss the reading in groups.

Coming to Your Own Conclusions

Often you will be asked to come to your own conclusions based on a reading that simply reports information. In other words, you have to think about and write about what it all means.

Read the following Royal Canadian Military Police report, reprinted from the book *Maritime UFO Files*. This is a real police report, written by RCMP Constable F.D. Chaisson, that documents a possible UFO sighting in Newfoundland.

On 10 October 1974 at approximately 10:45 P.M. [Atlantic Time], a report of a possible sighting of an Unidentified Flying Object in the Central Newfoundland area was made to the Gander Airport Detail Office ... by John Breen [of] Gander, Newfoundland. Breen, a three-year veteran Air Traffic Controller now employed at the Gander Air Traffic Control Centre, was at the time of the sighting flying a Cessna Aircraft [Canadian Registration C-GLCF]. Breen was flying at an approximate altitude of 5,000 ft. [1524 m], experiencing clear skies with occasional cloudy periods and was returning to Gander from Deer Lake, Newfoundland. When about 40 miles [64 km] northwest of Gander, Breen, along with his only passenger, sighted the possible UFO. Janice Gould [also of] Gander, Breen's passenger and girlfriend, sighted the object just as they passed over the town of Grand Falls, Newfoundland, a small town about 60 miles [100 km] west of Gander.

The object was described by Breen as a solitary, greenish, luminous light. When first noticed by Breen, the object was directly below his aircraft at approximately 3,000 feet [914 m]. Breen's first interpretation of this greenish light was that it was his right navigation light ... reflecting on something below. He turned off all his navigation lights for a moment; nevertheless, the greenish light continued directly below the aircraft. Breen at this time, along with Gould, attempted to determine whether or not the greenish light was part of a bigger unlighted mass; however, this met with negative results as nothing but the greenish light could be noted.

Breen further stated that at this time the Cessna was travelling at a speed of about 134 miles per hour [216 km/h], and that the greenish light could and did at times speed up and remain some distance ahead of the aircraft, still at approximately 3,000 feet [914 m]. This greenish light would then slow down and allow Breen to get directly above it. The light would continue to slow down, and as a result, lag some distance behind, and then go back to its original position below Breen's aircraft. Breen's observation period of this greenish light was about 25 minutes.

When approximately 5 to 6 miles [8 to 10 km] northwest of Gander, Breen contacted the Air Traffic Control Centre and advised them of what was taking place. The Controllers at ATC then attempted to pick up this object on their radar screen. One Robert Lawrence, the supervising Controller on duty at the time, advised that the object was picked up by their 6-mile [10-km] radar; however, the object remained on the screen for only two sweeps of the needle. The target did not show up on the screen as an aircraft. The target did, however, indicate while on screen that its course had changed from northwest to a westerly course, and the reason it could no longer be seen on radar was that it was now believed to be flying at tree-top level. Continued attempts to regain contact with the target met with negative results. Breen, upon arriving over the Gander area, circled his aircraft in an attempt to further identify the object; however, upon circling, all traces of the greenish light were gone.

Continual attempts to further identify the greenish light in question by both the Air Traffic Controllers and Breen met with negative results. ...

Upon the landing of Breen's aircraft at Gander International Airport, both Breen and Gould were immediately contacted. It was noted at this time that neither Breen nor Gould was under any sort of influence, from either alcohol or drugs. Their accounts of the incident are neither exaggerated nor dramatized, and both Breen and Gould appear to be of a mature and responsible nature.

Source: Don Ledger, *Maritime UFO Files* (Halifax: Nimbus Publishing, 1998), 102–3.

Assignment 16
WHAT ARE YOUR CONCLUSIONS?

Does the language used in the report suggest that the constable made any assumptions about the people (or objects) involved in this case? What kind of assumptions can you detect? Could the report be written any more objectively? What kind of conclusions might you arrive at about the witnesses, the reporting officer, and the whole incident?

WRITING 100-WORD SUMMARIES

One of the best ways to learn to read carefully and to write concisely is to write 100-word summaries. Writing 100 words sounds easy, but actually it isn't. Writing 200- or 300- or 500-word summaries isn't too difficult, but condensing all the main ideas of an essay or article into 100 words is a time-consuming task — not to be undertaken in the last hour before class.

A summary presents only the main ideas of a reading, *without including any reactions to it*. A summary tests your ability to read, understand, and *rephrase* the ideas contained in an essay, article, or book.

If you work at writing summaries conscientiously, you'll improve both your reading and your writing. You'll improve your reading by learning to spot main ideas and your writing by learning to construct a concise, clear, smooth paragraph. Furthermore, your skills will carry over into your reading and writing for other courses.

SAMPLE 100-WORD SUMMARY

First, read the following excerpt from an article about the life of Godtfred Christiansen, father of the Lego building block. It is followed by a student's 100-word summary.

Godtfred Christiansen: A Pioneer

Few of the children who play with Lego are likely to know that they are using a building method devised in ancient Greece. They will be unaware that the studs which enable the bricks to click together so satisfyingly are similar to those securing dry walls in Athens. Such happy ignorance is probably just as well. Godtfred Kirk Christiansen (1920–1995) developed Lego into one of the world's most popular toys without upsetting the boys and girls devoted to it by calling it "educational" or "improving." That message, though, is self-evident to the main buyers of Lego, the grown-ups who fondly watch their pride and joy absorbed for hours actually making things; so different from the junk toys which reflect passing fashion, designed merely as fodder for Christmas, here today, discarded tomorrow.

The simple facts of Mr. Christiansen's life are that he was born in Billund, in Jutland [Denmark], and at 12 went to work for his father who ran a small firm making wooden toys. In 1957, when he was 37, he took over the firm from his father and built it up to become the world's fifth largest toy-maker, measured by sales. He was a generous supporter of charities. He was married and he and his wife, Edith, had a son who now runs the business. That said, there is not a lot to add about Mr. Christiansen's personal life. ... He was perfectly amiable. Did you know, he would ask a visitor, that six Lego bricks of the same colour could be combined in more than 120 million ways? ... His father, he said, was keen on quality and gave his wooden toys three coats of varnish. The name Lego is a contraction of leg godt, which translates as "play well." Interesting, but that did not really help to explain how the uneducated Christiansen Junior became, according to some guesswork, one of the 100 wealthiest people in the world. ... Mr. Christiansen raised commonsense questions when a more sophisticated person might not risk displaying his ignorance.

Neither Mr. Christiansen nor his father invented interlocking plastic building bricks. They had to see off several rivals. It sounds obvious, but Lego seems simply to have made a better brick: better finished, better colour, neater fitting. ... It now sells about 11 billion of these little plastic bricks a year in more than 100 countries. Many analysts have tried to explain its success. But ... the secret of Lego's success [may lie] in its strategy of repeat-buying. The purchase of a first kit for, say, a 5-year-old, leads on to many more sales. There are ever more advanced kits to tempt children right up to the teens. Legoland, a theme park in Denmark full of Lego models, feeds the addiction. [There is now a Legoland just outside of London, England, and another opened in Carlsbad, California, in March 1999.]

Did Mr. Christiansen think up this clever marketing method? Probably not. Lego has recruited many talented managers whose education lasted beyond the age of 12. But Mr. Christiansen had an instinct for an opportunity to match the times, and the drive to carry it through. ...

Source: ©1995 The Economist Newspaper Group, Inc. Reprinted with permission. Further reproduction prohibited.

Here is a student's 100-word summary of the article:

> Godtfred Christiansen was a simple man who succeeded partly because of other people's good ideas. He didn't have a lot of education, but he had the kind of mind that it takes to become rich. His father's toy-making business in Denmark allowed Godtfred to sell Legos to children around the world. He loved talking about Legos more than about himself, and he passed on his company to his family. Legos have sold so well because parents have to keep buying more sets as their children grow. Today, the Lego company continues to expand because of smart business practices and Legolands.

Assignment 17

WRITE A 100-WORD SUMMARY

Your aim in writing the summary should be to give someone who has not read the article a clear idea of it. First, read the following excerpt, and then follow the instructions provided after it.

Why Write?

This is going to come as a shock to you, but being able to write well makes you sexy. What's more shocking is the fact that NOT being able to write well decreases your attractiveness to prospective mates. Intrigued? Read on!

Good writing is a skill that is necessary if you want to achieve three vital life objectives: communicate effectively and memorably, obtain and hold satisfying employment, and attract worthy sex partners. Once you come to appreciate these facts and fully understand the immense influence writing well can have on your life, then you will see how easily mastered trivia like faultless grammar, sound sentence structure, and an appealing style can transform you from road-kill on the Road of Life to a turbo-charged powerhouse.

While spoken communication is easy, natural and, for most of us, automatic (far too automatic for some) it doesn't have the lasting power of written language. Even e-mail, the most easily deleted, impermanent form of written language, can be reread, forwarded, and redirected, attaining a kind of permanence impossible for conversation. Who wants to be the author of a message remembered for its unintended but hilarious grammatical flaws or syntactical blunders ("Sisters reunite after 18 years at check-out counter!")?

In all business environments, good writing is a predictor of success. People who communicate well do well; this fact has been emphasized repeatedly in surveys of executives, panels of recruitment officers, and polls of employers. At one time there was an attitude among novices heading for a career on the corporate ladder that good writing was something that secretaries did and executives didn't need. In the current climate of instant and incessant electronic business communication and networked industries, very few people can rely on a subordinate to correct their grammar or polish their style before their colleagues or clients see their work.

Throughout evolutionary history, men and women have always sought mates who had the skills and attributes that suggested they could thrive in the environment of the times. Eons ago, female survival depended on choosing a man with a concrete cranium and huge biceps because he was most likely to repel predators and survive attacks. Prehistoric men selected women for their squat, sturdy bodies and thick fat layer because such females were more likely than their sinewy cousins to survive an ice-age winter and even provide some warmth. Skills such as spear-hurling and fire-tending are not much in demand these days. Now, men and women are biologically on the lookout for mates with updated thriving expertise. Your ability to communicate effectively is one of the skills that place you among the twenty-first century elite, those who will rise to the top of the corporate food chain, claiming the most desirable mates as you ascend! Besides, being able to write melting love notes or clever, affectionate e-mail is a far more effective turn-on these days than being able to supply a slab of raw mastodon or an exquisitely crafted loincloth. Go ahead — flex those writing muscles, flaunt that perfect grammar!

Why write? Excellent communication skills are the single most important attribute you can bring to the table when you're negotiating for power, profession, prestige, or partner.

Source: Adapted from Sarah Norton and Nell Waldman, *Canadian Content,* 4th ed. (Harcourt Brace & Company, Canada), 305–7.

A good way to begin the summary of an article is to figure out the thesis statement, the main idea the author wants to get across to the reader. Write that idea down now *before reading further.* How honest are you with yourself? Did you write that thesis statement? If you didn't, *write it now before you read further.* You probably wrote something like this:

Writing well is a skill that makes people more attractive.

Using that main idea as your first sentence, summarize the article by choosing the most important points. *Be sure to put them in your own words.* Your rough draft may be 150 words or more.

Now cut it down by including only essential points and by getting rid of wordiness. Keep within the 100-word limit. You may have a few words less but not one word more. (And every word counts — even a, and, and the.) By forcing yourself to keep within the 100 words, you'll get to the kernel of the author's thought and understand the article better.

When you have written the best summary you can, then and only then compare it with the summary on page 301. If you look at the model sooner, you'll cheat yourself of the opportunity to learn to write summaries because, once you read the model, it will be almost impossible not to make yours similar. So do your own thinking and writing, and then compare.

Assignment 18
WRITE A REACTION OR A 100-WORD SUMMARY

Respond to Chris Sasaki's article "ET Phone Earth: The Search for Extraterrestrial Intelligence" in any of the three ways we've discussed — in a reaction paragraph, an essay, or a 100-word summary. If you plan to respond with an essay, briefly summarize Sasaki's main ideas about the search for extraterrestrials in your introductory paragraph — how the search is conducted and what is hoped for. Then write about your reactions to his ideas in your body paragraphs. Save your final thought for your concluding paragraph.

ET Phone Earth: The Search for Extraterrestrial Intelligence

Huge "blips" appear on radar screens around the world as identified objects approach Earth from deep space. Strange craft enter the atmosphere and hover silently over cities around the world. The spacecraft lands. Doors open and mysterious creatures emerge. The aliens have arrived.

Is this how humans and intelligent creatures from another planet will first make contact? Maybe in movies like *Independence Day* and *Close Encounters of the Third Kind*. But chances are the first contact between humans and intelligent extraterrestrials will be nothing more than the detection of a faint radio signal coming from space.

Just as humans around the world communicate electronically, we can attempt to communicate with extraterrestrials by sending and listening for radio signals. In fact, that's pretty much all we can do for now. The Milky Way galaxy — the spiral collection of billions of stars we call home — is just too big for us to explore by spaceship. Even if we could build a starship that travelled at the speed of light, it would still take us thousands of years to explore even a small corner of our galaxy.

So for the time being, we're limited to interstellar telecommunication instead of interstellar travel. In 1974, scientists transmitted a radio message toward a star cluster called M13. The message was a picture showing a "map" of the solar system, mathematical and chemical information, and a representation of a human body.

Have any aliens received the message and replied? Not yet. In fact, the targeted star cluster is over 20 000 light years away. That means the radio message travelling at the speed of light won't get there for 20 000 years. And even if extraterrestrials receive the message and reply, we won't hear their answer for another 20 000 years! Stay tuned!

There's actually much more listening than transmitting going on. Around the world, researchers are using large radio antennas called radio telescopes to listen for signals from space. They hope to detect a message coming from an alien civilization with technology like ours. Such programs are called SETI: The Search for Extraterrestrial Intelligence. A number of programs, such as the SETI Institute's Project Phoenix, are scanning the skies right now.

Have SETI scientists found anything? Not yet. Still, they're hopeful that someday ET will phone us. In fact, it seems more and more likely that we're not alone in the galaxy. Recently, astronomers found planets in orbit around other stars and after all, without planets you can't have life. Scientists have also discovered evidence that there may have been life on Mars billions of years ago. If there was life on Mars, maybe there's life on other planets.

Perhaps, one day, an electronic signal will be received from space, a signal more important than any ever sent or received before. Perhaps, one day, we will hear a message from an alien civilization on a planet circling a distant star in the

Milky Way galaxy: "Greetings, inhabitants of Earth. We wish to communicate with you ... "

Source: Chris Sasaki, "ET Phone Earth: The Search for Extraterrestrial Intelligence," *Yes Magazine: Canada's Science Magazine for Kids*, Issue 3, 1996.

Answers

PART 1 SPELLING

WORDS OFTEN CONFUSED, SET 1 (PP. 8–12)

EXERCISE 1

1. Here, a
2. advises
3. It's
4. conscious
5. do, their

6. already, know, it's, accept, desserts
7. Choose, have
8. affect, clothes
9. feel, fill, courses
10. complementing, an, effect

EXERCISE 2

1. our, an, are
2. It's, feel
3. clothes, know
4. due, do
5. conscious, an, effect, our

6. break, conscience
7. course, an, dessert, feel
8. advice, forth, conscious
9. it's
10. know, no, already, chose

EXERCISE 3

1. its, chose, an
2. an
3. Its, it's
4. conscious, a
5. effect, due

6. accept, clothes
7. fill
8. new, complement
9. course, cloths, coarse, it's
10. course, fill, our, clothes, cloths

EXERCISE 4

1. advise
2. a, complement, already
3. chose, advice
4. an, effect
5. have, chose

6. clothes, accept
7. do
8. conscious, hear
9. compliment, already
10. except

EXERCISE 5

1. already
2. know, its
3. It's, an, have
4. a, conscience
5. accept

6. an
7. chose, accept, desert
8. clothes
9. except
10. due, break, it's, our

PROOFREADING EXERCISE

My dog had six puppies last night, and they were all strong and active ~~accept~~ *except* the littlest one born last—it was the runt. ~~It's~~ *Its* head and body were much smaller than those of ~~it's~~ *its* brother and sisters. We named him first and called him Pee-Wee because we were ~~all ready~~ *already* starting to ~~fill~~ *feel* that he was special. At first, the other puppies wouldn't let Pee-Wee eat, and we could ~~here~~ *hear* him cry for milk. It's almost as if the others were trying to get rid of him. We didn't know what to do, so we called the animal hospital to get some ~~advise~~ *advice*. They told us that we could make sure he got enough milk by taking the others out of the box after they seemed full and that eventually Pee-Wee would be ~~excepted~~ *accepted* by the others. The plan worked. By the second day, Pee-Wee was part of the family. We could ~~of~~ *have* lost ~~are~~ *our* favourite puppy if we hadn't received such good advice.

WORDS OFTEN CONFUSED, SET 2 (PP. 17–22)

EXERCISE 1

1. personal, women
2. there, led, than
3. past, than
4. woman, weather
5. Through, right, principal

6. to, they're, quite, too
7. their, through, their
8. piece
9. whether, lose
10. too, two, than

EXERCISE 2

1. your
2. You're, right, they're, quite
3. through, to, right
4. Their, wear, loose, there
5. to, quite, to, peace
6. than, their
7. who's, they're
8. piece
9. two
10. their, there

EXERCISE 3

1. where
2. were, wear, write, their
3. were, women
4. whether, principal
5. personnel
6. led, through, past
7. their, quiet, through
8. threw, lose
9. Then, loose, piece
10. whose, were

EXERCISE 4

1. where, your
2. two, piece
3. to
4. where
5. loose, than
6. two
7. quite, wear, your, piece
8. you're
9. their, peace, quiet
10. personal, you're

EXERCISE 5

1. their
2. who's, led, two
3. There, whose
4. Too
5. whether, right, than
6. women, wear, too, too
7. woman, to
8. principal, women, their
9. through
10. women

PROOFREADING EXERCISE

When I was in high school, the ~~principle~~ *principal* was always complaining about our homework record. The teachers had told him that about half the students didn't do ~~there~~ *their* homework on time, and some never did any at all. So one September he started the first-day assembly by saying, "This year ~~your~~ you're all going to do ~~you're~~ *your* homework every night for at least the first month of school. And if there is a schoolwide perfect homework record during September, I will ~~where~~ *wear* a swim-suit to school on the first of October and dive off the high diving board into the school pool in front of everyone no matter what the ~~whether~~ *weather* is like that day." We students were not about to ~~loose~~ *lose* a bet like that. September ~~past~~ *passed*, and on the first of October, the principal ~~lead~~ *led* us to the school pool; then he ~~through~~ *threw* off his heavy coat and climbed to the top of the diving board.

CONTRACTIONS (PP. 25–29)

EXERCISE 1
1. What's

2. I've, it's, I'd

3. aren't, we're

4. Let's, doesn't, that's

5. who's

6. shouldn't, can't

7. There's, I've, that's

8. no contractions

9. they'd

10. weren't, didn't

EXERCISE 2
1. don't, they've

2. You'll

3. can't, they've

4. They're, that's

5. can't, they're

6. it's, who's

7. there's, it's, that's

8. You'll

9. can't, they're

10. I'm, aren't

EXERCISE 3
1. I've, hasn't

2. they'd

3. it's, wouldn't

4. it's, they're

5. that's, there's

6. wouldn't

7. wasn't, it's

8. don't, wouldn't, that's

9. wouldn't

10. should've, wouldn't, that's

EXERCISE 4
1. I'm, you've

2. weren't

3. she's, he's, they're, who's

4. that's

5. no contractions

6. That's, we've, she's, wouldn't

7. wasn't

8. didn't, she's

9. he's

10. doesn't, she's

EXERCISE 5

1. Wouldn't, shouldn't

2. I'm

3. doesn't

4. Let's, who's, isn't

5. We've, it's

6. Where's, you're, they've

7. won't, I've

8. haven't, it's

9. I'm, we'll

10. They're, what's, let's, what's

PROOFREADING EXERCISE

~~Iv'e~~ *I've* had trouble ~~excepting~~ *accepting* the fact that I ~~cant~~ *can't* learn to speak German. I have taken first- and second-year German, but ~~their~~ *there* ~~was'nt~~ *wasn't* much speaking in either of those ~~too~~ *two* classes. My mouth doesn't make the ~~write~~ *right* sounds when I try to say German words. I think that my teeth get in the way. I have decided to ask my teacher for ~~advise~~ *advice* but ~~cant~~ *can't* bring myself to go see her because I know that ~~shes~~ *she's* going to ask me to tell her about my problem—in German.

POSSESSIVES (PP. 33–35)

EXERCISE 4

1. snowmobile's

2. Canada's, winter's

3. no possessives

4. snowmobile's, Bombardier's

5. invention's

6. Ski-Doo's

7. vehicle's

8. world's

9. public's

10. provinces'

EXERCISE 5

1. man's

2. saxophonist's

3. Kenny G's

4. no possessives

5. no possessives

6. Escalante's, man's

7. Escalante's

8. Guinness's

9. Escalante's

10. holder's

PROOFREADING EXERCISE

The Labelles are a family that has lived next door to me for twenty years. I have grown up with the ~~Labelle's~~ *Labelles'* daughter, Nicole. My family is bigger than ~~her's~~ *hers*. When I go to her house, ~~Nicoles~~ *Nicole's* favourite pastime is doing jigsaw puzzles. We always start off by separating a ~~puzzles~~ *puzzle's* pieces into different categories. She makes piles of edge pieces, sky pieces, flower pieces, and so on. Then I start putting the edge ~~piece's~~ *pieces* together to form the border. The Labelles' son is named Marc, and he usually shows up just in time to put the last piece in the puzzle.

REVIEW OF CONTRACTIONS AND POSSESSIVES (PP. 36–37)

1. I've, *Seinfeld's*

2. show's, wasn't

3. I'm, television's, series'

4. wasn't, wouldn't, show's

5. no contractions or possessives needing apostrophes

6. no contractions or possessives needing apostrophes

7. show's, they'd

8. characters', witnesses'

9. jury's, would've, they're

10. there's, it's

Going to the Globe

I was very fortunate to attend a high school where *there's* an English teacher, Ms. Evans, who absolutely loves Shakespeare. Ever since *she'd* heard that a new Globe Theatre was being built in London, England, *she'd* been saying, "*I'm* going to see it as soon as *it's* finished, and *I'll* take a group of students with me."

Shakespeare's original Globe Theatre had been destroyed by a fire in 1613 during a performance of one of his plays, and it *hadn't* been rebuilt since then. *I'm* one of the lucky students who accompanied Ms. Evans on her first trip to the new Globe.

When we arrived in London, Ms. *Evans'* excitement rubbed off on all of us. We found the *Globe's* location just across the Thames River from another of *London's* most famous landmarks—Big Ben.

The *theatre's* outside was just as beautiful as its inside, and it smelled like freshly cut lumber. In fact, *that's* what *it's* almost entirely made of. *There's* not a nail used in the whole outer frame structure. The huge wooden beams visible from the outside are held in place with more than 6000 wooden pegs, just as they *would've* been in *Shakespeare's* time.

We *didn't* get to see a performance at the Globe, but the tour *guide's* description of one of them made it possible to imagine an *audience's* excitement, an *actor's* challenges, and a *playwright's* satisfaction at the rebuilding of his Globe Theatre.

RULE FOR DOUBLING A FINAL LETTER (PP. 39–40)

EXERCISE 1

1. getting
2. trusting
3. tripping
4. planning
5. benefiting
6. missing
7. reading
8. occurring
9. skimming
10. screaming

EXERCISE 2

1. shopping
2. offering
3. wrapping
4. nailing
5. knitting
6. omitting
7. honouring
8. bragging
9. marking
10. hopping

EXERCISE 3

1. steaming
2. expelling
3. sipping
4. suffering
5. warring
6. wedding
7. stressing
8. flopping
9. spinning
10. differing

EXERCISE 4

1. creeping
2. subtracting
3. abandoning
4. drooping
5. happening
6. weeding
7. fogging
8. dropping
9. referring
10. submitting

EXERCISE 5

1. interpreting	**6.** inferring
2. preferring	**7.** guessing
3. betting	**8.** bugging
4. stooping	**9.** jogging
5. flipping	**10.** building

PROGRESS TEST (P. 41)

1. A. The Powells'

2. B. effect

3. A. choose

4. A. quiet

5. B. submitted

6. A. Who's

7. B. should have

8. A. passed

9. B. break

10. A. its

PART 2 SENTENCE STRUCTURE

FINDING SUBJECTS AND VERBS (PP. 51–53)

EXERCISE 1

1. Weather forecasts affect many people.

2. But they are not always correct.

3. Sometimes rain and wind arrive instead of sunny skies.

4. Travellers need accurate weather predictions.

5. There are many possible dangers in travelling.

6. A hurricane is never a welcome event on a vacation.

7. At times, the weather seems more enemy than friend.

8. Often the skies cooperate with people's travel plans.

9. At times like this, the sun shines as if by special request.

10. Then the weather is perfect and feels like a friend again.

EXERCISE 2

1. There is a long-standing tradition in aviation.

2. Passengers get peanuts and a drink as a mid-flight snack.

3. Any drink tastes better with peanuts.

4. And the tiny foil packages please people.

5. But peanuts are dangerous to passengers with peanut allergies.

6. Most people eat peanuts and feel fine.

7. A mildly allergic person gets watery eyes and hives.

8. In extreme cases, people with peanut allergies die.

9. So many airlines propose peanut-free zones on airplanes.

10. Needless to say, peanut companies are not happy about the proposal.

EXERCISE 3

1. I never knew much about curses and magic spells.

2. According to a magazine article, the Greeks and Romans used them all the time.

3. There were magicians for hire back then.

4. These magicians made money through their knowledge of the art of cursing.

5. Some people took revenge on their enemies with special curses for failure.

6. Others wanted only love and placed spells on the objects of their desires.

7. The magicians wrote the commissioned curses or love spells on lead tablets.

8. Then they positioned these curse tablets near their intended victims.

9. Archeologists found one 1700-year-old curse tablet over the starting gate of an ancient race course.

10. It named the horses and drivers of specific chariots and itemized the specifics of the curse.

EXERCISE 4

1. Plastic snow domes are popular souvenir items.

2. They are clear domes usually on white oval bases.

3. People display these water-filled objects or use them as paperweights.

4. Inside are tiny replicas of famous tourist attractions like the Eiffel Tower or Big Ben.

5. Snow or glitter mixes with the water for a snowstorm effect.

6. These <u>souvenirs</u> often <u>hold</u> startling combinations.

7. In a snow dome, even the <u>Bahamas</u> <u>has</u> blizzards.

8. There <u>is</u> also a <u>dome</u> with smog instead of snow.

9. Some <u>people</u> <u>consider</u> snow domes valuable collectables.

10. <u>Others</u> just <u>buy</u> them as inexpensive mementos.

1. In Canada, there <u>is</u> a widespread <u>concern</u> about endangered species.

2. Habitat <u>loss</u> <u>causes</u> about 80 percent of animal extinction.

3. The <u>International Fund for Animal Welfare</u> <u>designed</u> a survey to test the public response to plans for a new federal bill to <u>protect</u> the environment.

4. The proposed federal <u>bill</u> <u>protects</u> swamps, wetlands, and forests, and <u>safeguards</u> the animals that live there.

5. <u>It</u> <u>regulates</u> both public and private land.

6. In addition, <u>it</u> <u>guarantees</u> the right to government compensation to landowners who encounter <u>financial</u> hardship as a result of habitat protection measures.

7. Provincial <u>governments</u>, however, <u>argue</u> that land management is their jurisdiction.

8. Environmental <u>groups</u> <u>criticize</u> provincial governments for not doing enough to protect endangered species.

9. Sometimes habitat <u>protection</u> <u>requires</u> complete banning of industrial activity in a given area, but some <u>species</u> <u>have</u> less extensive requirements.

10. A <u>skylark</u>, for example, <u>needs</u> an open-field nesting site for only six weeks a year.

My <u>friend</u> <u>Maria</u> <u>spends</u> every weekday afternoon in the school library. <u>She</u> does her homework, <u>finishes</u> her reading assignments, and <u>organizes</u> her notes and handouts. <u>I</u> <u>envy</u> her good study skills. <u>She</u> <u>is</u> always ready for the next day of class. <u>I</u>, however, <u>go</u> back to my apartment in the afternoon. There <u>are</u> so many distractions at home. The <u>television</u> <u>blares</u>, and my <u>roommates</u> <u>invite</u> their friends over. <u>I</u> <u>am</u> usually too tired to do school work. Maybe the <u>library</u> <u>is</u> a better place for me too.

LOCATING PREPOSITIONAL PHRASES (PP. 56–59)

1. <u>Tornadoes</u> <u>are</u> the fiercest (of all weather patterns).

2. They <u>begin</u> (during thunderstorms) and <u>bring</u> (with them) rain, hail, and lightning.

3. The circling <u>winds</u> (of a tornado) often <u>achieve</u> speeds (of 320 km per hour).

4. <u>Most</u> (of the damage) and <u>many</u> (of the injuries) <u>come</u> (from flying debris).

5. <u>Tornadoes</u> normally <u>travel</u> (across the land) (at about 48 km per hour).

6. But <u>they</u> sometimes <u>move</u> as quickly (as a speeding car).

7. The <u>part</u> (like a vacuum cleaner hose) (at the centre) (of the tornado) <u>pulls</u> up anything (in its path)—automobiles, buildings, livestock.

8. (Among their amazing tricks), <u>tornadoes</u> <u>suck</u> the fish and frogs out (of small lakes) and <u>drop</u> them (on land) (in another location).

9. <u>I</u> like watching movies (about tornadoes), (like *The Wizard of Oz* and *Twister*).

10. But professional "storm chasers" <u>like</u> to watch the real ones.

EXERCISE 2

1. The many <u>cases</u> (of food poisoning) (in North America) (in the past few years) <u>alarm</u> people.

2. Some food <u>scientists</u> <u>point</u> (to food irradiation) (as one possible solution).

3. The <u>irradiation</u> (of food) <u>kills</u> bacteria (through exposure) (to gamma rays).

4. (With irradiation), <u>farmers</u> <u>would need</u> to spray fewer pesticides (on their crops).

5. And irradiated <u>food</u> <u>lasts</u> longer (on the shelf) or (in the refrigerator).

6. However, many <u>scientists</u> <u>worry</u> (about the risks) (of food irradiation).

7. <u>Irradiation</u> <u>reduces</u> vitamins and <u>alters</u> nutrients (in the food).

8. The radioactive <u>materials</u> (at the irradiation plants) <u>are</u> also potentially dangerous.

9. <u>Critics</u> <u>predict</u> accidents (in the transportation and use) (of these radioactive substances).

10. (In North America), the <u>controversy</u> (about food irradiation) <u>continues</u>.

EXERCISE 3

1. *Romeo and Juliet* <u>is</u> my favourite play (by William Shakespeare).

2. <u>It</u> <u>is</u> one (of the most famous love stories) (in the world).

3. Many <u>movies</u> <u>use</u> this story (as part) (of their plots).

4. One <u>thing</u> (about the story) <u>surprised</u> me.

5. Both <u>Romeo</u> and <u>Juliet</u> <u>have</u> other love interests (at some point) (in the play).

6. Romeo has his eyes (on another woman) (before Juliet).

7. And (after Tybalt's death,) Juliet promises (against her will) to marry Paris.

8. But (before that), Juliet marries Romeo (in secret).

9. Friar Lawrence helps the newlyweds (with a plan) (for them) to escape (without anyone's notice).

10. However, the complicated timing (of the plan) has tragic results (in the lives) (of Romeo and Juliet).

EXERCISE 4

1. (For a change) (of pace), I shopped (for my Mother's Day gift) (at an antique mall).

2. I found old jewellery (in every shade) (of yellow, red, blue, and green).

3. There were even linens (from all the way) back (to pre-Confederation).

4. One booth sold only drinking glasses (with advertising slogans and cartoon characters) (on them).

5. Another stocked old metal banks (with elaborate mechanisms) (for children's pennies).

6. (In the back corner) (of the mall), I found a light blue pitcher (with a dark blue design).

7. My mother had had one (like it) (in the early years) (of my childhood).

8. My sisters and I drank punch (from it) (on hot days) (in the summer).

9. I checked the price (on the tag) (underneath the pitcher's handle).

10. But (at a moment) (like that), money didn't matter.

EXERCISE 5

1. (Over the weekend), I watched a hilarious old movie, *Genevieve,* (on late-night television).

2. The whole story takes place (in the countryside) (of England).

3. It is a black-and-white movie (from the 1930s or 1940s).

4. The clothes and manners (of the characters) (in *Genevieve*) are very proper and old-fashioned.

5. Two young couples enter their cars (in a road rally) (for fun).

6. They participate (in the race) strictly (for adventure).

7. Genevieve is the name (of the main couple's car).

8. (During the road rally), the two couples' polite manners disappear (in the rush) (for the finish line).

9. Predictably, they begin to fight (with each other) and try to sabotage each other's cars.

10. But (like all good comedies), *Genevieve* and its ending hold a surprise (for everyone).

PARAGRAPH EXERCISE

Folklore (from all over the world) reveals that people (in many cultures) (throughout history) have believed (in some type) (of vampire). Many (of the ancient vampires), however, do not resemble the ones we are familiar with (from movies and books). ... [A]ncient vampires do not possess prominent canine teeth or fear garlic, the cross, and the dawn. These are modern touches, added (by the writers) (of horror novels and films) to intrigue and scare us.

UNDERSTANDING DEPENDENT CLAUSES (PP. 62–66)

EXERCISE 1

1. I am not a big talker in school.

2. Whenever a teacher asks me a question in class, I get nervous.

3. When I know the answer, I usually find the courage to speak.

4. If I don't know the answer, I look up at the ceiling as if I am thinking about it.

5. Usually, the teacher calls on someone else before I finish "thinking."

6. Obviously, when I take a public speaking class, I must talk sometimes.

7. In my last public speaking class, the assignment was to give a speech that demonstrated some sort of process.

8. The speech that I gave explained how crêpes are made.

9. Since I work at a French restaurant, I borrowed a crêpe pan to use in my demonstration.

10. The crêpes cooked quickly, and the teacher and students were so busy eating them that I didn't have to say much at all.

EXERCISE 2

1. Many of us remember when microwave ovens were first sold to the public.

2. People worried about whether they were safe or not.

3. Before we had the microwave oven, we cooked all of our food over direct heat.

4. At first, it was strange that only the food heated up in a microwave.

5. And microwave ovens cooked food so much faster than ordinary ovens did.

6. We had to get used to the possibilities that the microwave offered.

7. Since they are fast and don't heat up themselves, microwave ovens work well in offices, in restaurants, and on school campuses.

8. People who are on a budget can bring a lunch from home and heat it up at work.

9. Now that the microwave oven is here, we can even make popcorn without a pan.

10. As each new technology arrives, we wonder how we ever lived without it.

EXERCISE 3

1. When Canadians gather at sporting events, everyone sings "O Canada," while the Canadian flag proudly flies overhead.

2. "O Canada" is the song that Canada has chosen as its national anthem.

3. After Calixa Lavallée composed the music, the song was first performed at a banquet for skaters in Quebec City on June 24, 1880.

4. Adolphe-Basile Routhier wrote the French version, which he called "Chant national."

5. It was translated into English by Stanley Weir, who was a schoolteacher in Toronto.

6. Though French Canadians sang the anthem widely, English Canadians did not use it until the end of the nineteenth century.

7. When it gathered in 1967, the Parliament approved "O Canada" as the Canadian national anthem.

8. The words, which were altered somewhat after parliamentary debate, became official through the National Anthem Act, which was passed on June 27, 1980.

9. Canada's flag was hotly debated from Confederation to 1964, when the flag with the single red maple leaf became official.

10. Before that time, the United Kingdom's Union Jack was used for Canadian ceremonies, whether Canadian nationalists liked it or not.

EXERCISE 4

1. Since we all want our documents to look perfect, we have probably used a bottle of white correction fluid at some time in our lives.

2. Liquid Paper or, as it was first known, "Mistake Out" was invented by Bette Nesmith (later Graham).

3. After the young bank secretary noticed that sign painters always painted over their errors instead of erasing them, she had an idea.

4. Nesmith started filling up small bottles with white paint, which she used to cover her typing mistakes.

5. As soon as her friends saw how well Nesmith's paint worked, they all wanted their own bottles.

6. Once she realized that the idea was a success, she developed a liquid that was more than just paint.

7. She patented her formula and called it Liquid Paper.

8. She decided to sell the product to a big corporation.

9. After IBM turned down Nesmith's invention, she formed "The Liquid Paper Company" herself and earned a large fortune.

10. Michael Nesmith, who is Bette Nesmith's son, helped his mother in her business even after he became a member of the famous singing group called The Monkees.

EXERCISE 5

1. When I first heard the expression "white elephant," I didn't know what it meant.

2. Yesterday I finally learned what "white elephant" means.

3. A white elephant is an unwanted object that may be difficult to get rid of.

4. Most white elephants are gifts that friends or relatives give us.

5. As I read the story behind the expression, I understood it better.

6. The ruler of an ancient land received any white elephants born in his country; it was a custom that sometimes came in handy.

7. The ruler then gave the white elephants as presents to people who had angered him.

8. The elephants would eat so much and become so difficult to keep that they ruined the lives of the people who received them as "gifts."

9. That is why we now use the term to describe objects that cause us to feel responsible and burdened.

10. Whenever I give a present, I choose it carefully so that it will not become a white elephant.

PARAGRAPH EXERCISE

We can think about an eclipse of the Sun in another way. Since sunlight cannot pass through the Moon, the Moon casts a shadow. The shadow is cone-shaped. It usually does not touch the Earth. But sometimes it moves across the Earth. When that happens, there is an eclipse. Inside of the small place where the shadow touches, people can see a total eclipse. There is darkness. In places that are near the shadow, people can see only a partial eclipse. Farther away from the shadow, people can see no eclipse at all.

The Moon's shadow makes a circle when it touches the Earth. The circle moves as the Moon does. So an eclipse of the Sun can be seen in one place for only a few minutes.

CORRECTING FRAGMENTS (PP. 69–73)

EXERCISE 1
Answers may vary, but here are some possible revisions.

1. My car's compact disc player is difficult to use while driving.

2. The discs ~~reflecting~~ *reflect* the sunlight and ~~shining~~ *shine* in my eyes.

3. The old CD ejects from the slot with a hissing sound.

4. *There is* nowhere to put it while getting the new one.

5. Then *I try to insert* ~~inserting~~ the new CD without touching its underside.

6. Fumbling with those flat plastic cases can be really frustrating.

7. *There is* one case for the old one and one case for the new one.

8. Meanwhile I am driving along.

9. *I'm* not paying any attention to the road.

10. I hope I don't hit anything.

EXERCISE 2
Answers may vary, but here are some possible revisions.

1. The largest of the dinosaurs were vegetarians.

2. Tyrannosaurus rex *was* a meat-eater or carnivore.

3. *It was* supposed to be the biggest of the carnivorous dinosaurs.

4. In 1995 scientists discovered the remains of a carnivore bigger than T. Rex.

5. ~~In Africa living~~ *It lived in Africa* around 90 million years ago.

6. *It was* named for having sharklike teeth and living in the Sahara Desert.

7. It's called Carcharodontosaurus saharicus.

8. *It was* over fifteen metres long and ~~weighing~~ *weighed* eight tonnes.

9. Just its skull measured over one and a half metres in length.

10. T. Rex ~~being~~ *will always be* an easier name to remember.

EXERCISE 3
Answers may vary, but here are some possible revisions.

1. We shopped all day at the mall. We were looking for the perfect suitcases to take on our cruise this summer.

2. We were sure that one of the specialty stores would carry a good selection, with hard and soft luggage, large and small sizes, and lots of accessories to choose from.

3. We gave up and ate lunch after walking from store to store and getting tired.

4. We could not believe how crowded the mall was on a weekday. There were long lines in every shop and at the food court, too.

5. Everywhere we looked people stood around, crowding the walkways and window shopping.

6. Many teenagers gathered in groups. They laughed at each other but ignored the shoppers.

7. Pairs of older people walked briskly around the balconies, using the mall as an exercise track.

8. Actually, we did enjoy ourselves as we ate. We watched all the curious people around us.

9. We finally found the luggage we were looking for in a tiny shop near the elevators at the end of the mall.

10. Without the crowds and the poor selection, our shopping trip would have been a complete success.

EXERCISE 4

Answers may vary, but here are some possible revisions.

1. Thrift stores, yard sales, and flea markets have become very popular places to shop because they sell items that are not available anywhere else as cheaply.

2. Most thrift stores benefit charities, which use the profits to help people in need.

3. Although the styles of clothing and furniture found in thrift stores are often outdated, many people prefer the old styles over the new.

4. Modern shelving units are made of particle board or plastic, but thrift store shoppers can find more substantial ones, which are made of solid wood or thick metal.

5. There are also famous stories of people becoming rich because they visited yard sales and flea markets.

6. One man bought a framed picture for a few dollars at a flea market. He liked the frame itself but not the picture.

7. When he returned home, he removed the picture from the frame and found the signature of a famous artist.

8. At a yard sale, a woman bought a small table. She later discovered that it was worth half a million dollars.

9. Of course, collectors always shop at these places. They hope to find treasures like rare cookie jars, pens, paintings, records, toys, and other objects of value.

10. In a way, shopping at thrift stores, yard sales, and flea markets is a kind of recycling that benefits everyone.

EXERCISE 5

Answers may vary, but here are some possible revisions. (Added independent clauses are in italics.)

1. Because the car cost too much, *we bought a motorcycle instead.*

2. Then I asked him for directions to the museum.

3. Since the government protects endangered species, *eagles are not game birds.*

4. *My parents worry about* where I'll be in ten years.

5. *Photographers took pictures* while the spectators left the stadium and the players left the field.

6. She was a tough comic with a painful past.

7. Mozart did not live a very long life.

8. A Canadian family saw her story on the news.

9. If cars could fly, *rush-hour traffic would be no problem*.

10. Although we had no insurance at the time, *the officer did not give us a ticket*.

PROOFREADING EXERCISE
Answers may vary, but here are some possible revisions.

The information superhighway, or the Internet as it's called, was quick to arrive in our homes and businesses. ~~Bringing with it~~ *With it, we have* access to merchandise, movies, services, and much more. ~~Although~~ *However*, it is not clear yet exactly where this "highway" is going. Holding up the process are legal questions and software and hardware limitations. ~~And~~ *It is also unclear* whether everyone will have equal access to the benefits the Internet provides~~. Because~~ *because* fees for these services can be high. Also, people worry about credit card security. If and when these problems are solved~~. We~~ *, we* will be ready for the future.

CORRECTING RUN-ON SENTENCES (PP. 76–80)

EXERCISE 1
Your answers may differ depending on how you choose to separate the two clauses.

1. I planned a surprise party for my sister Nina's birthday; it was a disaster.

2. All of her friends arrived at our house on time; however, no one could find Nina.

3. The sentence is correct.

4. The sentence is correct.

5. An hour passed, but there was no sign of the birthday girl.

6. After two hours, we began to worry about Nina; she was usually home by dinnertime.

7. By nine o'clock the cake had almost disappeared, and most of Nina's friends had gone home.

8. Nina finally drove up at 10:30, so the remaining guests hid behind the furniture.

9. "Happy Birthday!" we all yelled. She looked more confused than surprised.

10. She had treated herself to a movie for her birthday; I treated myself to the last piece of her cake.

EXERCISE 2

Your answers may differ depending on how you choose to separate the two clauses.

1. I am writing a research paper on Margaret Laurence; she was one of Canada's most celebrated novelists and a pioneer in the world of Canadian literature.

2. She was born in Neepawa, Manitoba. In her novels *The Stone Angel, A Jest of God, The Fire-Dwellers,* and *The Diviners*, the town was called "Manawaka."

3. Laurence was encouraged to write by Jack McClelland. He also published the works of other Canadian writers such as Mordecai Richler and Farley Mowat.

4. Margaret and her husband, Jack, briefly lived in England; then they moved to Africa.

5. She became very interested in European/African relations. As a result, her early books, *This Side Jordan* and *The Tomorrow-Tamer,* deal with this issue.

6. Her husband wanted her to be a traditional wife and mother, but Margaret wanted to be a full-time writer.

7. The sentence is correct.

8. The sentence is correct.

9. Twice her books were condemned or banned in schools, yet today they are taught as Canadian classics.

10. In 1986, she was diagnosed with inoperable and fatal lung cancer. Several months later she took her own life.

EXERCISE 3

Your answers may differ since various words can be used to begin dependent clauses.

1. The sentence is correct.

2. The calls are made by companies whose salespeople try to interest us in the newest calling plan or credit card offer.

3. They don't call during the day when nobody is home.

4. I feel sorry for some of the salespeople since they're just doing their job.

5. When my father tells them to call during business hours, they hang up right away.

6. The sentence is correct.

7. When my mother answers, she is too polite, so they just keep talking.

8. Although we try to ignore the ringing, it drives us all crazy.

9. The sentence is correct.

10. Since we never buy anything over the phone, maybe these companies will all get the message and leave us alone.

EXERCISE 4
Your answers may differ since various words can be used to begin dependent clauses.

1. When Glenn Gould died, Canada lost a great musician.

2. Not only was Gould a sublime pianist, but he was also a composer of international fame.

3. The sentence is correct.

4. Because he was a child prodigy, he was put on the stage at a very young age.

5. When he was 14 years old, he became a soloist with the Toronto Symphony.

6. Though he began touring across Canada at age 19, in later years Gould stopped performing in public.

7. The sentence is correct.

8. Since he was an eccentric and a loner, few people knew much about his personal life.

9. The sentence is correct.

10. Gould's music continues to live on though he is no longer alive.

EXERCISE 5
Your answers may differ depending on how you choose to separate the two clauses.

1. There is a new way to find a date in Japan; singles use vending machines to sell information about themselves to others.

2. Men provide personal details in packets to be sold in the machines, but first the men swear they are not married.

3. If a woman chooses to purchase a packet for a couple of dollars, in it she will find a picture of the man, his age, and his employment status.

4. The packets also include the men's phone numbers so that the women can contact only the men they like.

5. The system seems to be working, and many of the couples are dating more than once.

6. A lot of Japanese businesspeople use the machines since they do not have time to meet people in other ways.

7. Employees have little opportunity to socialize in Japan, where it is normal to stay at work until late into the evening.

8. Although a man might pay almost $50 to put many of his packets into the machines, that doesn't mean that women will call him.

9. Japan is famous for its vending machines, which are even used to sell meat and clothes.

10. Whereas other countries might find it unusual to sell personal information in vending machines, they seem to be working well as matchmakers in Japan.

REVIEW OF FRAGMENTS AND RUN-ON SENTENCES (P. 81)

PROOFREADING EXERCISE
Your revisions may differ depending on how you chose to correct the errors.

Unlike the one-way communication of the mass media, personal interaction isn't something we do *to* others; rather, it is an activity we do *with* them. In this sense, person-to-person communication is rather like dancing — at least the kind of dancing we do with partners. Like dancing, communication depends on the involvement of a partner. And like good dancing, successful communication doesn't depend only on the person who takes the lead. A great dancer who forgets to consider and adapt to the skill level of his or her partner can make both people look bad. In communication and dancing, even two talented partners don't guarantee success. When two skilled dancers perform without coordinating their movements, the results feel bad to the dancers and look foolish to the audience. Finally, relational communication — like dancing — is a unique creation that arises out of the way in which the partners interact. The way you dance probably varies from one partner to another. Likewise, the way you communicate almost certainly varies with different partners.

IDENTIFYING VERB PHRASES (PP. 83–88)

EXERCISE 1

1. John Harrison has been tasting ice cream (for nearly twenty years).

2. He has recently hired an insurance company to protect his very valuable taste buds.

3. The new policy will pay $1 million (in the event) (of damage) (to his tongue).

4. Harrison knows that the ice cream's taste would be altered (by a metal or a wooden spoon).

5. So he always samples the different flavours (from a spoon) plated (with gold).

6. This professional taster does not smoke, drink caffeinated beverages, or eat hot chilis.

7. He never even gets to swallow the ice cream itself.

8. He just swishes it briefly (around his mouth).

9. Harrison may have inherited his special tasting talents.

10. Many (of his family members) have also worked (in the ice cream business).

EXERCISE 2

1. I have just discovered "The Farnsworth Chronicles," an Internet site devoted (to the life) (of Philo T. Farnsworth).

2. Thirteen-year-old Philo T. Farnsworth was ploughing a field (in 1922) when he visualized the concept that led (to television) as we know it.

3. Others were working (on the idea) (of sending images) (through the air), but Farnsworth actually solved the problem (in that open field).

4. He looked (at the rows) that the plough had made (in the earth).

5. And he reasoned that images could be broken down (into rows), and each row could be sent (through the air) and (onto a screen).

6. Farnsworth's idea made television a reality, but historically he has not been fully recognized (for this and his other accomplishments).

7. (In 1957), he was featured (as a guest) (on *I've Got a Secret,*) a television show that presented mystery contestants.

8. The panelists (on the show) were supposed to guess the guest's secret, which the audience was shown so that everyone knew the answer (except the people) asking the questions.

9. They asked if he had invented something painful, and he replied that he had; the panelists never guessed that he was the inventor (of television).

10. Farnsworth did receive a box (of cigarettes) and $80 (for being) (on the show).

EXERCISE 3

1. The theatre is known (for its excesses)— [you] take, (for example), a 1998 stage production (of *Beauty and the Beast)* (in London, England).

2. The set alone contained 64 automated props, including the Beast's castle, which weighed nearly thirteen tonnes.

3. Many (of the main characters' wigs) were fashioned (from human hair).

4. Nine kilograms (of hair)—some real and some artificial—were used to make the Beast's original costume, which took (over 400 hours) to complete.

5. Each (of the eight different wigs) [that] Belle's character wore (for every performance) required human hair that had grown (to a length) (of 75 cm or more).

6. An entirely new pyrotechnic device was invented (for this show); experts (in stage explosives) worked (for a year and a half) to perfect it.

7. They designed a hand-held fireball that could be thrown (by the enchantress character) when she turned the prince (into a beast).

8. The candelabra character wore a costume that included huge lighted candles (at the end) (of each hand).

9. Some people enjoy watching a play; others would rather watch a football game.

10. Coincidentally, the energy that one performance (of *Beauty and the Beast)* used was equivalent (to the amount) needed to light an entire sports stadium.

EXERCISE 4

1. Aspirin has recently turned 100 years old; Felix Hoffmann, a chemist, was trying to ease his own father's pain when he discovered aspirin (in 1897).

2. Although aspirin can cause side effects, each year people (around the world) give themselves 50 billion doses (of the popular painkiller).

3. But people (in different countries) take this medicine (in different ways).

4. The British like to dissolve aspirin powder (in water).

5. The French have insisted that slow release methods work best.

6. Italians prefer aspirin drinks (with a little fizz).

7. And North Americans have always chosen to take their aspirin (in pill form).

8. However it is taken, aspirin continues to surprise researchers (with benefits) (to human health).

9. It has been found to benefit people susceptible (to heart attack, colon cancer, and Alzheimer's disease).

10. Where would we be (without aspirin)?

EXERCISE 5

1. I like to walk (around the park) (with my two little poodles) (in the early evening).

2. The three (of us) have enjoyed this ritual (for several years) now.

3. (On Friday evening), we were just passing the duck pond, and a big dog (with no owner) ran over (to us).

4. It was obviously looking (for other dogs) to play with.

5. Yip and Yap have never barked so loudly before.

6. I had originally named them (for their distinct barking noises).

7. But lately I had not heard these short, ear-splitting sounds very often.

8. The big dog was shocked (by the fierceness) (of my little dogs' reply) and quickly ran to find other friends.

9. Even I could not believe it.

10. I will never worry (about their safety) (around big dogs) again.

REVIEW EXERCISE

(In October 1999), Adrienne Clarkson was appointed Canada's newest governor general. Most people do not know that the governor general outranks even the prime minister. The person who holds this office is, (in fact), the Queen's representative (to Canada). The governor general's responsibility entails signing bills passed (by Parliament), which is the final step a bill takes (before becoming a law). Today, however, this office is really a ceremonial post and symbolizes Canada's traditional ties (with the British Crown). Nevertheless, the position (of governor general) still comes (with a lot) (of responsibility). The person who fills this office must attend many functions and, (among other things), deliver countless speeches. This is definitely not a job (for somebody) who is afraid (of public attention).

When the prime minister introduced the new governor general, many were pleased (with his decision). Ms. Clarkson is the first Canadian (of Chinese descent) to hold such a position. Although she may now call the luxurious surroundings (of Rideau Hall)—the governor general's official residence—her home, her story is similar (to that of many other families) who have immigrated (to Canada).

Her mother and father, William and Ethel Poy, escaped (from Hong Kong) (during World War II) (with their two young children). When they arrived (in Ottawa), they had all (of their worldly possessions) (in just a few suitcases). Her high school teachers and fellow-students remember Adrienne as being especially bright and hard-working. While her brother, Neville, went on to become a successful surgeon, Adrienne devoted herself (to studying English literature and art). She was fascinated (by culture) and learned to speak French and Italian fluently.

Soon, others began to recognize her talents. She was asked to review books (on CBC radio), and eventually she began a career as a TV journalist (on *the fifth estate*), a news program. Here, she showed herself to be a strong-willed person who stood up (for her beliefs). The long hours and busy schedule (of a television career), however, were very demanding.

(In 1982), Clarkson left the world (of TV journalism) and began working as a Canadian diplomat (in France). Even when she performed her official duties there, she continued to show her fondness (for the arts). Clarkson was a hit (in Paris), where she managed to turn what was once a dreary diplomatic residence (into an exciting cultural centre). After completing her duties (in Paris), Clarkson moved back (to Canada) and began working (on a new TV program). (For her new show), she produced and directed hour-long documentaries that examined such subjects as film, music, and modern dance.

Her appointment (to the post) (of governor general) is the pinnacle (of a life) filled (with hard work). (In her nationally televised speech), she made clear her devotion (to the arts) and her commitment (to Canada). Clarkson compared Canada (to a work) (in progress). According (to her), Canada is a three-legged stool built (of French, English, and Aboriginal cultures) that has expanded to include all colours and religions. She said that Canada is made up (of many immigrant parents) like her own, "dreaming their children (into being Canadians)."

USING STANDARD ENGLISH VERBS (PP. 90–93)

EXERCISE 1

1. walk, walked
2. is, was
3. have, had
4. do, did
5. needs, needed

6. am, was
7. has, had
8. are, were
9. does, did
10. works, worked

EXERCISE 2

1. is, was
2. do, did
3. have, had
4. asks, asked
5. have, had

6. learn, learned
7. are, were
8. does, did
9. plays, played
10. am, was

EXERCISE 3

1. started, like
2. creates
3. are, have
4. finished, needed
5. owns, does

6. watches, follow
7. enjoys, was
8. completed, expected
9. have
10. have

EXERCISE 4

1. do, don't
2. am, is
3. need, explains
4. help, does
5. works, hope

6. did, dropped
7. was, do
8. work, check
9. learn, learns
10. expect, don't

EXERCISE 5

1. Last year our high school drama class *travelled* to London, England.

2. The sentence is correct.

3. We *were* all very excited about the trip.

4. Before the trip, we *learned* to read the London subway map.

5. We *discovered* that the people in London call the subway "the tube."

6. Once we *were* there, we understood why.

7. The underground walls *are* round just like a tube.

8. The sentence is correct.

9. We even *walked* right past the Crown Jewels.

10. The sentence is correct.

PROOFREADING EXERCISE

Everyday as we drive though our neighbourhoods on the way to school or to work, we see things that *need* to be fixed. Many of them cause us only a little bit of trouble, so we forget them until we face them again. Every morning, I *have* to deal with a truck that someone *parks* right at the corner of my street. It *blocks* my view as I try to turn onto the main avenue. I need to move out past the truck into the oncoming lane of traffic just to make my left turn. One day last week, I *turned* too soon, and a car almost hit me. This truck *doesn't* need to be parked in such a dangerous place.

USING REGULAR AND IRREGULAR VERBS (PP. 98–101)

EXERCISE 1

1. looked

2. look

3. looking

4. look

5. looked

6. look

7. looked

8. looking

9. looks

10. look

EXERCISE 2

1. drive, driven

2. thinking, thought

3. take, takes

4. told, telling

5. wrote, written

6. knew, know

7. teach, taught

8. torn, tearing

9. ridden, rode

10. made, make

EXERCISE 3

1. were, heard

2. seen, begun

3. flown, eaten

4. got, did

5. take, eating

6. written, coming, lost

7. swore, felt

8. bought, paid

9. getting, thought

10. saw, told, lay

EXERCISE 4

1. used, supposed

2. catch, came, heard

3. were, left

4. read, draw, build

5. felt, drew

6. did, slept

7. knew, spent

8. went, were

9. woke, stayed

10. forget, spent, were

EXERCISE 5

1. laid, lying, felt

2. know (or knew), been

3. broke, had

4. became, thought

5. was

6. read, frightened

7. kept, shook

8. worked, rose, sneaked (or snuck)

9. left, find

10. lose, stung

PROGRESS TEST (P. 102)

1. B. fragment (*He has ridden it* many times ...)

2. B. incorrect verb form (*were* taking)

3. B. incorrect verb form (were *lying*)

4. A. fragment (*The* sun is out and the birds are singing.)

5. B. incorrect verb form (was *supposed*)

6. A. unnecessary comma (I have saved my money and am finally taking ...)

7. B. missing comma to prevent misreading (And when she left, the restaurant ...)

8. A. incorrect verb form (We had already *gone* to the movies ...)

9. B. run-on sentence (I work hard at my job, but I enjoy it.)

10. B. fragment (*I will graduate* just as soon as I pass my last four classes.)

MAINTAINING SUBJECT/VERB AGREEMENT (PP. 105–9)

EXERCISE 1

1. is

2. fly

3. knows, stand

4. are

5. is

6. seem, go

7. are

8. take

9. have

10. have

EXERCISE 2

1. is

2. was

3. cling

4. make

5. soften

6. are

7. is

8. radiate

9. overlooks

10. enjoy

EXERCISE 3

1. has

2. have, have

3. love

4. makes

5. says

6. thinks

7. is, haven't

8. has

9. is

10. knows

EXERCISE 4

1. have

2. is

3. is

4. is, is

5. are

6. has

7. represent

8. are

9. comes

10. shine

EXERCISE 5

1. has

2. is

3. is

4. visits

5. travel

6. get

7. have

8. have

9. get

10. are

PROOFREADING EXERCISE

My courses for this academic year are really challenging. Each of the classes *is* difficult in a different way. Some of them *require* us to learn on our own in labs. And the others demand that students carefully *follow* the minute instructions of the professor. The assignments given by my geography instructor, for example, *are* harder than I expected. Everybody in the class *has* to prepare a scale model of a mountain range. All of the models so far have looked the same. But one of the models *was* a little out of scale, and the instructor failed it. The other students and I *have* decided to work together so none of us *make* the same mistake. I guess that all of this hard work *is* worthwhile. My instructors *say* it helps prepare us for our future careers.

AVOIDING SHIFTS IN TIME (PP. 111–12)

PROOFREADING EXERCISES

1. I loved travelling by train. The rocking motion *made* me so calm, and the clackety-clack of the railroad ties as we *rode* over them *sounded* like a heartbeat to me. I also *enjoyed* walking down the aisles of all the cars and looking at the different passengers. Whole families sat together, with children facing their parents. I noticed the kids liked to ride backward more than the adults. The food that we ate in the dining car was expensive, but it *was* always fancy and delicious. My favourite part of the train *was* the observation car. It *was* made of glass from the seats up so that we could see everything that we passed along the way.

2. People, especially those who have money, are sometimes wasteful. People *exhibit* wastefulness in different ways. Restaurants *waste* a lot of food every day. Homeowners *water* their lawns for too long and let the excess run down the street. People cleaning out their garages *throw* away their clothes and furniture instead of giving them to charities. I do admit that I am wasteful too, for I am a typical member of my society. I use three sheets of paper for a one-page assignment because I *make* tiny mistakes, and I order too much food at restaurants. We all *need* to start conserving our resources now while there is still time.

3. The paragraph is correct.

RECOGNIZING VERBAL PHRASES (PP. 114–17)

EXERCISE 1

1. [Choosing a program] is one of the most important decisions for students.

2. Many students take a long time [to decide about their programs].

3. But they fear [wasting time in the wrong courses] more than indecision.

4. They spend several semesters as undecided students [taking general education classes].

5. [Distracted by class work], students can forget [to pay attention to their interests].

6. Finally, a particular subject area will attract them [to study it further].

7. One student <u>might find</u> happiness in [doing a psychology experiment].

8. [Writing a poem in an English class] <u>may be</u> the assignment [to make another decide].

9. [Attracted by telescopes], a student <u>might choose</u> [to study astronomy].

10. [Finding the right program] <u>takes</u> time and patience.

EXERCISE 2

1. I <u>have learned</u> how [to manage my time] when I <u>am</u> not <u>working</u>.

2. I <u>like</u> [to go to the movies on Friday nights].

3. [Watching a good film] <u>takes</u> me away from the stress of my job.

4. I especially <u>enjoy</u> [eating buttery popcorn] and [drinking a cold pop].

5. It <u>is</u> the perfect way for me [to begin the weekend].

6. I <u>get</u> [to escape from deadlines and the pressure {to succeed}].

7. I <u>indulge</u> myself and <u>try</u> [to give myself a break]—nobody <u>is</u> perfect, and everybody <u>has</u> setbacks.

8. All day Saturday I <u>enjoy</u> [lounging around the house in my weekend clothes].

9. I <u>do</u> a little [gardening] and <u>try</u> [to relax my mind].

10. By Sunday evening, after [resting for two days], I <u>am</u> ready [to start my busy week all over again].

EXERCISE 3

1. Many people <u>dislike</u> [speaking in front of strangers].

2. That <u>is</u> why there <u>is</u> an almost universal fear of [giving speeches].

3. [Feeling insecure and {exposed}], people <u>get</u> dry mouths and sweaty hands.

4. Note cards <u>become</u> useless, [rearranging themselves in the worst possible order].

5. [To combat this problem], people <u>try</u> [to memorize a speech], only [to forget the whole thing] as the audience <u>stares</u> back at them expectantly.

6. And when they <u>do remember</u> parts of it, the microphone <u>decides</u> [to quit at the punch line of their best joke].

7. [Embarrassed] and [humiliated], they <u>struggle</u> [to regain their composure].

8. Then the audience usually <u>begins</u> [to sympathize with and encourage the speaker].

9. Finally [used to the spotlight], the speaker relaxes and finds the courage [to finish].

10. No one expects [giving a speech] [to get any easier].

EXERCISE 4

1. Canadian astronaut Roberta Bondar blasted off into space [to gather data] on how living things function in space.

2. Bondar was aboard the space shuttle *Discovery* in January 1992, [setting a record as Canada's first woman in space].

3. After [graduating from high school], Bondar assertively pursued her career, [obtaining five university degrees in science and medicine].

4. She applied to the new Canadian Space Agency [to become a candidate for astronaut].

5. The wait [to go into space] lasted nine years, but Bondar remained fit and ready.

6. When the astronauts finally left the launch pad on the *Discovery,* Bondar thrust her fists in the air, [shouting "Yes, yes, yes."]

7. Bondar and her six colleagues spent eight days in space, [investigating the effects of weightlessness on the human body].

8. Today Bondar does research at the University of Western Ontario, [travelling around the country] [to encourage young people in the sciences].

9. Bondar was appointed Chair of the Science Advisory Board, a board set up [to advise the federal health minister].

10. She believes that [protecting the environment] is one of the most important responsibilities we have today.

EXERCISE 5

1. We have all seen stage shows where magicians try [to hypnotize people], [beginning with the suggestion], "You are getting very sleepy. ... "

2. Then they order their [hypnotized] subjects [to cluck like chickens] or [to cry like babies].

3. Hypnotists can even convince subjects [to feel very cold] even if the room is actually warm.

4. More important, subjects have been able [to hallucinate on command] and [to control pain] through hypnosis.

5. Now researchers are studying the brains of supposedly [hypnotized] people [to see if there is such a thing as a real hypnotic state].

6. [Measuring the {altered} blood flow to different locations in the brain] <u><u>allows</u></u> scientists [to visualize the effects of hypnosis].

7. And studies <u><u>show</u></u> that these effects <u><u>can</u></u> indeed <u><u>be measured</u></u> by changes in the brains of [hypnotized] subjects.

8. [To identify people] only [pretending to be hypnotized], scientists secretly <u><u>filmed</u></u> all participants while only an audiotape <u><u>made</u></u> suggestions to the subjects.

9. Subjects genuinely able [to be hypnotized] <u><u>responded</u></u> to either the audiotape or the hypnotist himself.

10. Those who <u><u>did</u></u> not <u><u>respond</u></u> unless a hypnotist <u><u>was</u></u> in the room <u><u>were judged</u></u> [to be faking the effects of hypnosis], and their brain measurements <u><u>revealed</u></u> less change than the others.

PARAGRAPH EXERCISE

In the opinion of most westerners, "barkeeps <u><u>were</u></u> ... the hardest [worked] folks in camp. ... " One of these burdens <u><u>was</u></u> [to act as a human fire alarm]. Western saloons never <u><u>closed</u></u>, and whenever a fire <u><u>broke</u></u> out the saloon owner <u><u>would dash</u></u> into the street, [running up and down] [hollering] and [emptying his six-shooter at the moon]. The commotion <u><u>would send</u></u> the volunteer firemen [pouring into the street in their long johns] [to put out the fire]. [Having done so], all and sundry naturally <u><u>assembled</u></u> in the saloon [to mull over the event] while [imbibing a tumbler of {gut-warming} red-eye].

SENTENCE WRITING

Your sentences may vary, but make sure that your verbals are not actually the main verbs of your clauses. You should be able to double underline your real verbs, as was done here.

1. I <u><u>enjoy</u></u> [speaking French].

2. [Typing on a small keyboard] <u><u>hurts</u></u> my wrists.

3. [Driving to Regina from here] <u><u>takes</u></u> about three hours.

4. I <u><u>spent</u></u> the day [reading the final chapters of my book].

5. I <u><u>love</u></u> [to eat breakfast outside in the summer].

6. We <u><u>were invited</u></u> [to go out to dinner].

7. I <u><u>would like</u></u> [to chat with you], but I am late for a meeting.

8. [To cook like a real gourmet] <u><u>takes</u></u> practice.

9. [Impressed by my grades], my parents <u><u>bought</u></u> me a new car.

10. [Taken in small doses], aspirin <u><u>helps</u></u> prevent heart attacks.

CORRECTING MISPLACED OR DANGLING MODIFIERS (PP. 119–21)

Your answers may differ slightly.

EXERCISE 1

1. After *I ordered* pizza for dinner, my cellphone lost its signal.

2. I found a penny *as I jogged* around the park.

3. The sentence is correct.

4. One year *after he became manager*, the store went out of business.

5. The sentence is correct.

6. My *smiling sister* appeared with an armful of flowers for my graduation.

7. The dancer tripped *on his shoelace and fell*.

8. They sent us *an envelope full of postcards* from Bermuda.

9. The sentence is correct.

10. I bought a new dress *that has* gold buttons.

EXERCISE 2

1. The sentence is correct.

2. *Taking careful notes,* the students paid attention to each of the speakers.

3. *I was wearing my jogging suit when I* mailed your invitation.

4. The recruits listened to their new commander *giving directions in a booming voice.*

5. The sentence is correct.

6. *Sitting in their chairs,* the children ate the ice cream sandwiches.

7. She drove her new car home from the showroom; *the car had a full tank of gas.*

8. *After I made other plans*, the party went on without me.

9. My brother's car pulled into the driveway, *and he had a surprised look on his face.*

10. *As we flew to the Bahamas for a week's holiday, we realized that we had forgotten our sunglasses.*

EXERCISE 3

1. *Walking around the zoo*, the children saw lions and bears.

2. As team leaders, *you will have many responsibilities.*

3. The maid brought in *the neatly folded extra towels* we had requested.

4. *Reading their policy very carefully*, they noticed an error.

5. *As they entered the auditorium,* she kicked her friend by accident.

6. The *frowning* teacher handed the tests back to the students.

7. *As I talked with the guests,* the party finally got underway.

8. *For our mother*, we adopted a cat *with a fluffy tail.*

9. *Dressed in their overalls*, the farmers planted the new crop.

10. At the age of 18, *Canadian citizens are accorded* voting rights.

EXERCISE 4

1. *As I took tickets at the Tilt-a-Whirl*, the carnival quickly lost its appeal.

2. The sentence is correct.

3. *Still dressed in their costumes*, the actors opened their gifts.

4. The sentence is correct.

5. The dog pulled at its heavy leash *dragging along the floor.*

6. The sentence is correct.

7. *Going through her pockets*, she found a dollar bill.

8. The sentence is correct.

9. The sentence is correct.

10. After shouting "Happy New Year!" *everyone was* completely quiet.

EXERCISE 5

1. One day *after I turned 40*, my new car broke down on the freeway.

2. My brother lets his dog hang out the car window *because the dog likes* the rush of fresh air on his face.

3. The sentence is correct.

4. Studying in the writing lab, *I eliminated* my comma problems.

5. The sentence is correct.

6. *We saw a pair of squirrels chasing each other up and down a tree.*

7. The sentence is correct.

8. The sentence is correct.

9. Lifting the heavy television, *she became red in the face.*

10. The sentence is correct.

PROOFREADING EXERCISE

Corrections are italicized. Yours may differ slightly.

I love parades, so last year my family and I went to Toronto to see the Caribana parade. It turned out to be even more wonderful than I expected.

Although we arrived one day before the festivities, the city was already crowded with tourists. Early the next morning, people set up lawn chairs on Lakeshore Boulevard. We didn't want to miss one float in the parade, so we found our own spot and made ourselves at home. When the parade began, I had as much fun watching the spectators as *watching* the parade itself. I saw children *sitting on their parents' shoulders and* pointing at the breathtaking floats. *The costumes were* decorated extravagantly with feathers and sequins. I couldn't believe how beautiful *they* were.

The crowd was overwhelmed by the sights and sounds of the parade. Everyone especially enjoyed hearing the steel drum bands, *marching and playing their instruments with perfect rhythm.* They must have practised the whole year to be that good.

My experience didn't end with the parade, however. After the last float had passed, I found a $20 bill *as I walked up Yonge Street. I framed it as a souvenir of my Caribana experience, and now it hangs on my wall at home.*

FOLLOWING SENTENCE PATTERNS (PP. 125–29)

EXERCISE 1

S LV DESC.
1. I am afraid (of flying).

S   AV OBJ.
2. The engine sounds scare me.

S AV   AV   OBJ.
3. (During takeoff), I sit (in my seat) and close my eyes.

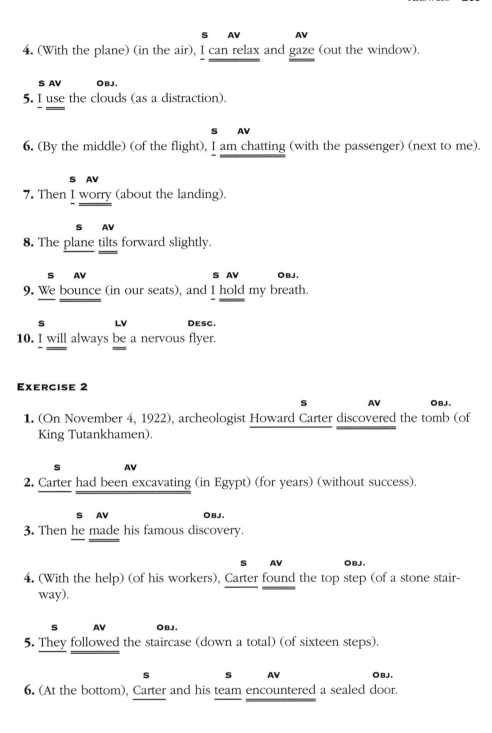

4. (With the plane) (in the air), <u>I</u> can <u>relax</u> and <u>gaze</u> (out the window).
                                   S   AV   AV

5. <u>I</u> <u>use</u> the clouds (as a distraction).
    S AV   Obj.

6. (By the middle) (of the flight), <u>I</u> <u>am chatting</u> (with the passenger) (next to me).
                                S   AV

7. Then <u>I</u> <u>worry</u> (about the landing).
       S AV

8. The <u>plane</u> <u>tilts</u> forward slightly.
        S   AV

9. <u>We</u> <u>bounce</u> (in our seats), and <u>I</u> <u>hold</u> my breath.
    S   AV   S AV   Obj.

10. <u>I</u> <u>will</u> always <u>be</u> a nervous <u>flyer</u>.
     S   LV   Desc.

EXERCISE 2

1. (On November 4, 1922), archeologist <u>Howard Carter</u> <u>discovered</u> the tomb (of King Tutankhamen).
                                          S   AV   Obj.

2. <u>Carter</u> <u>had been excavating</u> (in Egypt) (for years) (without success).
     S   AV

3. Then <u>he</u> <u>made</u> his famous discovery.
       S   AV   Obj.

4. (With the help) (of his workers), <u>Carter</u> <u>found</u> the top step (of a stone stairway).
                            S   AV   Obj.

5. <u>They</u> <u>followed</u> the staircase (down a total) (of sixteen steps).
     S   AV   Obj.

6. (At the bottom), <u>Carter</u> and his <u>team</u> <u>encountered</u> a sealed door.
                    S   S   AV   Obj.

          S   AV   OBJ.
7. They had found a tomb undisturbed (for thousands of years).

       S   AV   OBJ.
8. It held the personal belongings (of a young Egyptian king).

          S   LV   DESC.   S   LV
9. Some (of the objects) were precious; others were just ordinary household

       DESC.
effects.

           S   AV   OBJ.
10. The job (of cataloguing and removing the items) took ten years.

       S   AV
1. We live (in a world) (with photocopiers, scanners, and fax machines).

          S   AV   OBJ.   S   AV   OBJ.
2. If we need copies (of documents), these machines make them (for us).

                              S   AV   OBJ.
3. (Up until the late 1800s), people copied all documents (by hand).

                                       S   AV   OBJ.
4. (As a solution) (to this problem), Thomas Edison invented an electric pen.

                                    S   AV   OBJ.   S   LV
5. (Unlike ordinary pens), Edison's electric pen made stencils; the pen itself was

       DESC.
inkless.

            S   AV   OBJ.   S   AV   OBJ.
6. Its sharp tip poked holes (in the paper), and later a roller spread ink (over the
holes).

          S   AV
7. The ink went (through the holes) (onto another sheet) (of paper) underneath.

                   S   LV   DESC.   S   AV   OBJ.
8. And an exact copy was the result; in fact, one stencil produced many copies.

  S   S   AV   LV
9. The first <u>documents</u> [that] <u>Edison</u> <u>reproduced</u> (with his electric pen) <u>were</u> a

       DESC.   DESC.
speech (from *Richard III*) and the outline (of a photograph) (of Edison's wife,

Mary).

            S   AV   OBJ.
10. Although <u>Edison</u> <u>sold</u> many thousands (of his electric pens) (at the time), only

      S   AV
<u>six</u> (of them) <u>have survived</u>.

EXERCISE 4

      S   AV
1. <u>People</u> often <u>travel</u> (with their dogs, cats, or other pets).

       S   AV   OBJ.
2. <u>Airlines</u> <u>offer</u> some suggestions (about flying) (with pets).

             S   LV   DESC.
3. First, a <u>pet</u> <u>should be</u> old enough to fly—9 weeks old (at least).

        S   AV
4. All <u>pets</u> <u>must travel</u> (in approved carriers) (with food and water dishes).

                      S   AV   OBJ.
5. (During the flight), <u>airlines</u> <u>store</u> most pets (in the cargo areas).

              S   AV   S   AV
6. One small <u>pet</u> <u>can ride</u> (in the passenger area) if the pet's <u>carrier</u> <u>fits</u> (under a

seat).

                   S   AV
7. However, only one <u>pet</u> <u>may travel</u> (in the passenger area) (per flight).

               S   AV
8. Ordinary <u>water</u> (in a pet's dish) usually <u>spills</u> (during loading).

         S   AV   S
9. But <u>ice cubes</u> (in the water dish) <u>will melt</u> (after loading) so that the <u>pet</u>

       AV   OBJ.
<u>will have</u> water.

　　　s　**LV** **DESC.**　　　　　**s**　　**AV**　　　　　　　　　**s**
10. Sedatives are risky when the pet can't react normally if, for example, its carrier

　　　AV
overturns.

EXERCISE 5

　　　　　　　　　　　　s　　　　**AV**
1. The Hudson's Bay Company was established (in 1670) (with the development)
(of the fur trade) (in North America.)

　　　　　　　　　　s　　　**AV**
2. Originally, the company was controlled (by the British overseers)

　　　　　　　　　　　　　s　　　　**AV**　　　　　　**OBJ.**
(until May 1970), when Queen Elizabeth II granted Canadians ownership.

　　　　　　　　　　　　　s　　**Lv**　　**DESC.**　　　**s**　**AV**
3. The company's first Canadian headquarters were (in Winnipeg), but they moved
(to Toronto) (in 1987).

　　　　　　　　　　s　　**AV**　　**OBJ.**
4. The Hudson's Bay Company opened its first store (in downtown Calgary,
Alberta), (in 1884).

　　　　　　　　　　　　s　　**LV**　　　**DESC.**　　　　　　**DESC.**
5. (Today), the Hudson's Bay Company is Canada's oldest corporation and largest
department store retailer.

　　　　　　s　　　　　　**AV**
6. Many Bay shoppers never contemplate this company's most important historic
OBJ.
duty—to supply France and Russia (with food and munitions) (throughout
World War I).

　　　　　　　　　　　　　　　　　s　　**LV**　　　**DESC.**　　　**s**
7. (After the stock market crash of 1929), the company was badly shaken, but it
　　AV　　　　**OBJ.**
survived the Depression.

8. (In 1970), to celebrate the 300th anniversary (of the store), the company built
                                                                 (S) *(AV)*
OBJ.
a replica (of the sailing ship *Nonsuch*), the first ship to explore the Bay. It sailed *(S)* *(AV)*
(along the coasts) (of England, the Great Lakes, and the Pacific Northwest)
before being placed (in a museum) (in Manitoba).

9. To recognize the Hudson's Bay Company's 325th anniversary, (in February
1995), a commemorative silver dollar displaying the co-founders Radisson and *(S)*
des Groseilliers (with the *Nonsuch*) (in the background) was produced. *(AV)*

10. (In January 1994), the Provincial Archives (of Manitoba) became the permanent *(S)* *(LV)* *(DESC.)*
home (of the Hudson's Bay Company Archives). They consist of handwritten *(S)* *(LV)* *(DESC.)*
OBJ. *OBJ.* *OBJ.* *OBJ.* *OBJ.*
journals, ships logs, maps, photos, rare books, and much more.

PARAGRAPH EXERCISE

Nature Is a Cultural Phenomenon

Nature is so important (to many Canadians) that we devote a lot (of time and
S AV DESC.   *S AV OBJ.*
other resources) to caring for it. Love (of nature) flourishes (in cultures) that have
S   *AV*   *S AV*
highly developed technologies. (With rare exception), we are no longer afraid (of the
OBJ.   *S LV*   *DESC.*
forces) (of nature). We believe that nature can be controlled, so we see it (in a benev-
S AV   *S*   *AV*   *S AV OBJ.*
olent way), (as something to be enjoyed.) Nature is a source (of fantasies) (about a
S AV DESC.
way) (of life) different (from urban civilization); it is a source (of entertainment) (in
S LV DESC.
nature programs) (on television); and it provides a retreat (from alienating work). We
S AV OBJ.   *S*
tour (through nature), hike, mountain-bike, and cross-country ski.
AV   *AV*   *AV*   *AV*
So many people visit our national parks and other nature reserves (in the
S AV   *OBJ.*   *OBJ.*
summer) that we must control how we use them. (In a period) (of drought), we

       AV   OBJ.   S AV   OBJ.   S   LV

may have to accept restrictions on where we light campfires. ... Foreign visitors are

                DESC.   S   AV   OBJ.

sometimes surprised to learn that we voluntarily disarm ourselves before entering

                S   AV   AV OBJ.

places where bears can, and occasionally do, kill us.

                       S   AV   S   AV

(In our love) (of nature), we not only act to conserve it, we also actively manage

OBJ. S   AV   S   AV

it.   We may have to work hard to restore the "balance (of nature)" that was disturbed

       S   AV   S   LV   DESC.

when a park was created. Most provincial parks are too small to support a population

                              S   S   S   AV

(of wolves), but, (without predators), moose, deer, and elk can multiply (to the point)

      S   AV   OBJ.   S   AV

where they damage the vegetation. Parks managers may then decide to reduce their

numbers (by culling the herds), (through planned hunting).

AVOIDING CLICHÉS, AWKWARD PHRASING, AND WORDINESS (PP. 133–37)

Your answers may differ from these possible revisions.

EXERCISE 1

1. I compare prices before I buy.

2. I often try three or four stores.

3. I look for the lowest price.

4. I have saved $100 on one item this way.

5. Omit this sentence.

6. Prices may vary significantly on a single item.

7. But knowing when to buy is not easy.

8. Once I waited for a computer sale that never happened.

9. However, I am happy when I do find a bargain.

10. Looking for good prices is what I always try to do.

EXERCISE 2

1. I received a surprise in the mail today.

2. It was a small square brown box.

3. It came from Cape Dorset.

4. I wondered if I knew anyone in Cape Dorset.

5. Finally, I remembered that our former next-door neighbours had moved to Cape Dorset.

6. Their son Josh and I had been good friends, so I thought that it was from him.

7. As soon as I looked in the box, I knew Josh had sent it.

8. Josh had remembered that I collect snow domes as souvenirs.

9. Inside was a large snow dome with a polar bear and a man riding a dog sled; the nameplate said *Cape Dorset* in red letters.

10. When I shook the dome, it looked like a blizzard inside.

EXERCISE 3

1. I saw an exciting performance at the Shaw festival.

2. Each spring, many tourists come to the festival in Niagara-on-the-Lake.

3. People come from everywhere to see the classics.

4. It would be sufficient to see a good performance, but the enjoyment of travelling through the area is an extra surprise.

5. The town is beautiful at this time of year, since the orchards are in blossom.

6. There are many vineyards and wineries in the area.

7. Each winery has a tasting room, where you can sample a free glass of excellent wine.

8. Today, it's unusual to receive something for free.

9. All you have to do is buy a bottle of good Canadian wine.

10. The best way to end a visit to the Shaw Festival is to bring a picnic to the Niagara Escarpment and enjoy a view of the river.

EXERCISE 4

1. Old-fashioned places are hard to find these days.

2. Black Creek Pioneer Village, near Paramount Canada's Wonderland, is that kind of place.

3. The original Pioneer Village was settled in the early nineteenth century, mainly by German farmers from Pennsylvania.

4. The village has been carefully restored and is shown as it was in the 1860s.

5. The village has over 35 shops and homes.

6. Pioneer Village also has a blacksmith, a cabinet maker, and other tradespeople willing to discuss their crafts with visitors.

7. There are also a doctor's house, Roblin's Mill and water wheel, and a local schoolhouse.

8. The village's costumed hosts lead guests through a part of Canadian history.

9. People can even take a ride on a horse-drawn wagon.

10. Special events include a Pioneer Festival in September and Christmas celebrations in December.

Exercise 5

1. The other day I stayed home from work because I was sick.

2. I told my boss I needed one day of rest, but I almost didn't get it.

3. I had forgotten that Thursdays were gardeners' days.

4. These gardeners use power leaf blowers and tree trimmers.

5. Due to the noise, I couldn't sleep.

6. I tried watching television.

7. The daytime shows were worse than the noise.

8. Once the gardeners finished in the afternoon, I fell asleep.

9. Omit this sentence.

10. After sixteen hours of sleep, I felt better and went happily back to work.

Proofreading Exercise

Many people collect books, but one woman collected too many. She piled stacks of books around her house. She was 70 years old before her love of books led to her death. In 1977, the woman's neighbours called the police to tell them that she hadn't been seen at her house, and they were worried. When the police arrived, they found that a stack of books had collapsed on her in bed. She was alive when they found her, but she died as they took her to the hospital.

CORRECTING FOR PARALLEL STRUCTURE (PP. 139–43)

Exercise 1

1. The sentence is correct.

2. It doesn't look or act like other robots.

3. Its "head" contains a microphone for ears, a small screen for a face, and a video camera for eyes.

4. The sentence is correct.

5. The sentence is correct.

6. The difference between this and other robots is that the PRoP, as it's called, becomes an extension of anyone who controls it through the Internet.

7. A person in one city will be able to log on to the PRoP in another city and wander around—seeing what it sees, speaking to people it meets, and hearing what it hears.

8. The sentence is correct.

9. The inventors of the PRoP believe that research labs and businesses will be most interested in the PRoPs at first.

10. But in the future, PRoPs could make it possible to take a vacation or play a game of chess with a faraway friend without ever leaving your desk.

EXERCISE 2

1. I recently discovered the meaning and history of the word *trivia*.

2. The sentence is correct.

3. She would do spooky things to them on highways, at crossroads, and on country paths.

4. The sentence is correct.

5. The three roads came together and formed a "T" shape.

6. This type of place had two different ancient names: *triodos* in Greek and *trivium* in Latin.

7. The sentence is correct.

8. To please Hecate (Trivia), people placed statues of her with three faces or bodies wherever three roads met.

9. Because these landmarks were so easy to find, people began to use these decorated spots as gathering places to talk about daily business and to catch up on gossip.

10. The sentence is correct.

EXERCISE 3

1. The sentence is correct.

2. My mother, father, and I were all born on July 1.

3. My mother's name is Sarah Louisa; my girlfriend's name is Louisa Sarah.

4. Both my mother and her sister-in-law had their babies within months of each other.

5. The sentence is correct.

6. When my father was in high school, he had three jobs: waiter, babysitter, and newspaper carrier.

7. To earn extra money, I often deliver newspapers, work in a restaurant, and babysit for my neighbour.

8. My sister and I sometimes meet accidentally at the movies, wearing the same shirts.

9. Is this just a coincidence or do we have something in common?

10. My sister and I both hope to become veterinarians: I study science at school; she volunteers at an animal shelter.

EXERCISE 4

1. Many students worry about completing their assignments on time and about writing exams.

2. They feel stressed, both psychologically and physically.

3. On the physical level, they may experience loss of appetite, sleeplessness, headaches, sweating, or even ulcers or other illnesses.

4. On the psychological level, stress may involve feeling helpless, anxious, or afraid of losing control.

5. This sentence is correct.

6. This sentence is correct.

7. There are various personal factors that are related to a person's ability to handle stressful events effectively: having a sense of control over one's life, having a network of friends and family, having a flexible attitude to unexpected events, and having a hobby or a favourite sport.

8. Nevertheless, most people, at some time or other in their lives, feel stressed and unable to cope.

9. The best way to deal with such a situation is to put in place coping strategies, such as monitoring your responses to everyday demands and expectations, learning relaxation techniques, and maintaining a regular sleep routine.

10. If these strategies fail, talking to another person, such as a counsellor or health professional, is often extremely helpful.

EXERCISE 5

1. I've made a list of eight basic steps I can follow to improve my writing.

2. First, I need to accept that my writing needs work and that I can make it better if I try.

3. Second, I need to eliminate wordiness.

4. Third, I need to work on my vocabulary.

5. Fourth, I need to proofread my papers more carefully.

6. Fifth, I need to vary my sentence length.

7. Sixth, I need to use the active voice.

8. Seventh, I need to budget my time so that a first draft can sit for a while before I revise it.

9. Finally, I need to look at the overall structure of a paper, not just the words and sentences.

10. By following these eight steps, I hope to be a better writer.

PROOFREADING EXERCISE

Alfred Hitchcock was born in England in 1899, but he became a citizen of the United States in 1955. He hated his childhood nicknames, "Fred" and "Cocky." He did not have a close relationship with his brother, his sister, or any friends. When Hitchcock was only 6 years old, his father gave Alfred a note and told him to take it to the police station near their house. He delivered the note to one of the officers. The officer followed the directions in the note, put little Alfred in a holding cell for several minutes, and told him that was what happened to bad children. It was his father's way of keeping Alfred on the right track, but it had the opposite effect. Throughout his life, Hitchcock had an intense fear of doing something wrong. He made more than 50 films; the most successful of them was *Psycho*. In the opening credits of his television series, he used to step into a line drawing of his famous pro-file. Many people don't know that Alfred Hitchcock drew that sketch himself.

USING PRONOUNS (PP. 148–51)

EXERCISE 1

1. I

2. he

3. he and I

4. I

5. he and I

6. he

7. I

8. him and me

9. he

10. him

EXERCISE 2

1. its

2. his

3. their

4. its

5. their

6. their

7. her

8. Everyone in the class turned in *an* essay.

9. their

10. its

EXERCISE 3

1. me

2. He and she

3. I

4. their

5. their

6. I

7. Each of the new teachers has *a* set of books.

8. their

9. Everyone at the polling place had *an* opinion and expressed it with *a* vote.

10. she

EXERCISE 4

1. I finished typing my paper, turned off my computer, and put *my paper* in my backpack.

2. Elijah told his brother, "Your car has a new dent in it."

3. *They felt better* because they bought their textbooks early.

4. Lina's mother *said, "You can take your new calculator to school."*

5. When I put my jacket in the dryer, *the jacket* shrunk.

6. Ricardo told his counsellor, *"You don't understand me."*

7. While we were counting the money from our garage sale, *the money* blew away.

8. *When our dog runs away, we get angry.*

9. Sean asked his friend, *"Why wasn't I invited to the party?"*

10. The sentence is correct.

EXERCISE 5

1. The MacNeils bought some new trees, but *the trees* were too tall.

2. The sentence is correct.

3. I signed the credit card slip, put my card back in my wallet, and handed *the slip* to the cashier.

4. When students work in groups, *students* get a lot of work done.

5. As he took the lenses out of the frames, the *lenses* (or *frames*) broke.

6. Whenever I put gas in my car, I get a headache from the smell of *gasoline*.

7. Coupons help people save money on certain items.

8. The sentence is correct.

9. *The teacher asked Sheema* to copy her notes for another student. (or *Sheema was asked to copy the teacher's* notes for another student.)

10. The sentence is correct.

PROOFREADING EXERCISE (CORRECTIONS ARE ITALICIZED.)

I told my cousin Miles a secret at our last family reunion, and as soon as I did, I knew *the secret* would get out. I forgot that Miles is six years younger than *I* when I told him that I was taking a job overseas. Right before I told him the secret, I said, "Now this is just between you and *me*, and you're not going to tell anyone, right?" He assured me that the only person he would talk to about it was *I*. I made the mistake of believing him. If I had *printed my secret* in a full-page ad in the newspaper and delivered it to my family, *my secret* could not have been spread around faster. Miles and I are still cousins, but *he* and *I* are no longer friends.

AVOIDING SHIFTS IN PERSON (PP. 152–54)

PROOFREADING EXERCISES
Your revisions may differ depending on whether you choose to begin in first, second, or third person.

1. Those of us who drive need to be more aware of pedestrians. We can't always gauge what someone walking down the street will do. We might think that all pedestrians will keep walking forward in a crosswalk, but they might decide to turn back if they forgot something. We could run into them if that happens. People's lives could be affected in an instant. We all should slow down and be more considerate of others.

2. This paragraph is correct.

3. Scientists and others are working on several inventions that have not been perfected yet. Some of these developments seem like complete science fiction, but they're not. Each of them is in the process of becoming a real new technology. It's hard to imagine eating meat grown on plants. Scientists will feed the plants artificially made blood. Researchers are also working to produce animals (perhaps even humans) grown in artificial wombs. The most interesting development is selective amnesia (memory loss). Patients will be able to ask their doctors to erase painful memories as a mental-health tool. And, of course, computers will gain more and more personality traits to become more like human beings.

REVIEW OF SENTENCE STRUCTURE ERRORS (PP. 154–56)

Your corrections may differ.

1. A. not parallel (in the evenings, on weekends, and *during the holidays*)

2. B. subject/verb agreement error (Each ... *is* the same size)

3. A. fragment (The guest speaker's presentation was too long.)

4. A. pronoun reference error (The dogs wearing sunglasses ... were cute.)

5. B. wordiness (At 6:00 every morning, I get up and make a pot of coffee.)

6. A. cliché (I hate taking tests.)

7. B. dangling modifier (*After I took a coffee break,* the cash register ...)

8. A. incorrect pronoun (The teacher gave ~~my friend and~~ *me* extra credit ...)

9. B. run-on sentence (It was warm and dry; I hardly even felt the breeze.)

10. A. pronoun agreement (Everyone on the field trip brought *a lunch*.)

11. A. misplaced modifier (Speaking in a high voice, *the trainer annoyed the dog.*)

12. A. awkward phrasing (*Parents and teens can understand each other.*)

13. A. cliché (You have *really helped me.*)

14. B. subject/verb agreement (One of its pieces *is* missing ...)

15. B. shift in person (I like being self-employed because *I* can be *my* own boss.)

PROOFREADING EXERCISE
Corrections are italicized. Yours may differ.

Let's Get Technical

In my child development classes, I'm learning about ways to keep girls interested in technology. Studies *show* that girls and boys begin their school years equally interested in technology. After elementary school, *girls lose interest.* Because boys keep up with computers and other technology throughout their educations, *boys get ahead in these fields.* Experts have come up with some suggestions for teachers and parents to help *girls stay involved in technology.*

Girls need opportunities to experiment with computers. Girls spend time on computers, but they usually just do their *assignments; then* they log off. Since computer games and programs are often aimed at *boys, parents* and teachers need to buy computer products that will challenge girls not only in literature and art, but also in math, science, and *business.*

Another suggestion is to put computers in places where girls can socialize. One reason many boys stay interested in technology is that *they can do it on their own*. Girls tend to be more interested in working with others and *sharing* activities. When computer terminals are placed close to one another, girls work at them longer.

Finally, parents and teachers need to *provide positive role models. They need to teach girls* about successful women in the fields of business, *science*, and technology. And the earlier *girls get interested* in these fields, the better.

PART 3 PUNCTUATION AND CAPITAL LETTERS

PERIOD, QUESTION MARK, EXCLAMATION POINT, SEMICOLON, COLON, DASH (PP. 159–63)

EXERCISE 1

1. My friend Adam and I were late for class yesterday; it was a really important day. (or !)

2. We had stayed up past midnight the night before perfecting our speech.

3. The teacher had given us the best topic of all—food irradiation.

4. I wondered how the other students would react when they heard that they had been eating irradiated spices for years.

5. Would they be alarmed or think it was cool?

6. Adam and I had assembled several visual aids to accompany our speech: a poster-sized chart of an irradiation facility, a photo of the glowing rods of radioactive material used to irradiate the food, and jars of both irradiated and nonirradiated spices.

7. Adam thought that sterilizing food with radiation was a great idea.

8. I had mixed feelings—at least I think they were mixed—about radiation used on food.

9. By the time we arrived in class, another pair of students had started their speech.

10. Now we have to wait until next week's class to give our speech; this time we will not be late. (or !)

EXERCISE 2

1. People have not stopped inventing mousetraps; in fact, there are over 4000 different kinds!

2. Some are simple; however, some are complicated or weird.

3. Nearly 50 new types of machines to kill mice are invented every year.

4. The most enduring mousetrap was designed by John Mast; it is the one most of us picture when we think of a mousetrap: a piece of wood with a spring-loaded bar that snaps down on the mouse just as it takes the bait.

5. John Mast created this version of the mousetrap in 1903; since then no other mousetrap has done a better job.

6. There is a long list of technologies that have been used to trap mice: electricity, sonar, lasers, super glues, etc.

7. One mousetrap was built in the shape of a multi-level house with several stairways; however, its elaborate design made it impractical and expensive.

8. In 1878, one person invented a mousetrap for travellers; it was a box that was supposed to hold men's removable collars and at night catch mice, but it was not a success.

9. Who would want to put an article of clothing back into a box used to trap a mouse?

10. Can you guess the name of the longest running play in Toronto? It's *The Mousetrap*!

EXERCISE 3

1. People in Australia are asking themselves a question: why are some dolphins carrying big sponges around on their heads?

2. First it was just one dolphin; now several dolphins are doing it.

3. Marine biologists all over the world are trying to understand this unusual sponge-carrying behaviour.

4. They wonder about whether the sponges decrease the dolphins' ability to manoeuvre under water.

5. If they do, then why would the dolphins sacrifice this ability?

6. The dolphins might be using the sponges for a very important reason: to help them find food.

7. Some scientists think that the sponges may protect the dolphins' beaks in some way.

8. The sponges might indicate position in the social order; that's another explanation.

9. Or the dolphins could be imitating each other—a kind of dolphin "fad," in other words.

10. Only one group of experts knows whether these sponges are hunting tools or just fashion statements: (or ;) that is the dolphins themselves.

EXERCISE 4

1. Who would have thought that educators were a nomadic group?

2. In 1899, Frontier College was founded by Alfred Fitzpatrick and a group of university students; their aim was to make education available to the labourers in the work camps of Canada.

3. Labourer-teachers were trained and sent to the camps where they worked alongside the labourers during the day; then they taught reading and writing to them at night.

4. Frontier College was also involved in encouraging Canadians to take up farming; a woman by the name of Margaret Strang offered her tutorial and medical services for those who were interested at a model settlement at Edlund, Ontario.

5. The Department of National Defence made an agreement with Frontier College, which placed labourer-teachers in Depression relief camps to provide recreation and tutoring.

6. Some other projects that labourer-teachers were involved in were as follows: constructing the Alaska Highway, working in rail gangs after World War II, tutoring new Canadians, and working in long-term community development projects in northern settlements.

7. In the mid-1970s, Frontier College enlarged its focus to include urban frontiers; volunteers began working in prisons and with street youth, ex-offenders, and people with special needs.

8. More than a decade ago, Frontier College began doing work with children, teens, and families, while at the same time developing the workplace literacy program, called Learning in the Workplace.

9. The original idea — to help out those isolated in work camps across Canada — has changed a great deal since Frontier College's founding in 1899, but it continues to be an important aspect in today's education system.

10. In 1999, Frontier College celebrated its centenary — 100 Years of Teaching and Learning in Canada.

EXERCISE 5

1. Do you believe in ghosts?

2. On Aug. 14, 1999, the body of a young man was found on the Yukon and B.C. border by three teachers who went hunting for the day.

3. The man—he was named Kwaday Dan Sinchi by the Champagne and Aishihik First Nations—was found on a northern B.C. glacier.

4. Though the First Nations people of the area believed he was as old as 10 000 years, tests show the remains to be about 550 years old.

5. Discovered along with the hunter were various artifacts: a hat, a robe made of animal skins, and spear tools.

6. Radiocarbon dating was done on two samples: the hat and the cloak. The results are considered to be 95 percent accurate.

7. The "ghost" is believed to be a hunter who is estimated to have lived between the years 1415 and 1445, about the time Henry V was king of England and the Black Plague ravaged Europe.

8. This means the hunter died more than 300 years before the first known European contact on the northwest coast; however, it is still not known if he is an ancestor of the Champagne and Aishihik First Nations.

9. Scientists say that there are only two certainties: the "ghost" is a young male, and he was on a trading route between the coast and the interior.

10. The remains, which are now in the care of the Royal British Columbia Museum in Victoria, B.C., will be studied for further historic information.

PROOFREADING EXERCISE

In my design class, we are learning about the appeal of *packages*. Our instructor has asked us to think about the following *question*: do packages help sell products? During our last class meeting, we worked in groups to come up with examples of packages that have made us buy items in the past. The packages that my group thought of were book jackets, album and CD covers, water bottles, and candy wrappers. By the end of the semester, each group will try to design a new successful package based on what we've learned.

COMMA RULES 1, 2, AND 3 (PP. 165–70)

EXERCISE 1

1. Whenever I ask my friend Nick a computer-related question, I end up regretting it.

2. Once he gets started, Nick is unable to stop talking about computers.

3. When I needed his help the last time, my printer wasn't working.

4. Instead of just solving the problem, Nick went on and on about print settings and font choices that I could be using.

5. When he gets like this, his face lights up, and I feel bad for not wanting to hear the latest news on software upgrades, e-mail programs, and hardware improvements.

6. I feel guilty, but I know that I am the normal one.

7. I even pointed his problem out to him by asking, "You can't control yourself, can you?"

8. The sentence is correct.

9. Nick always solves my problem, so I should be grateful.

10. When I ask for Nick's help in the future, I plan to listen and try to learn something.

EXERCISE 2

1. Scientists have been studying the human face, and they have been able to identify 5000 distinct facial expressions.

2. The sentence is correct.

3. Winking is action number 46, and we do it with the facial muscle that surrounds the eye.

4. People around the world make the same basic expressions when they are happy, surprised, sad, disgusted, afraid, or angry.

5. These six categories of facial expressions are universally understood, but different societies have different rules about showing their emotions.

6. The smile is one of the most powerful expressions, for it changes the way we feel.

7. If we give someone a real smile showing genuine happiness, then our brains react by producing a feeling of pleasure.

8. If we give more of a polite imitation smile, then our brains show no change.

9. The sentence is correct.

10. A smile also wins the long-distance record for facial expressions, for it can be seen from as far away as several hundred feet.

EXERCISE 3

1. Edgar Allen Poe was born on January 19, 1809, in Boston, Massachusetts, and he lived a life as full of suffering and sadness as any of the characters in his stories.

2. Nevertheless, Poe became famous as an editor and as the author of short stories, novels, poems, and critical essays.

3. Poe died under mysterious circumstances in October 1849 and was laid to rest in Westminster Burying Ground in Baltimore, Maryland.

4. On the night of Poe's birth each year, a person wearing a dark hat and light-coloured scarf visits Poe's grave.

5. The stranger approaches the author's stone monument, lays down a small bunch of roses, and toasts Poe's memory with a half-empty bottle of cognac.

6. The sentence is correct.

7. Several years ago, the stranger wrote a message that this ritual would be continued by others.

8. Since that time, many people have taken the stranger's place at Westminster cemetery on Poe's birthday.

9. The sentence is correct.

10. Jerome has faithfully followed the movements of these strangers at the grave site for more than twenty years, so he knows that such stories are true.

EXERCISE 4

1. The sentence is correct.

2. Vinyl record albums may not be as easy to find as the other music formats, but many people think that they still sound the best.

3. The sentence is correct.

4. But there is no doubt that CDs are easier to package, to handle, and to maintain.

5. At the time CDs took over the music market, vinyl records almost disappeared.

6. In the past few years, musicians have begun releasing their work on CDs, cassettes, and LPs.

7. The sentence is correct.

8. There are even new models of turntables, but some are extremely expensive.

9. Most turntables are about the same price as a CD player, but some can cost up to $40 000.

10. People can buy new LPs in music/video stores, classic LPs in used-record stores, and old LPs in thrift stores.

EXERCISE 5

1. Gold is amazing, isn't it?

2. Unlike metals that change their appearance after contact with water, oil, and other substances, gold maintains its shine and brilliant colour under almost any circumstances.

3. When a miner named James Marshall found gold in the dark soil of California in 1848, the gold rush began.

4. Though few people are aware of it, the first gold in Canada was found in small deposits in central Nova Scotia and the Eastern Townships of Quebec.

5. Harry Oakes developed the deepest gold mine in North America at Kirkland Lake, Ontario.

6. Beginning with the Fraser River Gold Rush in 1858, a series of gold discoveries in British Columbia transformed the colony's history.

7. During the famous Klondike Gold Rush, the huge influx of people prompted the Canadian government to establish the Yukon Territory in 1898.

8. The sentence is correct.

9. Some people have become rich directly because of gold, and some have become rich indirectly because of gold.

10. For example, if it had not been for the gold rush, Levi Strauss would not have had any customers, and the world would not have blue jeans.

PROOFREADING EXERCISE

When you belong to a large family, holidays are a mixed blessing. They are certainly times to see one another, but how do you choose where to go and whom to see? For example, I have sets of relatives living in four different areas, and they all want to get together for the holidays. If I accept one group's invitation, I disappoint the others. If I turn them all down and stay home with my immediate family, I make them all mad. I guess I will just have to invite the whole clan to spend the holidays at my house, won't I?

SENTENCE WRITING

Here are some possible combinations. Yours may differ.

I like to swim, but I have never taken lessons.

When the alarm rings, I get up and get ready for school.

Although he is currently an elementary schoolteacher, he was a math tutor in college, and he worked as a ski instructor.

Since Tricia and James are both practical, organized university graduates, they are equal partners in their business.

COMMA RULES 4, 5, AND 6 (PP. 173–76)

EXERCISE 1

1. This year's class pictures, I believe, turned out better than last year's.

2. The sentence is correct.

3. There were, however, a few problems.

4. You may leave the sentence alone, or you may use a comma after *However*.

5. The sentence is correct.

6. My little brother, who is wearing a red sweater, is sitting on the left, but it's hard to see him.

7. Ms. Patel, the teacher who took the picture, needed to stand a little closer to the group.

8. The sentence is correct.

9. And no one, it seems, had time to comb the children's hair.

10. The sentence is correct.

EXERCISE 2

1. We hope, of course, that people will remember to vote on Tuesday.

2. The sentence is correct.

3. The sentence is correct.

4. The elementary school, which volunteers its gym as a polling station, make elections more convenient for voters in the neighbourhood.

5. We may, therefore, run into people that we know at the polling station.

6. You may leave the sentence alone, or you may use a comma after *Therefore*.

7. The voting booth, a small cubicle where each person casts a vote, is meant to be a private place.

8. The sentence is correct.

9. The sentence is correct.

10. No one, we trust, will influence our thoughts there.

EXERCISE 3

1. The sentence is correct.

2. Ms. Sousa, the geology teacher, looks like Ms. Riel, the chemistry teacher.

3. My clothes iron, which has an automatic shut-off switch, is safer to use than yours, which doesn't.

4. The sentence is correct.

5. The sentence is correct.

6. Claire and Andre, who ask a lot of questions, usually do well on their assignments.

7. The Ahmeds, who left before the concert was over, missed the grand finale.

8. The sentence is correct.

9. The sentence is correct.

10. The teacher posted the results of the exam, which we took last week.

EXERCISE 4

1. England's Prince Charles has two sons, William and Harry.

2. The sentence is correct.

3. William, whose full name is His Royal Highness Prince William Arthur Philip Louis of Wales, was named after William the Conqueror.

4. The princes' grandmother, Queen Elizabeth II, will pass the crown to her son Charles, who will then pass it on to William.

5. William, who was born in 1982, stands over six feet tall and has become as popular as a movie star.

6. The sentence is correct.

7. Charles and Harry have met the Spice Girls, who posed for pictures with them.

8. William is well read and intelligent; however, he is also athletic and fun-loving.

9. The sentence is correct.

10. However, it will probably be many years before William takes on his future title, which will be King William V.

EXERCISE 5

1. Jim Henson, who created the Muppets, began his television career in the mid-1950s.

2. He was, it seems, eager to be on TV, and there was an opening for someone who worked with puppets.

3. Henson and a buddy of his quickly fabricated a few puppets, including one called Pierre the French Rat, and they got the job.

4. Henson's next project, *Sam and Friends*, also starred puppets.

5. *Sam and Friends* was a live broadcast lasting only five minutes; however, it was on twice a day and ran for six years.

6. Kermit the Frog, a character that we now associate with *Sesame Street* and *The Muppet Show,* was part of the cast of *Sam and Friends*.

7. Henson provided the voice and animated the movements of Kermit and a few others from the beginning, and he worked with Frank Oz, who helped round out the cast of Muppet characters.

8. In 1969, the Muppets moved to *Sesame Street*; however, they graduated to their own prime-time program, *The Muppet Show,* in the late 1970s.

9. At the high point of its popularity worldwide, more than 200 million people, adults and children, tuned in to a single broadcast of *The Muppet Show*.

10. The sentence is correct.

PROOFREADING EXERCISE

Unlike my mom and my sister, who generally don't like dealing with food, I love to cook. I think I inherited this passion for cooking from my dad, who is always interested in trying out new recipes. He has a whole bookshelf full of cookbooks; what's more, he likes to read them, from cover to cover, in his spare time. Most of the meals we eat are, of course, prepared by him. But sometimes, when I have enough time and energy, I cook a special meal. My sister and her husband, Ted, have recently asked me to cook brunch for them and eight of their friends on New Year's Eve. Believe it or not, I can't wait!

SENTENCE WRITING

Here are some possible combinations. Yours may differ.

I have seen *Titanic*, the famous movie, several times.

I have seen the famous movie *Titanic* several times.

I could, I believe, learn a few more study skills.

I believe that I could learn a few more study skills.

My friend, who has curly hair and sits in the back of the class, wrote a good paper.

My curly-haired friend who sits in the back of the class wrote a good paper.

REVIEW OF THE COMMA (P. 177)

PROOFREADING EXERCSE

I am writing you this note, Helen, to ask you to do me a favour. [4] When you get home from work tonight, would you take the turkey out of the freezer? [3] I plan to get started on the pies, the rolls, and the sweet potatoes as soon as I walk in the door after work. [2] I will be so busy, however, that I might forget to thaw out the turkey. [5] It's the first time I've made the holiday meal by myself, and I want everything to be perfect. [1] My big enamel roasting pan, which is in the back of the cupboard under the counter, will be the best place to keep the turkey as it thaws. [6] Thanks for your help.

QUOTATION MARKS AND ITALICS/UNDERLINING (PP. 180–83)

EXERCISE 1

1. *The fifth estate* is still a popular television series.

2. "I don't explain," said Marshall McLuhan. "I explore."

3. "Do I have to do all of the dishes by myself?" my roommate asked.

4. Last night we watched the movie *Wag the Dog* on video.

5. Oscar Wilde wrote the play *The Importance of Being Earnest,* the novel *The Picture of Dorian Gray*, the poem "The Ballad of Reading Gaol," and the children's story "The Selfish Giant."

6. "Never use a big word if a little one will do," Emily Carr once said.

7. "The class period can't be over," said the student. "I haven't even started my concluding paragraph yet."

8. I found my friend in the library reading the latest issue of *Flare* magazine.

9. We were asked to read the essay "Thinking as a Hobby" for Wednesday's class.

10. The movie version of *The English Patient* was just as poetic as the book.

EXERCISE 2

1. "The Precambrian Shield" is a poem by E.J. Pratt.

2. "Once you fill in all the answers," the teacher said, "turn your quiz papers over on your desks."

3. I have a subscription to several magazines, including *Canadian Living*.

4. "Everything exists in limited quantities," Pablo Picasso perceived, "even happiness."

5. "How many times," she asked, "are you going to mention the price we paid for dinner?"

6. After Babe Ruth's death, his wife remarked, "I don't even have an autographed ball. You don't ask your husband for an autographed ball. He'd probably think you were nuts."

7. Sophocles, the Greek playwright, wrote the tragedy *Oedipus Rex* in the fifth century B.C.

8. "When you go by on a train, everything looks beautiful. But if you stop," Edward Hopper explained, "it becomes drab."

9. There is a Mexican proverb that says, "Whoever sells land sells his mother."

10. When Allan Lamport, who was mayor of the city, was asked about Toronto, he answered, "Nobody should visit Toronto for the first time."

EXERCISE 3

1. In her book *Orlando*, Virginia Woolf has this to say about art: "Green in nature is one thing, green in literature another."

2. Phil Hartman was the voice of Troy McClure on the animated TV series *The Simpsons*.

3. "Hold fast to your dreams," wrote Langston Hughes, "for if dreams die, then life is like a broken-winged bird that cannot fly."

4. David Suzuki wrote of his childhood in a chapter entitled "A New Generation"; it is part of his larger autobiography *Metamorphosis: Stages in a Life*.

5. Joan Didion describes her relationship with migraine headaches in her essay "In Bed."

6. "Where can I buy some poster board?" he asked.

7. "There is a school-supply store around the corner," his friend replied, "but I don't think that it's open this late."

8. Sylvia asked the other students if they had seen the Alfred Hitchcock movie called *The Birds*.

9. "I don't remember," James answered.

10. "It's not something you could ever forget!" she yelled.

EXERCISE 4

1. Kurt Vonnegut, in his novel *Slapstick*, describes New York City as "Skyscraper National Park."

2. "The past is still, for us, a place that is not safely settled," wrote Michael Ondaatje.

3. In her book *The Mysterious Affair at Styles*, Agatha Christie wrote that "Every murderer is probably somebody's old friend."

4. "Swear not by the moon," says Juliet to Romeo.

5. Pierre Trudeau told a U.S. audience, "Living next to you is like sleeping next to an elephant."

6. Norman Bethune stated that "The function of the artist is to disturb."

7. "Writers are always selling somebody out," Joan Didion observed.

8. The expression "All animals are equal, but some animals are more equal than others" can be found in George Orwell's novel *Animal Farm*.

9. A Swahili proverb warns, "To the person who seizes two things, one always slips from his grasp!"

10. Groucho Marx once remarked, "I wouldn't want to belong to any club that would accept me as a member."

EXERCISE 5

1. Ovid reminded us that we can learn from our enemies.

2. "We know what a person thinks not when he tells us what he thinks," said Isaac Bashevis Singer, "but by his actions."

3. The Spanish proverb "El pez muere por la boca" translated means "The fish dies because it opens its mouth."

4. "Ask yourself whether you are happy, and you cease to be so," John Stuart Mill wrote.

5. A Russian proverb states, "Without a shepherd, sheep are not a flock."

6. Stephen Leacock felt that "The essence of humour is human kindliness."

7. St. Jerome had the following insight: "The friendship that can cease has never been real."

8. Oscar Wilde found that "In this world there are only two tragedies. One is not getting what one wants, and the other is getting it."

9. "Self-respect," observed Joe Clark, "permeates every aspect of your life."

10. "Choose a job you love," Confucius suggested, "and you will never have to work a day in your life."

PROOFREADING EXERCISE

It may be decided, sometime off in the future, that the sum of Douglas Coupland's literary contribution equals the two words he used for the title of his 1991 debut as a novelist. In *Generation X*, Coupland pointed and clicked onto the generation born in the late 1950s and the 1960s as it stared into the future and tried to figure out what was going to fulfil it there. If the book didn't attract universally favourable reviews, it was a resounding commercial success and made Coupland an instant spokesman for his generation. It didn't matter so much that he didn't want the job—"I speak for myself," he's said, repeatedly, "not for a generation." No, he'd been deemed a sociological seer and, like it or not, each of his subsequent novels —books like *Microserfs* (1995) and *Girlfriend in a Coma* (1998)—would find itself judged less as fiction than as the words of an oracle between hard covers.

CAPITAL LETTERS (PP. 185–88)

EXERCISE 1

1. Mom and I have both decided to take classes next fall.

2. Fortunately, in Toronto we live near several colleges and universities.

3. Classes at the community colleges usually begin in late August or early September.

4. We could easily drive to the University of Toronto, Ryerson Polytechnic University, Humber College, George Brown College, or Sheridan College.

5. I want to take credit classes, and my mom wants to sign up for community education classes.

6. For instance, I will enroll in the academic courses necessary to transfer to a university.

7. These include English, math, science, and history classes.

8. My mother, on the other hand, wants to take noncredit classes with titles like "Learn to Play Keyboards," "Web Pages Made Easy," and "Be Your Own Real Estate Agent."

9. Mom already has a great job, so she can take classes just for fun.

10. I know that if I want to go to one of the colleges at the University of Toronto, I will have to be serious from the start.

EXERCISE 2

1. Born Alice Laidlaw in Wingham, Ontario, short story writer Alice Munro began to write fiction in her early teens.

2. After studying English for two years at the University of Western Ontario, she moved to British Columbia, where her husband established a bookstore.

3. Her early short stories were published in national magazines and broadcast on the CBC.

4. After the breakup of her marriage in 1976, she returned to southwestern Ontario.

5. Munro published her first book of short stories, *Dance of the Happy Shades*, for which she won her first Governor General's Award.

6. *Lives of Girls and Women*, one of Munro's most famous works, received the Canadian Booksellers Award.

7. When the CBC filmed a dramatization of this work, Munro's daughter Jenny was cast in the main role.

8. Some of the stories in *The Moons of Jupiter* previously appeared in *The New Yorker*, where Munro has continued to publish her work.

9. Munro sets some of her stories in British Columbia, in Toronto, and even in Albania, but her stories are mostly based in southwestern Ontario.

10. Students in literature classes study many of Munro's stories, including "Friend of My Youth" and "Lives of Girls and Women."

EXERCISE 3

1. Tom Cruise's family lived in Syracuse, New York, when he was born in 1962.

2. His original name was Thomas Cruise Mapother IV.

3. Before he became a famous actor, Tom Cruise didn't do as well in school as he wanted to because he had dyslexia, which causes reading problems.

4. Tom discovered acting when he was still a high school student in New Jersey.

5. He played the part of Nathan Detroit in Glen Ridge High School's production of the musical *Guys and Dolls*.

6. Tom Cruise then moved to New York City to find other jobs as an actor.

7. He was in a movie called *Endless Love* with Brooke Shields, but it was not successful.

8. The film that made Tom Cruise a star was *Risky Business*, in which he sang along to the Bob Seeger song "Old Time Rock & Roll."

9. *People* magazine has put Tom Cruise on its list of "Most Beautiful People" many times.

10. Cruise married another famous actor, Nicole Kidman, in December 1990, and they have adopted two children, Isabella and Connor.

EXERCISE 4

1. I grew up watching *The Wizard of Oz* once a year on TV before video stores like Blockbuster even rented movies to watch at home.

2. I especially remember enjoying it with my brother and sisters when we lived on Maple Drive.

3. Mom would remind us early in the day to get all of our homework done.

4. "If your homework isn't finished," she'd say, "you can't see the Munchkins!"

5. My favourite part has always been when Dorothy's house drops on one of the wicked witches and her feet shrivel up under the house.

6. The Wicked Witch of the West wants revenge after that, but Dorothy and Toto get help from Glinda, the Good Witch of the North.

7. Glinda tells Dorothy about the Emerald City and the Wizard of Oz.

8. On their way, Toto and Dorothy meet the Scarecrow, the Tin Man, and the Cowardly Lion.

9. Together they conquer the witch and meet Professor Marvel, the real man who has been pretending to be a wizard.

10. The ruby slippers give Dorothy the power to get back to Kansas and to her Aunt Em and Uncle Henry.

EXERCISE 5

1. Oscar Wilde was an Irish-born writer who lived and wrote in England for much of his life during the late 1800s.

2. He was famous for his refined ideas about art and literature.

3. While still a young man, Wilde travelled to America.

4. Contrary to what many people expected, he was well received in rough mining towns such as Leadville, Colorado.

5. He gave one particularly long speech to the miners who lived in Leadville.

6. Wilde spoke on the following topic: "The Practical Application of the Aesthetic Theory to Exterior and Interior House Decoration, with Observations on Dress and Personal Ornament."

7. During his stay in Leadville, Wilde had gained the miners' respect by visiting them down in the mines and by proving that he could drink as much whiskey as they could without getting drunk.

8. Wilde wrote about one incident that took place in Leadville.

9. Before giving a lecture he called "The Ethics of Art," Wilde was told that two criminals accused of murder had been found in town.

10. Earlier that evening, on the same stage where Wilde was about to give his speech, the two men were convicted of the crime and were then executed by Leadville officials.

REVIEW OF PUNCTUATION AND CAPITAL LETTERS (P. 189)

1. The height of the CN Tower, located in Toronto, is 553 m.

2. Have you ever read Helen Weinzweig's short story "A View from the Roof"?

3. We drove around the country all summer; now we're ready to stay right here.

4. "How much does a one-way ticket to Paris cost?" she asked.

5. We received your application, Ms. Kovac, and will contact you soon with our response.

6. The dog that receives the highest number of points wins the blue ribbon.

7. Mr. Michaels teaches Music 201, which is the intermediate voice class.

8. Whenever we eat there, we leave something behind at our table; then we have to drive back and get it.

9. We brought the plates, forks, cups, and napkins, but we forgot the bag with the food!

10. Hamlet doesn't *give* the famous advice "To thine own self be true," but he *follows* it.

11. I love to read the cartoons in *The Calgary Sun*; it's my favourite newspaper.

12. Packing for a long trip requires patience, planning, and previous experience.

13. Our French instructor gave us the following advice: "Think French when you speak French."

14. I wonder if we need to bring our English books to class today.

15. I think it was John Lennon who said, "Life is what happens when you're busy making other plans."

COMPREHENSIVE TEST (PP. 190–91)

1. (ww) I am delighted to *accept* an invitation to your wedding.

2. (sp) Our company is *committed* to excellence.

3. (awk) *Students should have* better food choices on campus.

4. (cap) The art class took a trip to the Museum of Civilization.

5. (pro) Our neighbour paid my brother and *me* to paint her fence.

6. (//) I knew that I had not studied for the test, that I missed several easy questions, and *that I* definitely wasn't going to pass it.

7. (c) The grass needs to be mowed, and the gutters need to be cleared before it rains.

8. (dm) *As I sat at the bus stop,* a car swerved and ended up facing the wrong direction.

9. (pro ref) He said, "Mr. Keely, I lost your notebook."

10. (shift) I eat pizza because it always *tastes* so good.

11. (p) I didn't know that you played the violin.

12. (apos) The *children's* toys were scattered around the room.

13. (mm) *When I was* 18, my parents bought me a car.

14. (ro) They didn't know what time it was*, for* (or *;*) neither of them wore a watch that day.

15. (cliché) *Finally*, nicotine patches help people *quit smoking*.

16. (wordy) With a little *planning,* it is easy to throw a *unique* party.

17. (pro agr) Everyone in the class forgot to bring *the* book. *or* All the students forgot to bring their books.

18. (frag) *The* gate was open, and music was playing in the backyard.

19. (cs) I enjoy buying birthday presents; they bring a special kind of joy.

20. (s/v agr) Each of the cookies *was* burned on the bottom.

WRITING

ORGANIZING IDEAS

EXERCISE 1 THESIS OR FACT? (P. 208)

1. FACT   **6.** FACT

2. THESIS   **7.** THESIS

3. THESIS   **8.** FACT

4. THESIS   **9.** THESIS

5. FACT   **10.** FACT

EXERCISE 2 ADDING TRANSITIONAL EXPRESSIONS (P. 210)

When I moved into my own apartment for the first time last month, I discovered the many hidden expenses of entering "the real world." *First of all*, I had no idea that utility companies needed a security deposit from anyone who hasn't rented before. Each utility required a $30 to $50 dollar deposit. *Therefore*, my start-up costs just for gas, electricity, and phone used up all the money I had saved for furnishings. *Next*, I found out how expensive it was to supply a kitchen with the basic staples of food and cleaning supplies. My initial trip to the grocery store cost $125, and I hadn't even bought my curtains at that point. *Finally*, I was able to budget my money and keep a little aside for any other unexpected expenses of living on my own.

WRITING ABOUT WHAT YOU READ

ASSIGNMENT 17 WRITE A 100-WORD SUMMARY (P. 225)

100-Word Summary of "Why Write?"

These days, writing well is a necessary skill for those who want to succeed—not only in business but also in personal life. In business, people who communicate well generally do well. Men and women have always looked for mates who had the skills that allowed them to thrive in their environment. Since writing well is such a predictor of success in the twenty-first century, it is one of the qualities people now seek when looking for a mate. So correct grammar, good sentence structure, and an appealing writing style are among the things that can make you sexy.

Index

Reader Reply Card

We are interested in your reaction to *The Least You Should Know about English, Form A*, First Canadian Edition, by Teresa Ferster Glazier, Page Wilson, and Kathleen A. Wagner. You can help us to improve this book in future editions by completing this questionnaire.

1. What was your reason for using this book?

    ☐ university course   ☐ college course   ☐ continuing education course
    ☐ professional   ☐ personal   ☐ other _____
      development   interest

2. If you are a student, please identify your school and the course in which you used this book.

3. Which chapters or parts of this book did you use? Which did you omit?

4. What did you like best about this book?

5. What did you like least?

6. Please identify any topics you think should be added to future editions.

7. Please add any comments or suggestions.

8. May we contact you for further information?

    Name: _____
    Address: _____
    Phone: _____
    E-mail:_____

(fold here and tape shut)

0116870399-M8Z4X6-BR01

The Publisher
HARCOURT CANADA
55 HORNER AVENUE
TORONTO, ONTARIO
M8Z 9Z9